STUDY GUIDE

for use with

BASIC STATISTICS FOR BUSINESS AND ECONOMICS

Douglas A. Lind
Robert D. Mason
Both of the University of Toledo

IRWIN
Burr Ridge, Illinois
Boston, Massachusetts
Sydney, Australia

Printed in the United States of America.

ISBN 0-256-15466-X

1 2 3 4 5 6 7 8 9 0 ML 0 9 8 7 6 5 4 3

Preface

This study guide is especially designed to accompany *Basic Statistics for Business and Economics* by Douglas A. Lind and Robert D. Mason. It can also be used alone, or as a companion to most other introductory statistics texts. It provides a valuable source of reinforcement for the material in the text. The chapters in the text and the study guide are parallel in topics, notation, and the numbering of formulas. The major features of the study guide include:

- **Chapter goals** are listed first. They stress the main concepts covered and the tasks students should be able to perform after having studied the chapter. It is recommended that students refer to the goals before reading the chapter to get an overview of the material to be studied and again after completing the chapter to confirm mastery of the material.

- Starting with Chapter 2, a brief **Introduction** follows the goals. In capsule form the material covered in previous chapters is tied with that covered in the current chapter, thus maintaining continuity throughout the book.

- Next there is a discussion of the relevant **statistical tools** described in the chapter.

- A **glossary** follows the chapter discussion. The glossary provides definitions of the key terms used in the chapter.

- **Chapter problems**, including solutions, come next. In this section the step-by-step method of solution is presented along with an interpretation of the results. The values are kept small to emphasize the concept.

- Following each chapter problem is an **exercise**. The student completes the exercise and checks the answer in the answer section at the end of the guide. Thus the student can check his/her comprehension of the material as they progress through the chapter.

Finally, **chapter assignments** cover the entire chapter and are intended to be completed outside the classroom. Part I of the assignment consists of matching questions, Part II is multiple-choice questions, and Part III problems, with space for students to show essential work. The pages are perforated, so that assignments can be torn out and handed in to the instructor for grading.

Students will attain the most benefit if they study the textbook first, and then read the corresponding chapter in the study guide.

Douglas A. Lind
Robert D. Mason

Contents

1

WHAT IS STATISTICS?

CHAPTER GOALS

After completing this chapter, you will be able to:

1. Define the word statistics and distinguish between descriptive statistics and inferential statistics.
2. List and describe the four levels of statistical measurement.

Introduction

No doubt you have noticed the large number of facts and figures, often referred to as *statistics*, that appear in the newspapers and magazines you read, the television you watch (especially sporting events) and in the grocery stores where you shop. As examples, a few statistics from the Sarasota (Florida) Herald-Tribune are:

1. Drug tests just conducted revealed that 8.8 percent of the 2.2 million American workers and job applicants surveyed failed their drug tests. This was down from 11.0 percent in the previous year.
2. Out of every 100,000 people in the United States, 455 are in prison. South Africa is next with 311 out of every 100,000.
3. In sports, the University of Minnesota upset Indiana 71–67, Colorado surprised Oklahoma State 57–53. And, Barry Bonds signed a 6-year contract with the San Francisco Giants for $43.0 million.
4. Stock prices jumped to record highs last week. The Dow Jones average of 30 industrials rose to over 3500.
5. Research findings revealed that 40 percent of American workers do not have health insurance as part of their job benefits. USDA choice beef boneless ribeye steak is $3.95 a pound, long stem roses $19.99 a dozen, and a Die Hard Sears battery $59.99.
6. According to the 1992 *World Almanac and Book of Facts*, 20,000 men are members of the Bald-Headed Men of America headquartered in Morehead, North Carolina.

The 455 persons in prison is a *statistic* (singular). Bond's $43.0 million is a *statistic*. A collection of all these figures is referred to as *statistics* (plural).

As a result, you may think of statistics simply as a collection of numerical information. However, statistics has a much broader meaning. We shall define **statistics** as a *body of techniques used to facilitate the collection, organization, presentation, analysis, and interpretation of numerical information for the purpose of making better decisions.*

Note in this definition of statistics cited above that the initial step is the collection of pertinent information. This information may come from newspapers or magazines, the companys' human relations director, the local, state, or federal government, universities, nonprofit organizations, the United Nations, and so on. A few actual publications of the federal government and others are:

- *Statistical Abstract of the United States,* published annually by the U.S. Department of Commerce.
- *Monthly Labor Review*, published monthly by the U.S. Department of Labor.
- *Survey of Current Business*, published monthly by the U.S. Department of Commerce.
- *Social Security Bulletin*, published annually by the U.S. Social Security Administration.
- *Crime in the United States*, published annually by the U.S. Federal Bureau of Investigation.
- *Hospital Statistics*, published annually by the American Hospital Association.
- *Vital Statistics of the United States*, published annually by the National Center for Health Statistics.

If the information is not available from company records or public sources, it may be necessary to conduct a **survey**. For example, the A.C. Nielsen Company surveys about 1,200 homes on an ongoing basis to determine which TV programs are being watched, and Gallup surveys registered voters before an election to estimate the percent that will vote for a certain candidate. These firms also sample the population regarding food preference, what features in automobiles are desirable, and what appliances consumers will most likely purchase next year. *Fortune* just surveyed 8,000 senior executives, outside directors, and financial analysts in 307 companies to find out the ten most admired firms, and the least admired firms. Each executive was asked to rate a list of firms on eight attributes, namely quality of management; quality of products or services; long-term investment value; financial soundness; ability to attract, develop and keep talented people; responsibility to the community and the environment; and wise use of corporate assets. Each attribute was rated on a scale of zero (poor) to ten (excellent). The ten most admired companies are:

RANK	LAST YEAR	COMPANY	SCORE
1	1	**Merck** Pharmaceuticals	9.02
2	2	**Rubbermaid** Rubber and plastic products	8.66
3	4	**Wal-Mart Stores** Retailing	8.58
4	10	**Liz Claiborne** Apparel	8.43
5	20	**Levi Strauss Associates** Apparel	8.26
6	8	**Johnson & Johnson** Pharmaceuticals	8.22
7	6	**Coca-Cola** Beverages	8.13
8	6	**3M** Scientific and photo equip.	8.12
9	5	**PepsiCo** Beverages	8.00
9	3	**Procter & Gamble** Soaps, cosmetics	8.00

Source: *Fortune*, February 10, 1992, p. 26.

Drug, apparel, and beverage companies dominate the top ten. After six years the No. 1 spot seems to be Merck's by divine right. Levi Strauss is the only newcomer.

Descriptive and Inferential Statistics

The definition of statistics referred to "collecting, organizing, and presenting numerical information." Data stored in a computer's memory or in a filing cabinet are of little value. Techniques are available that organize this information in a more meaningful form. Such aids are called **descriptive statistics**. A

statistical tool designed to describe the movement of a series of numbers over a long period of time—such as production, imports, wages and stock market trends—is called a *line chart*. The line chart below, for example, depicts the upward movement of the Dow Jones average of 30 industrials since 1987.

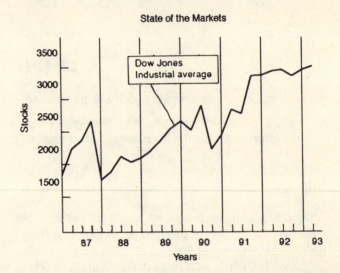

State of the Markets

Notice how easy it is to describe the trend of stock prices: The price of the 30 industrials, as represented by the Dow rose somewhat steadily from about 1,800 in 1987 to about 3,400 in early 1993.

Another descriptive measure is referred to as an average. Some examples are:

- In sports, for the 1992 Major League baseball season the New York Mets had the largest team salary with an average of $1.7 million per player. Walter Payton is the leading all-time rusher in professional football with 4.4 yards per carry.
- The National Center for Health Statistics reported that the average stay at short-stay hospitals is 8.9 days for persons 65 and over.
- The median age (an average) for men at the time of their first marriage is 26.1 years, and 23.9 for women according to the Bureau of the Census.

The Bureau of Labor Statistics describing the labor force in the United States reported that the average number of employed persons in 1993 was 116,712,000 and the average number of unemployed persons was 8,501,000. Averages and other descriptive measures are presented in Chapter 3.

A second aspect of statistics is called **inferential statistics**. This branch of statistics deals with problems requiring the use of a sample to infer something about the population. A **population** might consist of all the 3,336,000 people in Puerto Rico, or all 453,588 people in Wyoming. Or, the population might consist of all the teams in the Canadian Football League, the PE ratios for all chemical

2

stocks, and the total assets of the 20 largest banks in the United States. A population therefore, can be considered the total collection of people, prices, ages, the square footage of homes being constructed, and so on.

A **sample** is that part, or portion, of a population that is actually being studied. A sample might consist of 5,290 persons out of the 3,336,000 persons in Puerto Rico, 12 headlights selected for a life test, or the three scoops of grain selected at random to be tested for moisture content from a 15-ton truckload of grain. If we found that the three scoops of grain consisted of 1.50 percent moisture, we would infer that all the grain in the 15-ton load had 1.50 percent moisture. We start our discussion of inferential statistics in Chapter 4.

Types of Variables

There are two types of variables, quantitative and qualitative. When the characteristic being studied is *nonnumeric*, it is called a **qualitative variable**. A classification of students at your university by the state of birth, gender, or college affiliation (Business, Education, Liberal Arts, etc.) are examples of qualitative variables.

A variable that is reported *numerically* is called a **quantitative variable**. Examples include the balance in your checking account, the ages of the members of the United States Congress, the speeds of automobiles traveling along I–70 in Kansas, the number of customers served in the Commodore Barber Shop last week, or the number of new single family homes constructed by Reynolds Construction Company last year in Erie, Pennsylvania.

There are two types of quantitative variables, discrete and continuous. A **discrete variable** can only assume certain values and there is usually a "gap" between the values. Examples of discrete variables are: the number of children in a family, the number of customers in a carpet store in an hour, or number of commercials aired last hour on radio station WEND. A family can have 2 or 3 children, but not 2.456, or WEND can air 5 or 6 commercials, but not 5.75. Usually discrete variables result from counting.

A **continuous variable** can assume any value within a range. Examples of continuous variables are: the amount of snow for the winter of 1992-93 in Toronto, Ontario, the pressure in a tire, or a person's weight. Typically continuous variables are the result of measuring something. We can measure the pressure in a tire, or the amount of snow in Toronto.

Levels of Measurement

Data may be classified into four categories or levels of measurement. These categories are nominal, ordinal, interval, and ratio.

Nominal Level

When data can only be classified into categories, we refer to it as being **nominal** level of measurement. At this level the categories have no particular order or rank and are **mutually exclusive**, meaning that the characteristic can be tallied into only one category. For example, the Office of Special Education, U.S. Department of Education gave these counts of the number of handicapped children 3 to 21 years old who were in special educational programs.

Type of Handicapped	Number Served
Visual impairments	23,000
Serious emotional impairment	382,000
Speech impairments	974,000
Deaf-blindness	2,000
Learning disabilities	2,060,000
Mental retardation	565,000
Hearing impairments	58,000
Orthopedic impairments	48,000
All others	140,000
Total	4,252,000

The data is nominal level of measurement because it can only be classified into categories and it is immaterial what order the type of handicap is listed. Mental retardation could be listed first, serious emotional impairment second, and so on. The categories are mutually exclusive meaning that the type of handicap a child has can be counted into only one category. And such categories are said to be **exhaustive**, meaning that a handicapped child enrolled in the program must appear in one of the categories. Chapter 13 deals with data that is nominal level of measurement.

Ordinal Level

Ordinal level of measurement implies some sort of ranking. The Department of the Army gave these counts of females on active duty in 1992.

	Number
Commissioned officers	11,959
Warrant officers	505
Enlisted personnel	71,119

It is implied that female warrant officers are "higher" in rank than female enlisted personnel. And, commissioned officers are ranked higher than warrant officers. Further, the categories are mutually exclusive meaning that a female on active duty can only be counted in one category. She cannot be a commissioned officer and an enlisted personnel at the same time. Also, the categories are exhaustive meaning that a female *must* appear in one of the categories. Chapter 14 deals with tests involving ordinal level of measurement.

Interval Scale

For the **interval** scale of measurement the distance between numbers is constant. Temperature on the Fahrenheit scale is an example. Suppose the high temperature for the last 3 days was 85, 73, and 78 degrees Fahrenheit. We can easily put the readings in a rank order, but in addition we can study the difference readings. Why is this so? One degree on the Fahrenheit temperature scale is a constant unit of measure for all three days. Note in this example the zero point is just another point on the scale. It does not represent the absence of temperature, just that it is cold! Test scores are another example of the interval scale of measurement.

In addition to the constant difference characteristic, interval scaled data has all the features of nominal and ordinal measurements. Temperatures are mutually exclusive, that is the high temperature yesterday cannot be both 88 and 85 degrees. The "greater than" feature of ordinal data permits the ranking of daily high temperatures.

Ratio Scale

The **ratio** scale of measurement is the highest level. The zero point and the ratio of two observations are both meaningful. Weight, height, and money are examples of the ratio scale of measurement. If you have $20 and your friend has $10, then you have twice as much money as your friend. The zero point represents the absence of money. That is, the zero point is fixed and represents the absence of the characteristic being measured. If you have zero dollars you have none of the characteristic being measured.

GLOSSARY

Statistics—The body of techniques used to collect, organize, present, analyze, and interpret data to make better decisions.

Descriptive statistics—Techniques used to describe the data that have been collected.

Inferential statistics—A decision, estimation, prediction, or generalization about a population based on a sample.

Population—The total collection of people, individuals, objects, or measurements.

Sample—A portion or subset of the population.

Nominal scale—Data that are organized into categories the order of which is not important.

Ordinal scale—Data or categories that can be ranked, that is one category is higher than another.

Interval scale—The distance between numbers is a known or constant size, but the zero point is arbitrary.

Ratio scale—Data possessing a natural zero point and organized into measures for which differences are meaningful.

Mutually exclusive—If an object, item, or individual is classified in one category it is excluded from all others.

Exhaustive—Each object, item, or individual must fit in one of the categories.

CHAPTER ASSIGNMENT 1

What Is Statistics?

Name _____ Section _____ Score _____

PART I **Matching** Select the correct answer and write the appropriate letter in the space provided.

_____ 1. Statistics

_____ 2. Discrete data

_____ 3. Mutually exclusive

_____ 4. Ordinal scale

_____ 5. Ratio scale

_____ 6. Sample

_____ 7. Population

_____ 8. Nominal scale

_____ 9. Descriptive statistics

_____ 10 Inferential statistics

a. a part of the population

b. classification by hair color is an example

c. military ranks is an example

d. number of bedrooms in a house is an example

e. a sample item may be in only one category

f. pie charts are an example

g. weight is an example

h. the entire collection of objects

i. a generalization from a sample

j. a means of making better decisions

PART II **Multiple Choice** Select the correct answer and write the appropriate letter in the space provided.

_____ 11. The collection of all possible individuals, objects, or measurements is called a/an

    a. sample.
    b. exhaustive sample.
    c. population.
    d. ratio measurement.

_____ 12. Techniques used to determine something about a population, based on a sample, are called

    a. descriptive statistics.
    b. inferential statistics.
    c. robust statistics.
    d. mutually exclusive statistics.

_____ 13. An individual, object, or measurement that can appear in only one category is called

    a. exhaustive.
    b. nominal scale.
    c. interval scale.
    d. mutually exclusive.

_____ 14. The Equal Employment Opportunity Act requires employers to classify their employees by gender and by national origin. What level of measurement is this classification?

    a. Nominal
    b. Ordinal
    c. Interval
    d. Ratio

_____ 15. The number of auto accidents reported last month for each state is an example of which level of measurement?

    a. Nominal
    b. Ordinal
    c. Interval
    d. Ratio

_____ 16. The faculty at most universities is classified as Professors, Associate Professors, Assistant Professors and Instructors. This classification is an example of which level of measurement?

    a. Nominal
    b. Ordinal
    c. Interval
    d. Ratio

_____ 17. In your mathematics course last semester you received the following scores (out of 100) on the four tests: 88, 76, 92, and 86. These scores are examples of which level of measurement?

    a. Nominal
    b. Ordinal
    c. Interval
    d. Ratio

_____ 18. The difference between the interval and the ratio scale measurement is

    a. the zero point is meaningful for the ratio scale.
    b. all items fall into at least two categories.
    c. the items are *not* mutually exclusive.
    d. the data can be ranked.

_____ 19. In descriptive statistics we

    a. infer from a population to a sample.
    b. fit all the sample into at least one category.
    c. require the data to be interval scale.
    d. describe the conditions of the data.

_____ 20. Nominal data requires the categories to

    a. be mutually exclusive and exhaustive.
    b. be ranked.
    c. include zero.
    d. be divisible by 5.

_____ 21. Shoe sizes, such as 7B, 10AAA, and 12C, are examples of which level of measurement?

    a. Nominal
    b. Ordinal
    c. Interval
    d. Ratio

_____ 22. Which level of measurement is considered the "highest"?

    a. Nominal
    b. Ordinal
    c. Interval
    d. Ratio

2

SUMMARIZING DATA—FREQUENCY DISTRIBUTIONS AND GRAPHIC PRESENTATION

CHAPTER GOALS

After completing this chapter, you will be able to:

1. Organize raw data into a frequency distribution.
2. Develop a stem-and-leaf chart.
3. Draw a histogram, a frequency polygon, and a cumulative frequency polygon.
4. Summarize numerical information using charts, such as line charts, bar charts, and pie charts.

Introduction

This chapter begins our study of **descriptive statistics**. Recall from Chapter 1 that in descriptive statistics we describe a set of data. For example, suppose we want to describe the average entry level salary for a select group of professions. We find that the entry level salary for accountants is $28,000, for systems analysts $30,000, for infectious disease specialists $70,000, and so on. This unorganized data provides little insight into the pattern of entry salaries making conclusions difficult.

This chapter presents a technique that is used to organize raw data into a meaningful form. It is called a **frequency distribution**. Then the frequency distribution will be portrayed in the form of a frequency polygon, a histogram, or a cumulative frequency polygon to assist visualizing the salary structure of the various professions.

Frequency Distributions

A **frequency distribution** is a grouping of data into categories, showing the number of observations in each category. As noted, a frequency distribution is used to summarize large amounts of data into some meaningful form.

The steps to follow in developing a frequency distribution are:

1. Decide on the number of classes or the class interval.
2. Tally the observations into the appropriate classes.
3. Count the number of tallies in each class.

As an example, suppose the lengths of service, in years, of a sample of eight employees are:

4	3	2	6
5	8	4	4

The eight observations are the **raw data**. The first step is to arrange the data into an array. An **array** is an ordering of the data from low to high or high to low. Next, the number of years and the number of tallies for each year are determined.

Number of Years	Tallies	Number of Tallies
2	/	1
3	/	1
4	///	3
5	/	1
6	/	1
7		0
8	/	1

Then we condense this information. The values that occur within a particular interval are totaled. These intervals or groups are called **classes**. How many classes should there be? A common guideline is from 5 to 15. Having too few or too many classes gives little insight into the data. The size of the class interval may be a value such as 3, 5, 10, 15, 20, 50, 100, 1,000, and so on. The size, or width, of the **class interval** can be approximated by the formula:

$$\text{class interval} = \frac{\text{highest value} - \text{lowest value}}{\text{number of classes}}$$

Each class has a stated lower class limit and a stated upper class limit. The stated lower limit of the first class is usually slightly below the smallest value. Often it is a multiple of the class interval. Similarly, the upper stated class limit of the largest class is usually slightly larger than the largest value. In the previous example, the smallest number of years of service is 2. Therefore, we selected 1, which is slightly below 2, as the lower stated limit of the first class. The lower stated limit of the second class is 4 years. Six years is the upper stated limit of that class.

Note two employees have 1, 2, or 3 years of service. So the number of tallies in the 1–3 class is 2. There are 5 employees with 4, 5, or 6 years of service. So the class frequency for the 4–6 class is 5. The frequency distribution for the lengths of service is: (to simplify, only three classes are used):

Years of service	Class frequency
1–3	2
4–6	5
7–9	1

The number of tallies that occur in each class is called the **class frequency**. The class frequency of the lowest class is 2. For the next higher class it is 5.

The **class midpoint** divides a class into two equal parts. In the example, the class midpoint of the 7–9 class is 8, found by (7 + 9)/2. The **class interval** is the distance between the lower limit of two consecutive classes. It is 3, found by subtracting 1 (the lower stated limit of the first class) from 4 (the lower stated limit of the second class).

When constructing frequency distributions follow these guidelines:
1. Whenever possible, the width of the class intervals should be equal.
2. Avoid classes that overlap, such as 4–6 and 6–8. We would not be able to determine in which class to tally 6.
3. Avoid open-ended classes, such as "over 6."

Stem-and-Leaf Displays

This technique is a combination of sorting and graphing. It is an alternative to the frequency distribution for highlighting the pattern in the data. The first step is to locate the largest value and the smallest value. This will provide the range of the stem values. The stem is the leading digit or digits of the number, and the leaf is the trailing digit. For example, the number 15 has a stem value of 1 and a leaf value of 5. The number 231 has a stem value of 23 and a leaf value of 1.

The following are the amounts spent (in dollars) in the grocery store by a sample of 12 people.

$12	$28	$32	$24	$17	$06
34	18	22	42	36	26

The range of values is from $6 to $42. The first digit of each number is the stem and the second digit is the leaf. The first customer (upper left) spent $12. Hence, the stem value is 1 and the leaf value is 2. The completed display follows:

Leading Digit	Trailing Digit
0	6
1	278
2	2468
3	246
4	2

Graphically Portraying a Frequency Distribution

To get reader attention a frequency distribution is often portrayed graphically in a histogram or some other type of chart.

Histogram

The simplest type of a statistical chart is called a **histogram**. A histogram employs bars, whose heights correspond to the number of frequencies in each class. For the years of service for the sample of eight employees a histogram would appear as:

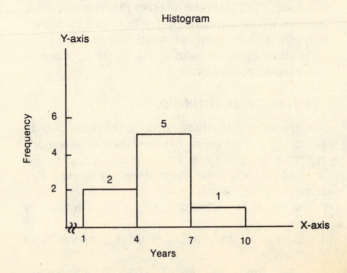

8

Frequency Polygon

A second type of chart used to portray a frequency distribution is the **frequency polygon**. For the frequency polygon, the assumption is that the observations in any particular class interval are represented by the class midpoint. For a frequency polygon, a dot is placed at the class midpoint opposite the number of frequencies in that class. For the distribution of years of service, the first plot is made by going to 2 years on the X-axis (the midpoint) and then going vertically on the Y-axis to 2 and placing a dot. This process is continued for all classes. Then the dots are connected.

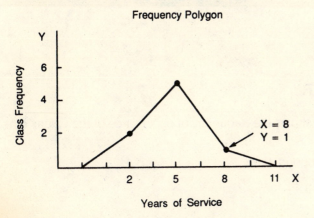

Frequency Polygon

Normal practice is to anchor the frequency polygon to the X-axis. This is accomplished by extending the graph lines to the midpoint of the class below the lowest class and to the midpoint of the class above the highest class.

Cumulative Frequency Polygon

A **cumulative frequency polygon** or **ogive** is used to show the number and percent of observations that occur less than a given value. Before we can draw a cumulative frequency polygon we must convert the frequency distribution to a cumulative frequency distribution. To construct a cumulative frequency distribution we add the frequencies from the lowest class to the highest class.

Years of Service	Class Frequency		Cumulative Frequency
1–3	2	add	2
4–6	5	down	7
7–9	1	↓	8

Notice in the cumulative frequency column that two workers had three or less years experience and

that seven had six or less years experience, and all eight had nine or less years of service. The cumulative frequencies are plotted on the vertical axis of the polygon.

The cumulative frequencies may also be converted to a percent. In the following chart the cumulative frequencies are on the left vertical axis, the cumulative percents on the right.

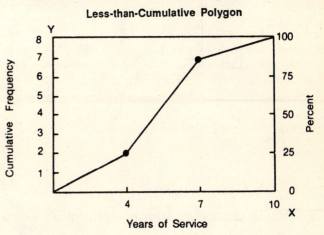

Less-than-Cumulative Polygon

Charts

Several charts are discussed in this chapter and each is designed to emphasize certain characteristics in the data. The **simple line chart** and the **simple bar chart** are often used when data are displayed over a period of time. In the line chart the values for the various periods are connected by a line. For a bar chart the data for each time period are represented by bars. Examples of the two charts using the total revenues, in millions of dollars for Ameritech Corporation for the years from 1987 to 1992.

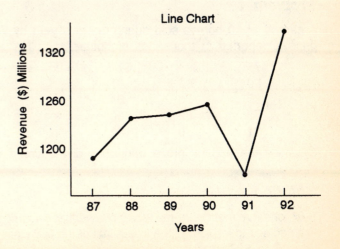

Line Chart

9

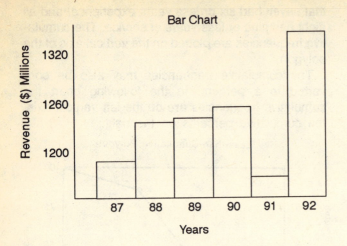

Bar Chart

A **pie chart**, widely used, is particularly useful if the relative size of the components are to be emphasized. (See Problem 8.)

GLOSSARY

Frequency distribution—An arrangement of the data that shows the frequency of occurrence of the values of interest.

Raw data—Numerical information presented in an ungrouped form.

Array—An ordering of the data from low to high or high to low.

Class—An interval between which data are tallied.

Class frequency—The number of observations or tallies that appear in each class.

Midpoint—A point that divides a class into two equal parts.

Histogram—A chart using bars to graphically portray the frequency distribution.

Frequency polygon—A chart using straight lines to graphically portray the frequency distribution.

Stem-and-leaf displays—A histogram in which tallies are replaced by digits in order to present data.

CHAPTER PROBLEMS

Problem 1

A sample of 30 homes sold during the past year by Waite Realty Company was selected for study. (Selling price is reported in thousands of dollars.)

$76	$94	$71	Low ———→ $67	$80		$78
80	82	67 ↙	88	72	High ———→	99
85	76	84	82	98		80
72	82	90	95	94		78
91	70	82	86	78		77

Organize these data into a frequency distribution and interpret your results.

Solution

First, observe that the home with the lowest selling price was $67 thousand and the highest was $99 thousand. We decided to let $65 be the lower limit of the first class and the class interval to be $5. Thus, the first class will be $65 to $69, and the second class $70 to $74, and so on.

10

Next, the selling prices are tallied into each of the classes. The first home sold for $76, therefore the price is tallied into the $75 thousand to $79 thousand class. The procedure is continued, resulting in the following frequency distribution.

Selling Price ($000)	Tallies	Number of Homes
$65 to $69	//	2
70 to 74	////	4
75 to 79	⊬ /	6
80 to 84	⊬ ///	8
85 to 89	///	3
90 to 94	////	4
95 to 99	///	3
		30

Observe that the largest concentration of the data is in the $80 to $84 thousand class.

As noted before, the class frequencies are the number of observations in each class. For the $65 to $69 class the class frequency is 2, and for the $70 to $74 class the frequency is 4. This indicates that two homes sold in the $65 to $69 thousand price range and four in the $70 to $74 thousand range. The smallest value that could be placed in the second class is $70 and the largest value is $74. Thus, $70 and $74 are the *stated limits* of the second class.

Recall that the selling prices are in thousands of dollars. For a house that sold for $70,389 the selling price would be given to the nearest thousand ($70 thousand). A home that sold for $69,832 would also be rounded to $70 and placed in the $70 to $74 class. Therefore, any house selling for $69,500 or more but less than $74,500 would be placed in the $70 to $74 class. The values of $69,500 and $74,500 are called the *true limits*.

The *class midpoint* is determined by going halfway between the stated limits, or halfway between the true limits. Using the second class as an example, the true limits are $69.5 to $74.5, halfway between these limits is $72.0, found by ($69.5 + $74.5)/2. The class midpoint may also be determined by using the stated limits. Again, using the second class as an example, the stated limits are $70 to $74, and halfway between these points is $72, found by ($70 + $74)/2.

The class interval is the difference between successive stated lower limits. In this case the class interval is $5, found by $70 − $65 = $5.

Stated Class Limits (in $000)	True Class Limits (in $000)	Midpoint (in $000)	Class Frequency
$65 to $69	$64.5 to $69.5	$67	2
70 to 74	69.5 to 74.5	72	4
75 to 79	74.5 to 79.5	77	6
80 to 84	79.5 to 84.5	82	8
85 to 89	84.5 to 89.5	87	3
90 to 94	89.5 to 94.5	92	4
95 to 99	94.5 to 99.5	97	3
			30

Exercise 1

Check your answers against those in the ANSWER section.

This is the first in a series of exercises designed to check your comprehension of the material just presented. It is suggested that you work all parts of the exercise. Then check your answers against those given in the answer section of this study guide.

The Jansen Motor Company has developed a new engine designed to further reduce gasoline consumption. The new engine was put in 20 mid-sized cars and the number of miles per gallon recorded (to the nearest mile per gallon).

29	32	19	30	40
27	28	21	36	20
27	18	32	37	29
30	23	25	19	30

Develop a frequency distribution. (Use a class interval of 10, with 15 the stated lower limit.)

Problem 2

Based on the information from Waite Realty in Problem 1, develop a histogram.

Solution

The class frequencies are scaled on the vertical axis (Y-axis) and the selling price on the horizontal (X-axis). A vertical line is drawn from the two true class limits of a class to a height corresponding to the number of frequencies. The tops of the lines are then connected. Two observations are in the $64.5 to $69.5 class. Thus, a vertical line is drawn at $64.5 and $69.5 up to 2. These lines are then connected to form the first bar. The remaining bars are constructed similarly.

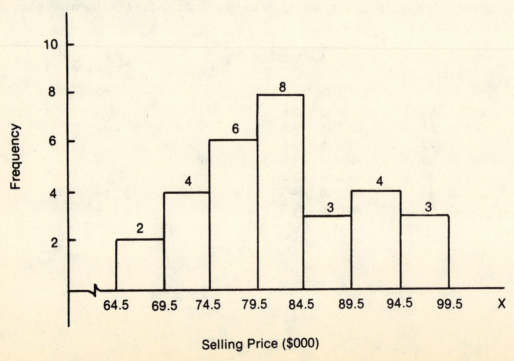

Selling Price ($000)

Problem 3

Based on the information from Problems 1 and 2, construct a frequency polygon.

Solution

The class frequencies are scaled on the vertical axis (Y-axis) and the class midpoints along the horizontal axis (X-axis). The first plot is at the point 67 on the X-axis and 2 on the Y-axis. To complete the frequency polygon, the midpoint of the class below the first class and above the last class are added. This allows the graph to be anchored to the X-axis at zero frequencies.

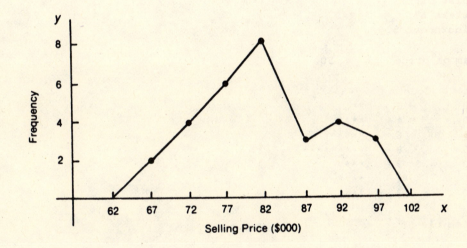

13

There are many computer software packages currently available. These packages will speed up the analysis and remove some of the likelihood of errors in computations. The package used most frequently in this study guide and the accompanying text is MINITAB. Following is the output for both a histogram and a stem-and-leaf display for the data in Problems 1, 2, and 3.

```
MTB >   set c1
DATA>   76, 80, 85, 72, 91, 94, 82, 76, 82, 70, 71, 67, 84, 90, 82, 67, 88, 82, 95, 86
DATA>   80, 72, 98, 94, 78, 78, 99, 80, 78, 77
DATA>   end
MTB >   name c1 'Price'
MTB >   hist c1;
SUBC>   start 67;
SUBC>   increment 5.

Histogram of price    N  =  30

Midpoint      Count
   67.00        2     **
   72.00        4     ****
   77.00        6     ******
   82.00        8     ********
   87.00        3     ***
   92.00        4     ****
   97.00        3     ***


MTB>    stem c1

Stem-and-leaf of price  N  =  30
Leaf Unit  =  1.0

    2        6    77
    6        7    0122
   12        7    667888
   (8)       8    00022224
   10        8    568
    7        9    0144
    3        9    589
```

The output for the histogram and the stem-and-leaf display from the MINITAB system is slightly different than that discussed earlier. Note the histogram is turned on its side. The stem-and-leaf display breaks the stem values into increments of 5 rather than 10. The left-hand column gives the number of observations less than the upper limit of the class, up to the middle value. That is, there are 12 homes selling for less than $79. The (8) indicates there are 8 observations between $80 and $94. The numbers below (8) indicate, for example, that 10 homes sold for more than $84, and that 7 sold for more than $90. Note using an increment of 5, the shape of the distribution is clearly revealed. A further discussion is presented in Problem 4.

Problem 4

Based on the information in Problems 1, 2, and 3, develop a stem-and-leaf chart.

Solution

As noted previously an observation is broken down into a leading digit and a trailing digit. Recall that the leading digit is called the *stem*, and the trailing digit the *leaf*. The first home sold for $76,000. The $000 were dropped, so the stem value is 7 and the leaf value is 6. The actual data range from $67 to $99, so the stem values range from 6 to 9 using an increment of 10.

Stem	Leaf
6	77
7	0122667888
8	00022224568
9	0144589

The display shows that there is a concentration of data in the $70–79 and the $80–89 groups.

Stem-and-leaf charts have several advantages over frequency distributions. First, recall that in Problem 1 we had to set up an array, then tally the values into the frequency distribution. The array is not required and the problem of establishing a class interval is eliminated. Second, if our initial class intervals prove to be unsatisfactory, changing the class intervals can be time consuming. Third, by keeping the spaces allotted to the leaves equal, a stem-and-leaf display provides a visual picture of the number of observations in each class. Finally, the general pattern as well as the actual data is presented. In a frequency distribution actual values are lost.

Exercise 4

Check your answers against those in the ANSWER section.

Use the Jansen Motor Company data in Exercise 1 to construct a stem-and-leaf chart.

Problem 5

Based on the information in Problem 1, construct a cumulative frequency polygon or ogive.

a. Estimate the price below which 75 percent of the homes were sold.
b. Estimate the number of homes sold for less than $72,000.

Solution

A cumulative frequency distribution (also called an ogive) is constructed by using the true upper class limits. The first step is to determine the number of observations "less than" the true upper limit of each class. Two homes were sold for less than $69.5 and six were sold for less than $74.5. The six is found by adding the two that sold for $65 to $69 thousand and the four that sold for between $70 and $74 thousand. The cumulative frequency for the fourth class is obtained by adding the frequencies of the first four classes. The total is 20, found by 2 + 4 + 6 + 8. The cumulative frequency distribution would appear as:

True Limits ($000)	Class Frequency		Cumulative Frequency
64.5—69.5	2	ADD	2
69.5—74.5	4		6
74.5—79.5	6		12
79.5—84.5	8		20
84.5—89.5	3		23
89.5—94.5	4		27
94.5—99.5	3		30

To construct a cumulative frequency polygon the upper true limits are scaled on the X-axis and the cumulative frequencies on the Y-axis. The cumulative percents are placed along the right-hand scale (vertical) scale. The first plot is X = 69.5 and Y = 2. The next plot is 74.5 and 6. As shown, the points are connected with straight lines. (See the following chart.)

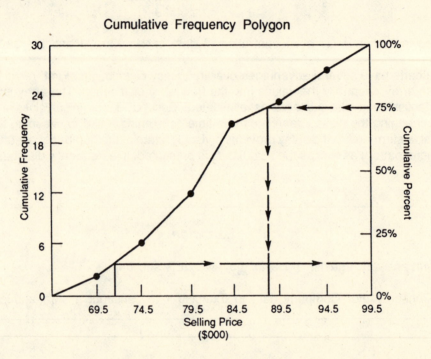

Cumulative Frequency Polygon

To estimate the amount for which less than 75 percent of the homes were sold, a horizontal line is drawn from the cumulative percent (75) over to the cumulative frequency polygon. At the intersection, a line is drawn down to the X-axis giving the approximate selling price. It is about $88 thousand. Thus, about 75 percent of the homes sold for $88,000 or less.

To estimate the percent of the homes that sold for less than $72,000 first locate the value of $72 on the X-axis. Next, draw a vertical line from the X-axis at 72 up to the graph. Draw a line horizontally to the cumulative percent axis and read the cumulative percent. It is about 12%. Hence, we conclude that about 12 percent of the homes sold for less than $72,000.

Exercise 5

Check your answers against those in the ANSWER section.

Use the Jansen Motor Company data in Exercise 1 to construct a less-than-cumulative frequency polygon. (a) Estimate the percent of the automobiles getting less than 30 miles per gallon. (b)Twenty percent of the automobiles obtain how many miles per gallon or less?

Problem 6

The percentage of disposable income (disposable income is the amount left after taxes) spent for groceries for the period 1970 to 1990 is shown below. Draw a simple line chart to depict the trend.

Year	Percent of Disposable Income on Groceries
1970	13.0%
1975	12.3
1980	11.2
1985	10.1
1990	9.5

Source: *Your Money, Personal Financial News for GMAC*, Vol. 2 No 2.

Solution

Time (five year intervals in this problem) is scaled on the horizontal axis, and the percent of disposable income spent for groceries on the vertical axis. Note that the vertical axis is broken. That is, some of the values are omitted. In this case the first value reported is 13.0%. The first plot therefore, is at 1970 and 13.0%. To plot move vertically from 1970 to 13.0% and place a dot. The next plot is 1975 and 12.3%. Continue this process for the remaining three periods. The dots are then connected with straight lines. What information does the chart convey? It appears we are spending a smaller percent of disposable income for groceries.

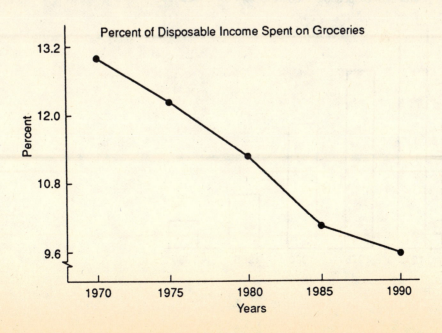

Percent of Disposable Income Spent on Groceries

17

Problem 7

Refer to Problem 6. Develop a simple bar chart for the percent of disposable income spent for groceries.

Solution

The usual practice is to scale time along the horizontal axis. The height of the bars corresponds to percent of disposable income spent for groceries. To form the first bar, draw parallel vertical lines from 1970 up 13.0%. Draw a line parallel to the *X*-axis at 13.0% to connect the lines. This process is continued for the other periods. The intrepretation of the chart is the same as **Problem 6**, we are spending a smaller and smaller proportion of disposable income for groceries.

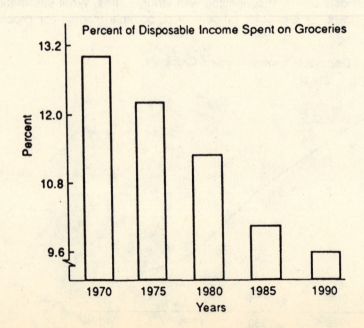

18

Problem 8

The purpose of home equity loans and the percent of each type of loan relative to the total is shown below:

Loan Purpose	Percent of Total	Cumulative Percent
Home Improvement	32%	32%
Debt Consolidation	30	62
Car Purchase	11	73
Education	10	83
Other	9	92
Investments	8	100

Portray the home equity loans information in the form of a pie chart.

Solution

The first step is to draw a circle. Next draw a line from 0 to the center of the circle and another from the center of the circle to 32%. Adding the 32% for home improvements and the 30% for debt consolidation gives 62%. A line is drawn from the center to 62%. The area between 32% and 62% represents the percent of equity loans for debt consolidation. The process is continued for the remaining cumulative percents.

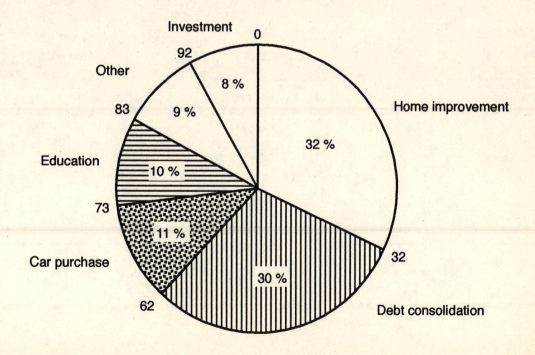

Source: *Your Money, Personal Financial News for GMAC*, Vol. 2, No. 2.

Exercise 8

Check your answers against those in the ANSWER section.

New cars sold in the United States in 1993 are classified into the following categories.

Manufacturer	Cars sold (Millions)
General Motors	3.2
Ford	1.8
Chrysler	2.5
Foreign	2.5

Portray these data in the form of a pie chart.

CHAPTER ASSIGNMENT 2

Summarizing Data: Frequency Distributions and Graphic Presentation

Name _____ Section _____ Score _____

PART I **Matching** Select the correct answer and write the appropriate letter in the space provided.

_____	1.	raw data
_____	2.	class
_____	3.	class midpoint
_____	4.	histogram
_____	5.	frequency distribution
_____	6.	interval
_____	7.	array
_____	8.	pie chart
_____	9.	class frequency
_____	10	Stem-and-leaf chart

a. tallies replaced by digits

b. these data are ordered from low to high

c. ungrouped data

d. chart that portrays a frequency distribution

e. a chart to portray nominal scale data

f. arrangement of data to show the frequency of occurrence

g. an interval between which data are tallied

h. number of tallies in a class

i. distance within a class

j. point that divides a class into two parts

PART II **Multiple Choice** Select the correct answer and write the appropriate letter in the space provided.

_____ 11. A grouping of data into categories giving the number of observations in each category is called a(n)

    a. array.
    b. frequency distribution.
    c. pie chart.
    d. component bar chart.

_____ 12. A listing of all the observations in a sample from smallest to largest is called a(n)

    a. array.
    b. histogram.
    c. frequency distribution.
    d. class interval.

_____ 13. The distance between the largest and the smallest value in a class is called the

    a. class interval.
    b. class midpoint.
    c. class frequency.
    d. histogram.

_____ 14. The class midpoint is

    a. obtained by adding the upper and lower class limits and dividing by 2.
    b. used to represent the class.
    c. obtained by adding the true lower limit and the true upper limit of a class and dividing by 2.
    d. All of the above.

_____ 15. The number of observations in a particular class is called the class

   a. interval.
   b. midpoint.
   c. frequency.
   d. None of the above.

_____ 16. In a less-than-cumulative frequency distribution the class frequencies are added from the

   a. largest frequency to the smallest.
   b. smallest frequency to the largest.
   c. first class to the last.
   d. last class to the first.

_____ 17. In constructing a frequency distribution, it is usually good practice to

   a. avoid open-ended classes.
   b. have more than 20 classes.
   c. have unequal class intervals.
   d. All of the above.

_____ 18. A difference between a histogram and a stem-and-leaf display is

   a. the identity of the original data is lost in a histogram.
   b. a histogram cannot be used for more than 30 observations.
   c. a stem-and-leaf display must have an interval of 100.
   d. All of the above are correct.

_____ 19. A pie chart requires

   a. only the nominal scale of measurement.
   b. at least ranked data.
   c. at least interval scale of measurement.
   d. at least the ratio scale of measurement.

_____ 20. A graphic representation of a frequency distribution constructed by erecting vertical bars is called a

   a. histogram.
   b. line chart.
   c. pie chart.
   d. pictogram.

PART III Problems Record your answer in the space provided. Show essential calculations.

21. A sample of 30 students at Ivy Tech were asked the one way distance in miles they travel to class. The information is reported below.

10	14	9	8	11	1	6	10	8	12
7	5	7	6	8	8	5	12	10	7
2	13	10	12	10	11	8	10	9	3

a. Organize the data into a frequency distribution. Use an interval of 3 and 0 as the stated lower limit of the first class.

b. Determine a cumulative frequency distribution.

23

22. The following stem-and-leaf display is given for the length of service, in months, for a sample of accountants at a large electronics firm.

Stem	Leaf
5	147
6	33689
7	1123459
8	011234458
9	122499

a. How many accountants were studied? _____

b. What was the shortest and the longest length of service? _____ shortest _____ longest

c. How many accountants have been with the company less than 70 months? _____

d. How many accountants have been with the company 80 months or more? _____

e. List the lengths of service for accountants with 50 to 59 months of service. _____

23. The following is a breakdown of the marital status of U.S. residents over the age of 18. Develop a pie chart to graphically portray the data.

Marital Status	Millions of People
Married	107.0
Single	36.0
Widowed	12.8
Divorced	12.0

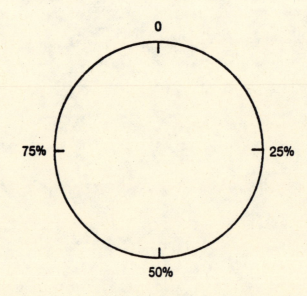

24

3

DESCRIBING DATA—MEASURES OF CENTRAL TENDENCY AND DISPERSION

CHAPTER GOALS

After completing this chapter, you will be able to:

1. Compute the mean, median, and mode for both upgrouped (raw) data and grouped data.
2. Describe the characteristics of the mean, the median, and the mode.
3. Compute the geometric mean and the weighted mean.
4. Compute measures of dispersion.
5. Explain Chebyshev's Theorem and the Normal rule.
6. Compute and interpret the coefficient of variation and the coefficient of skewness.

Introduction

What is an **average**? It is a single number used to describe the central tendency of a set of data. Examples of an average are:

1. The average stock traded on the New York Stock Exchange (NYSE) gained 23¢ yesterday.
2. The Treasury Department sold $10.6 billion in three month treasury bills this week at an average discount of 5.19%.
3. The Perrysburg Yellow Jacket football team averaged 6.3 yards each time they ran the football during the 1993 season.

There are several different types of averages. We will consider five: the **arithmetic mean**, the **median**, the **mode**, the **weighted mean**, and the **geometric mean**.

A comparison of two sets of data based only on two measures of central tendency can be misleading. For example, suppose a statistics instructor had two classes, one in the morning and one in the evening; each with six students. In the morning class the students' ages are: 18, 20, 21, 21, 23, and 23 years. In the evening class the ages are 17, 17, 18, 20, 25, and 29 years. Note that for both classes the mean age is 21 years but there is more variation or dispersion in the ages of the evening students. This chapter considers several measures of dispersion, namely, the **range**, the **mean deviation**, the **variance**, the **standard deviation**, the **interquartile range**, and the **quartile deviation**.

Measures of Central Tendency

The most widely used measure of central tendency is the **arithmetic mean** or simply the **mean**. It is calculated by summing the observations and dividing the total by the number of observations. Last year the dividends paid for three stocks were: $0.45, $0.75, and $1.11 per share. The sum of these three values is $2.31. The mean dividend is $0.77, found by $2.31/3. Notice that all three of the stocks were included in the calculation.

In some situations the arithmetic mean may not be representative of the data. For example, the mean annual income of a group of five executives is $94,800. Their salaries were: $40,000, $42,000, $44,000, $48,000, and $300,000. Notice how the one extreme value ($300,000) pulled the mean upward. Four of the five executives earned less than the mean, raising a question whether the arithmetic mean value of $94,800 is typical of the five executives.

The **median** is a useful average when a problem with an extreme value is encountered. To determine the median, the values are ordered from low to high or high to low and the middle value selected. Hence, half the observations are above the median and half are below it. For the above executive incomes, the middle value is $44,000, the median. It is a more representative value in this problem than the mean of $94,800.

Note that there were an odd number of executive incomes (5). For an odd number of ungrouped values we just order them and select the middle value. To determine the median of an even number of ungrouped values, the first step is to arrange them from low to high as usual, and then determine the value half way between the two middle values. Thus, the median may not be one of the values in the set of data. As an example, the final grades of the six students in Mathematics 126 were: 87, 62, 91, 58, 99, and 85. Ordering these from low to high: 58, 62, 85, 87, 91, and 99. The median grade is halfway between the two middle values of 85 and 87. The median is 86. The location of the median is found by $(n + 1)/2$.

A third measure of central tendency is the **mode**. The mode is the value that occurs most often in a set of ungrouped data. The dividends per share declared on five stocks were: $3, $2, $4, $5, and $4. Since $4 occurred twice, which was the most frequent, the mode is $4.

The **weighted mean** is another average. It is particularly useful when various classes or groups contribute differently to the total. For example, the coronary care unit of a certain hospital consists of nurses' aides, practical nurses, and registered nurses. If their hourly wages are $6, $7, and $11, respectively, it would not be accurate to say the average hourly wage is $8, found by ($6 + $7 + $11)/3, unless there was the same number in each group. Suppose the care unit consisted of ten employees. The one aide earns $6, the two practical nurses earn $7, and seven registered nurses earn $11 an hour. The $6 is weighted by 1, the $7 by 2, and the $11 by 7 to determine the weighted mean. The weighted mean is $9.70. That is:

$$[\$6 \times 1 + \$7 \times 2 + \$11 \times 7]/10 = \$9.70$$

The **geometric mean** is used to determine the mean percent increase from one period to another.

Skewness

The mean, median, and mode represent only the central tendency of a set of data. They do not suggest anything about the shape of the distribution. All frequency distributions do not have the same shape. Some may have a long tail to the right, or a long tail to the left. Such distributions are referred to as being **skewed**. If the long tail is to the right, the distribution is said to be **positively skewed**. If there is a long tail to the left, the distribution is said to be **negatively skewed**. A distribution that has the

same shape on either side of the center is **symmetrical**. This information is summarized in the following diagrams.

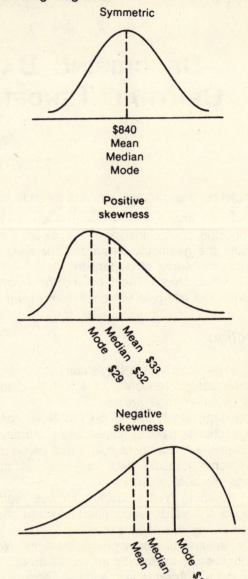

Where are the various averages located in the data? If the distribution is symmetrical and bell-shaped, the mean, median, and mode are equal. When the distribution is positively skewed, the mean is largest of the three averages and the mode is smallest. When the distribution is negatively skewed, the mean is smallest and the mode largest. The mode always appears on the apex (tallest point) on the curve, and the mean is pulled in the direction of the tail. The median always appears between the mode and the mean, regardless of the direction of the tail.

Measures of Dispersion

Perhaps the simplest measure of dispersion is the range. The **range** is the difference between the largest and the smallest observation. Recall that the oldest student in the morning statistics class was 23, the youngest 18. The range is 5 years, found by 23 – 18. For the evening class it is 12, found by 29 – 17. Thus we can say that there is more spread in the ages of the students enrolled in the evening class compared with the day class (because 12 years is greater than 5 years). The advantages of the range are that it is easy to compute and easy to understand.

The range has two disadvantages. It can be distorted by a single extreme value. Suppose the same statistics instructor has a third class of five students. The ages of these students are 20, 20, 21, 22, and 60 years. The range of ages is 40 years, yet four of the five students' ages are within two years of each other. The 60-year-old student has distorted the spread. Another disadvantage is that only two values, the largest and the smallest, are used in its calculation.

In contrast to the range, the **mean deviation** considers all the data. It is computed by first determining the difference between each observation and the mean. These differences are then averaged without regard to their signs. For the evening statistics class the mean deviation is 4.0 years, found by $(|17 - 21| + |17 - 21| + |18 - 21| + |20 - 21| + |25 - 21| + |29 - 21|)/6$. The parallel lines | | indicate absolute values. To interpret, 4.0 years is the average amount by which the ages differ from the mean age of 21.0 years.

The disadvantage of the mean deviation is that the absolute values are difficult to manipulate mathematically. The problem of absolute values is eliminated by squaring the differences. These squared differences are used in the computation of the **variance** and the **standard deviation**.

Squaring units of measurement, such as dollars or years, makes the variance cumbersome to use since it yields units like "dollars squared" or "years squared." However, by calculating the standard deviation, which is the positive square root of the variance, we can return to the original units, such as years or dollars. Because the standard deviation is easier to interpret, it is more widely used than is the mean deviation or the variance.

Chebyshev's Theorem and the Normal Rule

The standard deviation can be used to estimate the proportion of the observations that lie within a specified number of standard deviations from the mean. **Chebyshev's Theorem** states that, regardless of the shape of the distribution, at least $1 - 1/k^2$ of the observations will be within k standard deviations of the mean. k must be greater than 1.

If the distribution is approximately symmetrical and bell shaped then the **Normal Rule** is applied. This rule states that the mean, plus and minus one standard deviation will include about 68 percent of the observations. The mean plus and minus two standard deviations includes about 95 percent of the observations. Virtually all (99.7%) of the observations will lie within three standard deviations of the mean.

The Interquartile Range and the Quartile Deviation

Two other measures of dispersion are the **interquartile range** and the **quartile deviation**. Both are concerned with the middle 50 percent of the observations. How are they computed? First, we order the data from smallest to largest. Recall that the median divides these ordered values so that half are below it and half are above it. The lower half of the values can be further subdivided so that one-fourth are less than a particular value. This value is called the *first quartile*, designated Q_1. Similarly, the upper half of the observations is divided in half at the third quartile, Q_3.

The interquartile range is the distance between the first and the third quartiles. The quartile deviation is half that distance. What are the advantages of these measures? Both are easy to compute and not affected by extremely large or extremely small values. The disadvantage is that not all observations are used.

Relative Dispersion and Skewness

The **coefficient of variation** is used to compare the variability of two sets of data that are measured in different units. It is a measure of relative dispersion. To compute the coefficient of variation, the standard deviation is divided by the mean and the result is multiplied by 100. This measure reports the standard deviation as a percent of the mean.

For example, suppose in a study of executives the coefficient of variation for incomes is 29 percent and for their ages is 12 percent. We would conclude that there is more relative dispersion in the incomes of the executives than in their ages.

Another characteristic of a distribution is its **skewness**. A **symmetric** distribution has the same shape on either side of the median and it has no skewness. For a *positively skewed* distribution the long tail is to the right, the mean is larger than the median or the mode, and the mode appears at the highest point on the curve. For a *negatively skewed* distribution the mode is the largest value and is at the highest point of the curve, while the mean is the smallest.

The **coefficient of skewness**, designated sk, measures the amount of skewness and may range from –3.0 to +3.0. It is computed by subtracting the median from the mean, multiplying the result by 3, and dividing by the standard deviation.

GLOSSARY

Measure of central tendency—A value that is typical or representative of the data.

Mean—The sum of the observations divided by the total number of observations.

Median—The value of the observation in the center after they have been arranged from the smallest to the largest, or vice versa.

Mode—The value that appears most frequently in a set of data.

Symmetrical—A distribution that has the same shape on either side of the median.

Positively skewed—The distribution is not symmetrical. The long tail is to the right, that is, in the positive direction. The mean is larger than the median or mode. The mode occurs at the apex of the curve.

Negatively skewed—The distribution is not symmetrical. The long tail is to the left, or in the negative direction. The mean is smaller than the median or mode. The mode occurs at the apex of the curve.

Geometric mean—The nth root of the product of n observations.

Weighted mean—The value of each observation is multiplied by the number of times it occurs. The sum of these products is divided by the total number of observations to give the weighted mean.

Dispersion—The degree of variation in the data.

Range—The difference between the largest and smallest value in a set of data.

Mean deviation—The mean of the absolute values of the deviations from the arithmetic mean.

Variance—The mean of the squared deviations between each observation and the mean.

Standard deviation—The positive square root of the variance. A measure of dispersion reported in the same units as the original data.

Interquartile range—The difference between the values of the first and third quartile, indicating the range of the middle fifty percent of the observations.

Quartile deviation—Half of the interquartile range.

Chebyshev's Theorem—The proportion of observation in any data set that occurs within k standard deviations of the mean. It is equal to $[1 - (1/k^2)]$, where k is greater than 1.0.

Normal Rule—About 68 percent of the observations will lie within one standard deviation of the mean; about 95 percent of the observations will lie within two standard deviations of the mean; and virtually all (99.7%) will lie within three standard deviations of the mean.

Coefficient of variation—A measure of relative dispersion, which expresses the standard deviation as a percent of the mean. It is useful for comparing distributions in different units.

Coefficient of skewness—A measure of the lack of symmetry of a distribution. It relates the difference between the mean and the median to the standard deviation.

CHAPTER PROBLEMS

Problem 1

A comparison shopper employed by a large grocery chain recorded these prices for a 340-gram jar of Kraft blackberry preserves at six supermarkets selected at random.

Supermarket	Price X
1	$1.31
2	1.35
3	1.26
4	1.42
5	1.31
6	1.33
	$7.98

Compute the mean, median, and mode.

Solution

The *arithmetic mean* price of this raw data (ungrouped data) is determined by summing the prices for the six jars and dividing the total by six. This is a sample. The formula for the arithmetic mean of a sample is:

$$\bar{X} = \frac{\Sigma X}{n} = \frac{\$7.98}{6} = \$1.33 \qquad [3-1]$$

where $\bar{X}$ (read X bar) represents the sample mean, X is a particular value, Σ is the Greek capital letter sigma and it signifies the operation of adding all the values. (Note: The formula for the sample mean is numbered 3-1. This corresponds the formula in the text. This makes it easy to refer to it.)

Note: Had the Kraft blackberry preserve prices represented a population, that is, all the supermarkets in the area, the calculations would be the same but the notation would be somewhat different. Using formula 3-2 the calculation are:

$$\mu = \frac{\Sigma X}{N} = \frac{\$7.98}{6} = \$1.33 \qquad [3-2]$$

where μ (mu) represents the population mean, and N is the total number in the population.

The *median* is the middle value of the set of data after they have been ordered from smallest to largest. Note below for this set of ungrouped data there are six prices. There are an **even** number of prices. The median price is half way between the third and fourth price.

$$\text{Median} = \frac{\$1.31 + \$1.33}{2} = \$1.32$$

Prices Arranged
from
Low to High

$1.26
1.31
1.31 ⎫
1.33 ⎭ ◄——————— median
1.35
1.42

Suppose there are an **odd** number of prices such as, $1.31, $1.31, $1.33 , $1.35, and $1.42. The median is the middle value ($1.33). Of course, the values must first be ordered from low to high.

The *mode* is the price that occurs most often. The price of $1.31 per jar occurs twice and is the mode.

Exercise 1

Check your answers against those in the ANSWER section.

The number of miles driven to class by a sample of seven college students is: 8, 5, 4, 10, 8, 3, and 4.

Compute the mean, median, and mode.

Problem 2

The hourly wages for a sample of plumbers were grouped into the following frequency distribution. Since the wages have been grouped into classes, we refer to the following distribution as being *grouped data*.

Hourly Wages	Number f
$ 8–$ 9	3
10– 11	6
12– 13	12
14– 15	10
16– 17	7
18– 19	2
	40

Compute the arithmetic mean, the median, and the mode.

Solution

The arithmetic mean of the data grouped into a frequency distribution is computed by formula 3–8:

$$\bar{X} = \frac{\Sigma fX}{n} \qquad [3\text{--}8]$$

where X is the class midpoint, f is the frequency of occurrence, and n is the total number of observations.

It is assumed that the observations in each class are represented by the midpoint of the class. Using either the stated class limits, or the true class limits, the midpoint of the first class is $8.50 found by ($8.00 + $9.00)/2. For the next higher class, the midpoint is $10.50. Using formula 3–8, the arithmetic mean hourly wage is $13.40.

Wage Rate	Frequency f	Class Midpoint X	fX
$ 8–$ 9	3	$ 8.50	$ 25.50
10– 11	6	10.50	63.00
12– 13	12	12.50	150.00
14– 15	10	14.50	145.00
16– 17	7	16.50	115.50
18– 19	2	18.50	37.00
Total	40		$536.00

Determining the arithmetic mean hourly wage:

$$\bar{X} = \frac{\Sigma fX}{n} = \frac{\$536.00}{40} = \$13.40$$

The median of data grouped into a frequency distribution is found by applying formula 3–9.

$$\text{Median} = L + \frac{\frac{n}{2} - CF}{f} \, (i) \qquad [3\text{–}9]$$

where L is the lower true limit of the class containing the median, n is the total number of frequencies, CF is the cumulative number of frequencies in the class immediately preceding the class containing the median, and i is the width of the class containing the median.

The hourly wage distribution is repeated and a column giving the cumulative frequencies included.

	Hourly Wages	Frequency f	Cumulative Frequency CF
	$ 8–$ 9	3	3
	10– 11	6	9
Median Class	12– 13	12	21
	14– 15	10	31
	16– 17	7	38
	18– 19	2	40

The *median class* is located by dividing the total number of observations by 2. Thus, 40/2 = 20. The class containing the 20th plumber can be located by referring to the cumulative frequency column. Notice that 9 plumbers earn less than $11.50 (the true upper limit of the $10–$11 class). And, 21 plumbers earn less than $13.50, the true upper limit of the $12–$13 class. Thus, the 20th plumber earns some amount between $11.50 and $13.50. The lower true limit (L) of that class is $11.50. The class in the middle is designated as the *median class*.

The cumulative number of frequencies (CF) in the class preceding the median class is 9. The number of frequencies (f) in the median class is 12. The width of the median class (i) is $2.00. Solving for the median:

$$\text{Median} = L + \frac{\frac{n}{2} - CF}{f} = \$11.50 + \frac{\frac{40}{2} - 9}{12} \, (\$2.00) = \$13.33$$

The mode is the value that occurs most often. For data grouped into a frequency distribution, the mode is the midpoint of the class containing the most observations. There are more observations (12) in the $12.00 to $13.00 class than in any other class. The midpoint of the class is $12.50 which is the mode.

We computed three measures of central tendency for the hourly wage data. Observe that the mean ($13.40), the median ($13.33), and the mode ($12.50) are all different. Generally, this is the case. What measure of central tendency to select to represent the data will be discussed shortly.

Problem 3

At Sarasota College there are 10 instructors, 12 assistant professors, 20 associate professors, and 5 professors. Their annual salaries are instructor $32,000, assistant professors $35,000, associate professors $38,000, and professors $44,000 respectively. What is the weighted mean salary?

Solution

The number of faculty within each rank is not equal. Therefore, it is not appropriate simply to add the average salaries of the four ranks and divide by 4. We have a better method for weighting the averages. In this problem the salaries for each rank are multiplied by the number of faculty in that rank, the products totalled, then divided by the number of faculty. The result is the weighted mean.

The calculations using formula 3–4 are:

$$\overline{X}_w = \frac{w_1 X_1 + w_2 X_2 + w_3 X_3 + w_4 X_4}{w_1 + w_2 + w_3 + w_4} \qquad [3\text{--}4]$$

$$= \frac{10(\$32,000) + 12(\$35,000) + 20(\$38,000) + 5(\$44,000)}{10 + 12 + 20 + 5}$$

$$= \frac{\$1,720,000}{47}$$

$$= \$36,596$$

Problem 4

Croquet as a sport grew rapidly of the 80s. From 1977 to 1991 the number of croquet clubs in the United States increased from 5 to 300[1]. Compute the mean annual percent increase in the number of croquet clubs.

---

[1]Source: *Vitality*, August 1991, page 24.

32

Solution

The geometric mean annual percent increase from one time period to another is determined from text formula 3–7.

$$GM = \sqrt[n-1]{\frac{\text{Value at the end of the period}}{\text{Value at the start of the period}}} - 1 \qquad [3\text{--}7]$$

Note that there are 15 years involved. However, there are only 14 annual rates of change. That is, we compute the changes from 1977 to 1978, from 1978 to 1979, and so forth. So, n is 15 and $n - 1 = 15 - 1 = 14$ annual percent increases.

$$GM = \sqrt[15-1]{\frac{300}{5}} - 1 = \sqrt[14]{60.0} - 1$$

The 14th root of 60 is 1.33971, found by

$$\sqrt[14]{60} = \frac{\log \text{ of } 60}{14} = \frac{1.77815125}{14} = 0.127010803$$

The antilog of 0.127010803 is 1.33971. The value 1 is subtracted, according to formula 3–7, so the rate of increase is .33971, or 33.971% per year. Croquet clubs are increasing at a rate of almost 34% per year.

Exercise 3

Check your answers against those in the ANSWER section.

In 1945, there were 51 countries with membership in the United Nations. In 1990 there were 159 countries. What was the geometric mean annual percent increase?

Source: *USA Today*, September 17, 1991, Section A, page 1.

Problem 5

A sample of the amounts spent in November to heat all-electric homes of similar sizes in Scarsdale revealed these amounts (to the nearest dollar):

$212, $191, $176, $129, $106, $92, $108, $109, $103, $121, $175, $194

What is the range? Interpret your results.

Solution

The range is the difference between the largest and the smallest observation.

$$\text{Range} = \text{Highest-Lowest}$$
$$= \$212 - \$92 = \$120$$

This indicates that there is a difference of $120 between the largest and the smallest heating cost.

Problem 6

Using the heating cost data in Problem 5, compute the mean deviation.

Solution

The mean deviation is the mean of the absolute deviations from the mean. For raw, or ungrouped data, it is first computed by determining the mean. Next, the difference between each value and the mean is determined. Finally, these differences are totaled and the total divided by the number of observations. The formulas for sample mean (3–1) and for the mean deviation formula (3–10) are shown below.

Sample Mean

$$\overline{X} = \frac{\Sigma X}{n}$$

Mean Deviation

$$MAD = \frac{\Sigma |X - \overline{X}|}{n}$$

where X is the value of each observation, $\overline{X}$ is the arithmetic mean of the values, n is the number of observations, and $|\;|$ indicates the absolute value. In other words, the signs of the deviations from the mean are disregarded.

Payment X	$X - \overline{X}$		Absolute Deviations
$ 212	|$+69|	=	$ 69
191	| +48|	=	48
176	| +33|	=	33
129	| −14|	=	14
106	| −37|	=	37
92	| −51|	=	51
108	| −35|	=	35
109	| −34|	=	34
103	| −40|	=	40
121	| −22|	=	22
175	| +32|	=	32
194	| +51|	=	51
$1,716			$466

$$\overline{X} = \frac{\Sigma \overline{X}}{n} = \frac{\$1,716}{12} = \$143.00$$

$$MAD = \frac{\Sigma |X - \overline{X}|}{n} = \frac{\$466}{12} = \$38.83$$

Indicating that on the average the electric bills deviate $38.83 from the mean of $143.00.

Problem 7

Using the same heating cost data in Problem 5, compute the variance and the standard deviation.

Solution

The sample variance, designated s^2, is based on squared deviations from the mean. For ungrouped data it is computed using formula 3–14 or 3–15.

Formula 3–14

$$s^2 = \frac{\Sigma(X - \overline{X})^2}{n - 1}$$

Formula 3–15

$$s^2 = \frac{\Sigma X^2 - \frac{(\Sigma X)^2}{n}}{n - 1}$$

Computing the sample variance both ways:

X	X − $\overline{X}$	(X − $\overline{X}$)²	X²
$ 212	$69	4,761	44,944
191	48	2,304	36,481
176	33	1,089	30,976
129	−14	196	16,641
106	−37	1,369	11,236
92	−51	2,601	8,464
108	−35	1,225	11,664
109	−34	1,156	11,881
103	−40	1,600	10,609
121	−22	484	14,641
175	32	1,024	30,625
194	51	2,601	37,636
$1,716	0	20,410	265,798

$$s^2 = \frac{\Sigma(X - \overline{X})^2}{n - 1} = \frac{20,410}{12 - 1} = 1,855.45$$

Computed using the actual values:

$$s^2 = \frac{\Sigma X^2 - \frac{(\Sigma X)^2}{n}}{n - 1}$$

$$= \frac{265,798 - \frac{(\$1,716)^2}{12}}{12 - 1}$$

$$= 1,855.45$$

The standard deviation of the sample, designated by s, is the square root of the variance. The square root of 1,855.45 is $43.07. Note that the standard deviation is in the same terms as the original data, that is, dollars.

Exercise 4

Check your answers against those in the ANSWER section.

The manager of a fast-food restaurant selected several checks at random. The amounts spent by customers were $2, $5, $6, $4, and $3. Compute the range, mean deviation, sample variance, and sample standard deviation.

Problem 8

The office manager of the Mallard Glass Company is investigating the ages in months of the company's word processing equipment currently in use. The ages of 30 units selected at random were organized into a frequency distribution. Compute the range:

Age to the Nearest Month	Number of Word Processors
20–24	3
25–29	5
30–34	10
35–39	7
40–44	4
45–49	1

Solution

The range is the difference between the lower stated limit of the lowest class and the upper stated limit of the highest class.

Range = 49 − 20 = 29 months

Problem 9

Using the ages of the word processing equipment in Problem 8, compute the variance and the standard deviation.

Solution

Formula 3–18 is used to compute the standard deviation of grouped data.

$$s_1 = \sqrt{\frac{\Sigma fX^2 - \dfrac{(\Sigma fX)^2}{n}}{n-1}}$$

where X is the midpoint of a class, f is the class frequency, and n is the total number of sample observations.

Applying this formula to the distribution of the ages of the word processing equipment in Problem 8, the standard deviation is 6.39 months.

Age	f	Class Midpoint X	fX	fX²
20–24	3	22	66	1,452
25–29	5	27	135	3,645
30–34	10	32	320	10,240
35–39	7	37	259	9,583
40–44	4	42	168	7,056
45–49	1	47	47	2,209
	30		995	34,185

$$s = \sqrt{\frac{\Sigma fX^2 - \dfrac{(\Sigma fX)^2}{n}}{n-1}}$$

$$= \sqrt{\frac{34,185 - \dfrac{(995)^2}{30}}{30-1}}$$

$$= 6.39 \text{ months}$$

The variance is the square of the standard deviation.

$$s^2 = (6.39)^2 = 40.83$$

Problem 10

Use the ages of the Mallard Glass word processing equipment (Problem 7) to compute the interquartile range and the quartile deviation.

Solution

The interquartile range and the quartile deviation are computed by:

Formula 3–19

Interquartile range $= Q_3 - Q_1$

Formula 3–22

Quartile deviation, $Q.D. = \dfrac{Q_3 - Q_1}{2}$

where Q_3 is the third quartile and Q_1 is the first quartile.

The formulas for the first and third quartiles are:

Formula 3–20

$$Q_1 = L + \frac{\dfrac{n}{4} - CF}{f}\,(i)$$

Formula 3–21

$$Q_3 = L + \frac{\dfrac{3n}{4} - CF}{f}\,(i)$$

where:

    L is the lower true limit of the class containing the first (or third) quartile.
    n is the total number in the sample.
    CF is the cumulative number of frequencies occurring prior to the class containing the first (or third) quartile.
    f is the number of frequencies in the class containing the first (or third) quartile.
    i is the width of the class interval containing the first (or third) quartile.

36

The calculations for Q_1 and Q_3 are quite similar to those for the median (Q_2) discussed earlier in this chapter. To find Q_1: The first step is to search for the class in which Q_1 is located. Note there are 30 word processors. One-fourth of 30 is 7.5. Refer to the following table. Count down in the class frequency column. The first cumulative frequency is 3, the next 8, found by 3 + 5, the next is 18, found by 3 + 5 + 10, and so on.

Note in the cumulative frequency column that 3 word processors have been in use less than 24.5 months (the 24.5 months is the true upper limit of the first class). Eight processors have been in use less than 29.5 months. The 7.5 processors must be in the 24.5–29.5 age class.

Age (Stated Limits)	True Limits	Class Frequency f		Cumulative Frequency CF
20–24	19.5–24.5	3	COUNT	3
25–29	24.5–29.5	5	DOWN	8
30–34	29.5–34.5	10		18
35–39	34.5–39.5	7		25
40–44	39.5–44.5	4		29
45–49	44.5–49.5	1		30
		30		

Using the formula (3–20) for the values for first quartile (Q_1) are:

L = 24.5, the lower limit of the class containing the first quartile.
n = 30, the total number of word processors in the sample.
CF = 3, the cumulative number of frequencies occurring prior to the class containing the first quartile.
f = 5, the number of frequencies in the class containing the first quartile.
i = 5, the width of the 24.5–29.5 class.

Computing the first and third quartiles:

$$Q_1 = L + \frac{\frac{n}{4} - CF}{f}(i) \qquad Q_3 = L + \frac{\frac{3n}{4} - CF}{f}(i)$$

$$= 24.5 + \frac{\frac{30}{4} - 3}{5}(5) \qquad = 34.5 + \frac{\frac{3(30)}{4} - 18}{7}(5)$$

$$= 29.0 \text{ months} \qquad = 37.71 \text{ months}$$

Fifty percent of the word processors have been in use more than 29.0 months but less than 37.71 months. The interquartile range is 8.71, found by $Q_3 - Q_1 = 37.71 - 29.0 = 8.71$ months. The quartile deviation is:

$$Q.D. = \frac{Q_3 - Q_1}{2} = \frac{37.71 - 29.0}{2} = \frac{8.71}{2} = 4.355 \text{ months}$$

Exercise 5

Check your answers against those in the ANSWER section.

The weekly incomes of a sample of 60 employees of a fast-food restaurant chain were organized into the following frequency distribution.

Weekly Incomes	Number of Employees
$100–$149	5
150– 199	9
200– 249	20
250– 299	18
300– 349	5
350– 399	3

Compute (a) standard deviation and (b) quartile deviation.

Problem 11

A sample of the business faculty at state supported institutions in Ohio revealed the mean income to be $52,000 for 9 months with a standard deviation of $3,000. Use Chebyshev's Theorem to estimate the proportion of faculty that earn more than $46,000 but less than $58,000.

Solution

To find the proportion of faculty who earn between $46,000 and $58,000 we must first determine k; k is the number of standard deviations above or below the mean.

$$k = \frac{X - \overline{X}}{s} = \frac{\$46,000 - \$52,000}{\$3,000} = -2.00$$

$$k = \frac{X - \overline{X}}{s} = \frac{\$58,000 - \$52,000}{\$3,000} = 2.00$$

Applying Chebyshev's Theorem: $1 - \dfrac{1}{k^2} = 1 - \dfrac{1}{2^2} = 0.75$

This means that at least 75 percent of the faculty earn between $46,000 and $58,000.

The Normal Rule states that about 68 percent of the observations fall within one standard deviation of the mean, 95 percent are within plus and minus two standard deviations of the mean, and virtually all (99.7%) will lie within three standard deviations from the mean. Hence, about 95 percent of the observations fall between $46,000 and $58,000, found by $\overline{X} \pm 2s = \$52,000 \pm 2\,(\$3,000)$. Compare these results with those obtained from Chebyshev's Theorem.

Problem 12

Recall from Problem 11 that the study of business faculty at state supported institutions in Ohio revealed that the arithmetic mean salary for nine months is $52,000 and the standard deviation of the sample is $3,000. The study also showed that the faculty had been employed an average (arithmetic mean) of 15 years with a standard deviation of 4 years. How does the relative dispersion in the distribution of salaries compare with that of the lengths of service?

38

Solution

The coefficient of variation measures the relative dispersion in a distribution. In this problem it allows for a comparison of two distributions expressed in different units (dollars and years). Formula 3–23 is used:

$$CV = \frac{s}{\overline{X}} \ (100)$$

For the salaries:

$$CV = \frac{\$3,000}{\$52,000} \ (100)$$
$$= 5.8\%$$

For the length of service:

$$CV = \frac{4 \text{ years}}{15 \text{ years}} \ (100)$$
$$= 26.7\%$$

The coefficient of variation is larger for length of service than for salary. This indicates that there is more dispersion in the distribution of the lengths of service relative to the mean than for the distribution of salaries.

Problem 13

The research director of a large oil company conducted a study of the buying habits of consumers with respect to the amount of gasoline purchased at full-service pumps. The arithmetic mean amount is 11.50 gallons, and the median amount is 11.95 gallons. The standard deviation of the sample is 4.5 gallons. Determine the coefficient of skewness. Comment on the shape of the distribution.

Solution

The coefficient of skewness measures the general shape of the distribution. A distribution that is symmetrical has no skewness and the coefficient of skewness is 0. It ranges from –3 to +3. The direction of the long tail of the distribution points in the direction of the skewness. If the mean is larger than the median, the skewness is positive. If the median is larger than the mean, the skewness is negative. The coefficient of skewness is found by formula 3–24:

$$sk = \frac{3(\overline{X} - \text{median})}{s} = \frac{3(11.50 - 11.95)}{4.5} = -0.30$$

This indicates that there is a slight negative skewness in the distribution of gasoline purchases from full-service pumps.

Exercise 6

Check your answers against those in the ANSWER section.

An automobile dealership pays its salespersons a salary plus a commission on sales. The mean monthly commission is $990, the median $950, and the standard deviation $70. Is the distribution of commissions positively skewed, negatively skewed, or symmetrical? To verify your answer compute the coefficient of skewness.

CHAPTER ASSIGNMENT 3

Describing Data—Measures of Central Tendency and Dispersion

Name _____ Section _____ Score _____

PART I Matching Select the correct answer and write the appropriate letter in the space provided.

_____ 1. mean

_____ 2. median

_____ 3. mode

_____ 4. symmetrical distribution

_____ 5. negatively skewed

_____ 6. range

_____ 7. coefficient of variation

_____ 8. variance

_____ 9. coefficient of skewness

_____ 10 quartile deviation

a. has the same shape on both sides of the median

b. value that occurs most often

c. 50% of the values are larger

d. is affected by a very large value

e. long tail of distribution to the left

f. measure of relative dispersion

g. ranges from −3.00 to 3.00

h. difference between the largest and smallest values

i. based on the middle fifty percent of the observations

j. square of the standard deviation

PART II Multiple Choice Select the correct answer and write the appropriate letter in the space provided.

_____ 11. The arithmetic mean is determined by

    a. selecting the value in the middle.
    b. summing the values and dividing by the number of values.
    c. finding the value that occurs most often.
    d. selecting the value half way between the two middle observations.

_____ 12. For a symmetric bell-shaped distribution the

    a. mean, median, and mode are equal.
    b. mean is greater than the median and mode.
    c. mode is greater than the median and mean.
    d. None of these are correct.

_____ 13. In a negatively skewed distribution the

    a. mean is smaller than the median.
    b. mean is the same as the median.
    c. mean is larger than the median.
    d. median is larger than the mode.
    e. None of these is correct.

_____ 14. The Dow Jones Industrial Average increased from 961 in 1980 to 3461.19 in 1993. The mean annual rate of increase is best described by the

    a. arithmetic mean.
    b. geometric mean.
    c. weighted mean.
    d. median.

_____ 15. The mean deviation is based on

 a. squared deviations from the mean.
 b. squared deviations from the median.
 c. absolute deviations from the mean.
 d. the difference between the largest and smallest value.
 e. None of these is correct.

_____ 16. A coefficient of skewness of 2.85

 a. cannot occur, a mistake was made in arithmetic.
 b. indicates a large degree of positive skewness.
 c. indicates a large degree of negative skewness.
 d. indicates that the distribution is symmetrical.
 e. None of these is correct.

_____ 17. The quartile deviation and the interquartile range

 a. are based on the middle 25% of the observations.
 b. use the arithmetic mean in their calculations.
 c. are based on deviations from the mode.
 d. are based on the middle 50% of the observations.

_____ 18. The coefficient of skewness

 a. may range from 0 to 1.0 inclusive.
 b. is always positive.
 c. is a measure of relative dispersion.
 d. may range from −3.00 to 3.00.

_____ 19. The coefficient of variation

 a. is a measure of relative dispersion.
 b. is reported in the same units as the variance.
 c. is similar to the range.
 d. can assume negative values.

_____ 20. A study of the length of time, in days, that a traffic light will operate was conducted by the city traffic engineer. The variance of the length of time the traffic light will operate is in

 a. days.
 b. days squared.
 c. hours.
 d. percent.
 e. None of these is correct.

PART III Problems Record your answer in the space provided. Show essential calculations.

21. The weights of a sample of eight UPS outgoing packages, to the nearest pound, are:

14, 16, 24, 9, 13, 7, 11, 10

a. Compute the mean weight.

a. [   ]
Answer

b. Compute the median weight.

b. [   ]
Answer

c. Determine the modal weight.

c. [   ]
Answer

d. Compute the standard deviation of the weights.

d. [   ]
Answer

22. Forty unemployed persons applying for benefits were asked by the counselor at the employment office how many hours he or she spent searching for suitable employment last week. The survey responses were tallied as follows:

Hours Spent Searching	Number of Unemployed
0– 9	3
10–19	7
20–29	15
30–39	10
40–49	5

a. Determine the arithmetic mean number of hours spent searching for employment last week.

a. [_____]

Answer

b. What was the median number of hours spent?

b. [_____]

Answer

c. Determine the standard deviation of the distribution of number of hours spent searching for employment.

c. [_____]

Answer

23. The mean number of gallons of gasoline pumped per customer at Ray's Marathon Station is 9.5 gallons with a standard deviation of 0.75 gallons. The median number of gallons pumped is 10.0 gallons. The mean amount of time spent by a customer in the station is 6.5 minutes with a standard deviation of 2 minutes.

a. According to Chebyshev's Theorem, what proportion of the customers spend between 3.30 minutes and 9.70 minutes at the station?

a. [ ]
Answer

b. According to the Normal Rule, what proportion of the customers pump between 8.00 gallons and 11.00 gallons?

b. [ ]
Answer

c. Compute coefficient of variation for both the time spent at Ray's Marathon and the gasoline pumped. Comment on the relative dispersion of the two distributions.

c. [ ]
Answer

d. Compute the coefficient of skewness for the number of gallons pumped. Interpret this value.

d. [ ]
Answer

4

A SURVEY OF PROBABILITY CONCEPTS

CHAPTER GOALS

After completing this chapter, you will be able to:

1. Define what is meant by a probability.
2. Explain the three classifications of probability.
3. Calculate probabilities using the rules of addition and multiplication.
4. Calculate a probability using Bayes' Theorem.

Introduction

Chapters 2 and 3 emphasized **descriptive statistics**. In those chapters we described methods used to collect, organize, and present data, as well as measures of central tendency, dispersion, and skewness used to summarize data. In this chapter, we begin our study of **inferential statistics**.

An inference is defined as a *generalization about a population based on information obtained from a sample*. Probability plays a key role in inferential statistics. It is used to measure the reasonableness that a particular sample could have come from a particular population. Probability also allows us to measure effectively the risks in selecting one alternative over the others.

Probability Defined

A **probability** is *a measure of the likelihood that a particular event will happen*. It may be expressed either as a percent or as a decimal. The likelihood of any particular event may assume values between 0 and 1.0. A value close to 0 indicates the event is unlikely to occur, whereas a value close to 1.0 indicates that the event is quite likely to occur. To illustrate, a value of .60 might express your degree of belief that tuition will be increased at your college, and .05 the likelihood that your first marriage will end in divorce.

In our study of probability we will make extensive use of several key words: experiment, outcome, and event. An **experiment** is an *observation of some activity, or the act of obtaining some type of measurement*. For example, you roll a die and observe the number of spots that appear face up. The experiment is the act of rolling the die. Your survey company might be hired by Ford to find out how many consumers plan to buy a new American made car this year. You contact 5,000 consumers. The act of counting the consumers who indicated they would purchase an American made car is the experiment. The *particular result of an experiment* is called an **outcome**.

One outcome of the die-rolling experiment is the appearance of a 6. In the experiment of counting the number of consumers who plan to buy a new American-made car this year, one possibility is that 2,258 plan to buy one, another outcome is that 142 plan to buy one. *A collection of one or more outcomes* is called an **event**. Thus, the *event* that the number appearing face up in the die-rolling experiment is even is the *collection of the outcomes* 2, 4, or 6. Similarly the event that more than half of those surveyed plan to buy a new American-made car is the collection of the outcomes 2,500, 2,501, 2,502, and so on all the way up to 5,000.

Types of Probability

There are three types or classifications of probability: classical, relative frequency, and subjective. The **classical** type is based on the assumption that there are several *equally likely outcomes* for an experiment. The probability of a particular outcome is obtained by dividing the number of favorable outcomes by the total number of possible outcomes. For example, suppose you take a multiple-choice examination in which each question has four possible answers. Assume you did not study for the examination and have no idea which one of the choices is correct. In desperation you decide to guess the answer to each question. The four choices for each question are the outcomes. They are equally likely, but only one is correct. Thus the probability that you guess a particular answer correctly is .25, found by 1/4.

A probability obtained using the **relative frequency** approach is computed by dividing the number of times the event has occurred in the past by the total number of observations. Suppose the Civil Aeronautics Board maintained records on the number of times planes arrived late at the Newark International Airport. If 54 flights in a sample of 500 were late, then, according to the relative frequency definition, the probability a particular flight will be late is .108, found by 54/500.

Subjective probability is based on whatever information is available—personal judgment, intuition, or "hunches." The likelihood that the horse Sir Homer will win the race at Perry Downs today is based on the subjective view of the racetrack oddsmaker.

Probability Rules

In the study of probability it is often necessary to combine the probabilities of events. This is accomplished through both **rules of addition** and **rules of multiplication**. There are two rules for addition, the **special rule of addition** and the **general rule of addition**.

Special Rule of Addition

The special rule of addition states that the probability of the event A or the event B occurring is equal to the probability of event A plus the probability of event B. The rule is expressed by:

$$P(A \text{ or } B) = P(A) + P(B) \qquad [4\text{--}2]$$

To apply the special rule of addition the events must be **mutually exclusive**. This means that when one of the events occurs, *none of the others can occur at the same time*. When a single die is rolled

once, for example, a 2 and a 6 cannot both appear at the same time.

Venn Diagram

Venn diagrams, developed by English logician J. Venn, are useful for portraying events and their relationship to one another. They are constructed by enclosing a space, usually in the form of a rectangle, which represents the possible events. Two mutually exclusive events such as A and B can then be portrayed—as in the following diagram—by enclosing regions that do not overlap (that is, they have no common area).

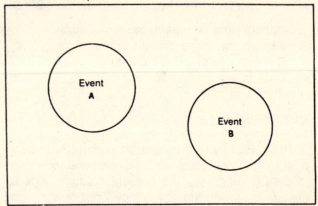

The **complement rule** states that the probability of the event A not occurring written $P(\sim A)$, is equal to one minus the probability of the event A occurring. This is written $P(\sim A) = 1 - P(A)$ or it could be written $P(A) = 1 - P(\sim A)$.

General Rule of Addition

What if the events are *not* mutually exclusive? In that case the **general rule of addition** is used. The probability is computed using the text formula 5–4.

$$P(A \text{ or } B) = P(A) + P(B) - P(A \text{ and } B) \qquad [4\text{--}4]$$

where $P(A)$ is the probability of the event A, $P(B)$ the probability of the event B, and $P(A \text{ and } B)$ the probability that both events A and B occur. For example, suppose that a study had shown 15 percent of the work force to be unemployed, 20 percent of the work force to be minorities, and 5 percent to be both unemployed *and* minorities. What percent of the work force are either minorities or unemployed? Note that if P (unemployed) and P (minority) are totalled, the 5 percent who are both minorities and unemployed are counted in both groups—that is, they are double-counted. They must be subtracted to avoid this double counting. Hence,

$$P \text{ (unemployed or minority)}$$
$$= P \text{ (unemployed)} + P \text{ (minority)}$$
$$- P \text{ (unemployed and minority)}$$
$$= .15 + .20 - .05$$
$$= .30$$

These two events are not mutually exclusive and would appear as follows in a Venn diagram:

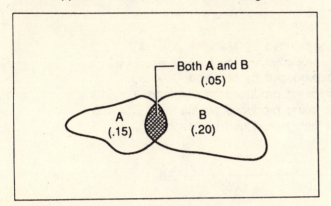

Special Rule of Multiplication

The **special rule of multiplication** is used to combine events where the probability of the second event does not depend on the outcome of the first event. Two events are **independent** *if the occurrence of one event does not affect the probability that the other event will occur.* The probability of two independent events A and B occurring is found by multiplying the two probabilities. It is written as shown in text formula 4–5.

$$P(\text{A and B}) = P(\text{A})P(\text{B}) \qquad [4\text{–}5]$$

As an example a nuclear power plant with two independent safety systems. The probability the first will not operate properly in an emergency $P(\text{A})$ is .01, and the probability the second will not operate $P(\text{B})$ in an emergency is .02. What is the probability that in an emergency both of the plants will not operate? The probability both will not operate is:

$$P(\text{A and B}) \quad = P(\text{A})P(\text{B})$$
$$= (.01)\ (.02)$$
$$= .0002$$

The probability .0002 is called a **joint probability**, which *is the simultaneous occurrence of two events.* It measures the likelihood that two (or more) events will happen together (jointly).

General Rule of Multiplication

The **general rule of multiplication** is used to combine events that are *not* independent—that is, they are dependent on each other. For two events, the probability of the second event is affected by the outcome of the first event. Under these conditions, the probability of both A and B occurring is given in formula 5–6, where $P(\text{B}|\text{A})$ is the probability of B occurring given that A has already occurred.

$$P(\text{A and B}) = P(\text{A})P(\text{B}|\text{A}) \qquad [4\text{–}6]$$

where $P(\text{B}|\text{A})$ is a **conditional probability**. A conditional probability is the *likelihood of a second event occurring, given that the first has already happened.*

For example, suppose that among a group of twelve prisoners, four had been convicted of murder. If two of the twelve are selected for a special rehabilitation program, what is the probability that both of those selected are convicted murderers? Let A_1 be the first selection (a convicted murderer) and A_2 the second selection (also a convicted murderer). Then $P(A_1) = 4/12$. After the first selection, there are 11 prisoners, 3 of whom are convicted of murder, hence $P(A_2|A_1) = 3/11$. The probability of both A_1 and A_2 happening is:

$$P(A_1 \text{ and } A_2) \quad = P(A_1)P(A_2|A_1)$$
$$= 4/12 \times 3/11$$
$$= .0909$$

Bayes' Theorem

Bayes' Theorem is used to revise the probability of a particular event happening based on the fact that some other event had already happened. For example, we have three machines each producing the same items. Machine A produces 10 percent defective and Machines B and C each 5 percent defective. Suppose each machine produces one-third of the total production. Since Machine A produces one-third of all the parts we naturally expect that prior to any experiment the probability of a defective being produced by Machine A is .33. Logically, the .33 is called a **prior probability**.

A part is selected at random. It was found to be defective. The question is: what is the probability that it was produced by Machine A? As noted above, Machine A produces twice as many defective parts as Machines B and C. (A produces 10%, B and C 5% each.) Since we discovered that the part selected was defective, the probability it was manufactured by Machine A is now greater than .33. Bayes' Theorem will give us this revised probability. The formula is: (See formula 4–7)

$$P(A_1|B) = \frac{P(A_1) \times P(B|A_1)}{P(A_1)P(B|A_1) + P(A_2)P(B|A_2) + P(A_3)P(B|A_3)} \qquad [4\text{--}7]$$

The probabilities to be inserted in the formula are:

$P(A_1)$ = Probability the part was produced by Machine A = .33
$P(A_2)$ = Probability the part was produced by Machine B = .33
$P(A_3)$ = Probability the part was produced by Machine C = .33
$P(B|A_1)$ = Probability of a defect being produced by Machine A = .10
$P(B|A_2)$ = Probability of a defect being produced by Machine B = .05
$P(B|A_3)$ = Probability of a defect being produced by Machine C = .05

Solving:

$$P(A_1|B) = \frac{.33\,(.10)}{.33\,(.10) + .33\,(.05) + .33\,(.05)} = .50$$

Hence, the probability that the defective part was manufactured by Machine A is increased from 0.33 to 0.50. We revised upward the probability that the part was produced by Machine A, because we obtained the additional information that the part selected was defective.

GLOSSARY

Probability—A measure of the degree of belief that a particular outcome will happen. Probabilities may range from 0 to 1.0, inclusive where 0 indicates that the event will not happen and 1.0 indicates it will definitely happen.

Experiment—The observation of some activity, or the act of taking some type of measurement.

Outcome—A particular result of an experiment.

Event—A collection of one or more outcomes of an experiment.

Classical probability—Each of the possible outcomes is equally likely. If there are *n* outcomes, the probability of a particular outcome is 1/*n*.

Relative frequency—The total number of times the event has occurred in the past, divided by the total number of observations.

Subjective probability—The assignment of probabilities based on whatever information is available—personal opinion, hunches, etc.

Mutually exclusive—If one of the outcomes of an experiment occurs, then none of the others can occur at the same time.

Venn diagram—A diagram useful for portraying the relationship of events.

Special rule of addition—If two events are mutually exclusive, the probability that one or the other will happen is $P(A \text{ or } B) = P(A) + P(B)$.

General rule of addition—If two events are *not* mutually exclusive: $P(A \text{ or } B) = P(A) + P(B) - P(A \text{ and } B)$ where $P(A \text{ and } B)$ is the joint probability of the occurrence of the events A and B.

Independent events—The occurrence of one event does not affect the probability the other event will occur.

Complement Rule—The probability of an event not happening can be determined by subtracting the probability of it happening from 1. That is, $P(\sim A) = 1 - P(A)$.

Conditional probability—The probability of the occurrence of a second event given the first event has occurred.

Joint probability—The simultaneous occurrence of two events.

Special rule of multiplication—A rule for combining two or more independent events. The probability of events A and B occurring is $P(A \text{ and } B) = P(A)P(B)$.

General rule of multiplication—A rule for combining two dependent events. The probability of the event A and B occurring is the probability of the event A times the probability of the event B, given that the event A occurred. $P(A \text{ and } B) = P(A)P(B|A)$.

Bayes' Theorem—A method for revising a probability based on obtaining additional information.

Prior probability—The original or initial probability determined prior to conducting the experiment.

CHAPTER PROBLEMS

Problem 1

Dunn Pontiac has compiled the following sales data regarding the number of cars sold over the past 60 selling days.

Number of Cars Sold	Number of Days
0	5
1	5
2	10
3	20
4	15
5 or more	5
Total	60

Answer the following questions:

What is the probability that two cars are sold during a particular day?
What is the probability of selling 3 or more cars during a particular day?
What is the probability of selling at least one car during a particular day?

Solution

This problem is an example of the relative frequency type of probability, because the probability of an event happening is based on the number of times the particular event happened in the past relative to the total number of observations.

The events are mutually exclusive. That is, if a total of two cars are sold on a particular day, four cannot be sold. The probability that exactly two cars are sold is:

$$P(2 \text{ cars}) = \frac{\text{Number of days two cars were sold}}{\text{Total number of days}} = \frac{10}{60} = .1667$$

The probability of selling three or more cars is obtained by using the special rule of addition given in formula 4–2. Let X represent the number of cars sold ($\geq$ is read "greater than or equal to." The notation > would be just greater than), then

$$P(X \geq 3) = P(3) + P(4) + P(5 \text{ or more})$$

$$= \frac{20}{60} + \frac{15}{60} + \frac{5}{60} = \frac{40}{60} = .67$$

Interpreting, three cars or more are sold 67 percent of the days.

The probability of selling *at least* one car is determined by adding the probabilities of selling one, two, three, four, and five or more cars. Again let X be the number of cars sold, then

$$P(X \geq 1) = P(1) + P(2) + P(3) + P(4) + P(5 \text{ or more})$$

$$= \frac{5}{60} + \frac{10}{60} + \frac{20}{60} + \frac{15}{60} + \frac{5}{60} = \frac{55}{60} = .92$$

The same result can also be obtained by using the complement rule. The probability of the occurrence of a particular event is obtained by computing the probability it did *not* occur and then subtracting that value from 1.0. In this example, the probability of not selling any cars is 5/60 = .08, and 1 − .08 = .92.

$$P(X \geq 1) = 1.0 - P(0)$$

$$= 1.0 - \frac{5}{60} = 1 - .08 = .92$$

52

Problem 2

A local community has two newspapers. The *Morning Times* is read by 45 percent of the households. The *Evening Dispatch* is read by 60 percent of the households. Twenty percent of the households read both papers. What is the probability that a particular household in the city reads at least one paper?

Solution

If we combine the three probabilities (.45, .60, and .20), they exceed 1.00. The group that reads both papers, of course, is being counted twice and must be subtracted to arrive at the answer. Letting T represent the *Morning Times*, and D the *Evening Dispatch*, and using the general rule of addition, formula 4–4:

$$
\begin{aligned}
P(\text{T or D}) &= P(\text{T}) + P(\text{D}) - P(\text{T and D}) \\
&= .45 + .60 - .20 \\
&= .85
\end{aligned}
$$

Thus, 85 percent of the households in the community read at least one paper.

Problem 3

The probability that a bomber hits a target on a bombing mission is .70. Three bombers are sent to bomb a particular target. What is the probability that they all hit the target? What is the probability that at least one hits the target?

Solution

These events are independent since the probability that one bomber hits the target does not depend on whether the other hits it. The special rule of multiplication formula 4–5 is used to find the joint probability. B_1 represents the first bomber, B_2 the second bomber, and B_3 the third bomber.

$$P(\text{all 3 hit target}) = P(B_1)P(B_2)P(B_3)$$
$$= (.70)\ (.70)\ (.70)$$
$$= .343$$

Hence the probability that all three complete the mission is .343.

The probability that at least one bomber hits the target is found by combining the complement rule and the multiplication rule. To explain: The probability of a miss with the first bomber is .30, found by $P(M_1) = 1 - .70$. The probability for M_2 and M_3 is also .30. The multiplication rule is used to obtain the probability that all three miss. Let X be the number of hits.

$$P(X > 0) = 1 - P(0)$$
$$= 1 - P(M_1)P(M_2)P(M_3)$$
$$= 1 - [(.30)(.30)(.30)]$$
$$= 1 - .027 = .973$$

So the probability that at least one bomber hits its target is .973.

Exercise 3

Check your answers against those in the ANSWER section.

A side effect of a certain anesthetic used in surgery is the hiccups, which occurs in about 10 percent of the cases. If three patients are scheduled for surgery today, and are to be administered this anesthetic, compute the probability that all three get hiccups, that none get hiccups, and that at least one gets hiccups.

Problem 4

The Bunte Auto Repair Shop has received a shipment of four carburetors. One is known to be defective. If two are selected at random and tested: (a) What is the probability that neither one is defective? (b) What is the probability that the defective carburetor is located by testing two carburetors?

Solution

(a) The selections of the two carburetors are *not* independent events because the selection of the first affects the second outcome. Let G_1 represent the first "good" carburetor and G_2 the second "good" one; then using formua 4–6:

$$P(G_1 \text{ and } G_2) = P(G_1)P(G_2|G_1)$$

| 3 out of 4 are good |
| 2 out of 3 are good |

$$= \left(\frac{3}{4}\right)\left(\frac{2}{3}\right) = .50$$

Hence, the probability that neither of the two selected carburetors is defective is .50.

(b) The probability that the defective carburetor is found requires the general rule of multiplication and the general rule of addition.

In this case the defect may be detected either in the first test or in the second one. The general rule of multiplication is used. Let D_1 represent a defect on the first test and D_2 on the second test. The probability is:

$$P(\text{find the defect}) = P(G_1)P(D_2|G_1) + P(D_1)P(G_2|D_1)$$

$$= \left(\frac{3}{4}\right)\left(\frac{1}{3}\right) + \left(\frac{1}{4}\right)\left(\frac{3}{3}\right) = .50$$

To explain further, the probability that the first carburetor tested is good is $P(G_1) = 3/4$. If the first one selected is good, then to meet the requirements of the problem the second one sampled must be defective. This conditional probability is $P(D_2|G_1) = 1/3$. The joint probability of these two events is 3/12 or 1/4. The defective part could be found on the first test [$P(D_1)$]. Since there is one defect among the four carburetors the probability found on the first test is 1/4. If the defect is found on the first test then the three remaining parts are good. Hence the conditional probability of selecting a good carburetor on the second trial is 1.0 [$P(G_2|D_1)$]. The joint probability of a defective part being followed by a good part is 1/4, found by $P(D_1) \times P(G_2|D_1) = (1/4)(3/3) = 1/4$. The sum of these two outcomes is .50.

Exercise 4

Check your answers against those in the ANSWER section.

Ten students are being interviewed for a class office. Six of them are female and four are male. Their names are all placed in a box and two are selected to be interviewed tomorrow. (a) What is the probability that both of those selected are female? (b) What is the probability that at least one is male?

Problem 5

A large department store is analyzing the per-customer amount of purchase and the method of payment. For a sample of 140 customers the following table presents the findings.

Payment Method	Amount of Purchase			Total
	B_1: Less than $20	B_2: $20 up to $50	B_3: $50 or more	
A_1 Cash	15	10	5	30
A_2 Check	10	30	20	60
A_3 Charge	10	20	20	50
Total	35	60	45	140

(a) What is the probability of selecting someone who paid by cash or made a purchase of less than $20?
(b) What is the probability of selecting someone who paid by check and made a purchase of more than $50?

Solution

(a) If we combine the events "Less than $20" ($B_1$) and "Cash payment" ($A_1$), then those who paid cash for a purchase of less than $20 are counted twice. That is, these two events are *not* mutually exclusive. Therefore the general rule of addition formula 4–4 is used:

$$P(A_1 \text{ or } B_1) = P(A_1) + P(B_1) - P(A_1 \text{ and } B_1)$$

$$= \frac{30}{140} + \frac{35}{140} - \frac{15}{140} = \frac{50}{140} = .36$$

The probability of selecting a customer who made a cash payment or purchased an item for less than $20 is .36.

(b) Conditional probability is used to find the probability of selecting someone who paid by check (A_2) and who made a purchase of over $50 ($B_3$).

There are two qualifications: "paid by check" and "made a purchase of over $50." Referring to the table, 20 out of 140 customers meet both qualifications, therefore, $20/140 = 0.14$.

This probability could also be computed in a three-step process:

1. The probability of selecting those who paid by check (A_2) is $60/140 = .43$.

2. Of the 60 persons who paid by check, 20 made a purchase of over $50. Therefore $P(B_3|A_2) = 20/60 = .33$.

3. These two events are then combined using the general rule of multiplication, formula 4–6:

$$P(A_2 \text{ and } B_3) = P(A_2)P(B_3|A_2)]$$

$$= (.43)(.33) = .14$$

Problem 6

The probability that a person has "BLEEBS," a rare disease that occurs in young baseball players, is .02. If a person has BLEEBS, the probability that the individual is diagnosed as having it is .80. On the other hand, if an individual does not have BLEEBS, the probability of being diagnosed as having it is .05. Given that a person is diagnosed as having BLEEBS, what is the probability that the person really does *not* have it?

Solution

This problem is solved using Bayes' Theorem. The various parts of the problem are as follows:

P(B) is the probability of having BLEEBS. It is .02.
P(NB) is the probability of not having BLEEBS. It is .98
P(D|B) is the probability of being diagnosed as having BLEEBS, given that the person has the disease. It is .80.
P(D|NB) is the probability of being diagnosed as having BLEEBS, given that the person does *not* have the disease. It is .05.
P(NB|D) is the revised probability of not having BLEEBS, given that the diagnosis is that of having BLEEBS.

A useful device for displaying conditional and joint probabilities is called a tree diagram. The tree diagram will be used to solve the above problem. The initial relationships are as follows:

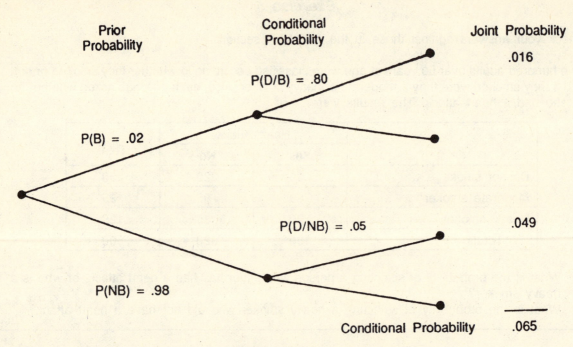

Prior Probability   Conditional Probability   Joint Probability

$P(D/B) = .80$

.016

$P(B) = .02$

$P(D/NB) = .05$

.049

$P(NB) = .98$

Conditional Probability   .065

The computational form of Bayes' Theorem formula 4–7 is repeated below.

$$P(NB|D) = \frac{P(NB) \times P(D|NB)}{P(B) \times P(D|B) + P(NB) \times P(D|NB)}$$

$$= \frac{(.98)\,(.05)}{(.02)\,(.80) + (.98)\,(.05)} = .754$$

Interpreting, this means that even though a person is diagnosed as having BLEEBS, the probability that he or she is not actually affected is .754.

To explain this problem further, note that all people fall into two categories, that is they have BLEEBS or they don't. Only two percent of the population actually have the condition [$P(B) = .02$] and 98 percent do not [$P(NB) = .98$]. Of those having BLEEBS, 80 percent are correctly diagnosed [$P(D|B) = .80$], but some people are diagnosed as having BLEEBS, when they actually do not [$P(D|NB) = .05$]. These are actually false positive readings.

The denominator of Bayes' Theorem computes the fraction of the population that are diagnosed as having BLEEBS. That fraction is obtained by combining the two joint probabilities as follows:

$$P(B) = P(B) \times (D|B) + P(NB) \times P(D|NB) = (.02)(.80) + (.98)(.05)$$

$$= .065$$

The .065 is the fraction of the population that will be diagnosed as having BLEEBS. However, some of those diagnosed actually have the condition [$P(B) \times P(D|B) = (.02)\,(.80) = .016$] and some while diagnosed as having BLEEBS actually do *not* [$P(NB) \times P(D|NB) = (.98)\,(.05) = .049$]. We are interested in the fraction that are diagnosed as having the condition but really don't [$(.049/.065) = .754$]. This result may seem rather startling, because more than 75 percent of the time the test results are actually incorrect. This indicates that the test for BLEEBS is not very discriminating.

Exercise 6

Check your answers against those in the ANSWER section.

A test on probability is to be given next week. Suppose 75 percent of the students study for the test and 25 percent do not. If a student studies for the exam the probability that he or she will pass is .90. If the student does not study, the probability that he or she will pass is 20 percent. Given that the student passed the test what is the probability he or she studied?

CHAPTER ASSIGNMENT 4

A Survey of Probability Concepts

Name _____ Section _____ Score _____

PART I **Matching** Select the correct answer and write the appropriate letter in the space provided.

_____ 1. Event

_____ 2. Outcome

_____ 3. Experiment

_____ 4. Classical probability

_____ 5. Joint probability

_____ 6. Mutually exclusive

_____ 7. Independent

_____ 8. Complement rule

_____ 9. Probability

_____ 10 Subjective probability

a. may range from 0 to 1

b. observing some activity

c. a particular result of an experiment

d. 1 minus the probability of the event happening

e. if one event happens another cannot

f. a probability based on whatever information is available

g. a collection of outcomes

h. two events occur at the same time.

i. the occurrence of one event does not affect the probability of another.

j. Outcomes are equally likely

PART II **Multiple Choice** Select the correct answer and write the appropriate letter in the space provided.

_____ 11. A probability is

    a. a measure of the likelihood an event will happen.
    b. never negative.
    c. never greater than 1.0.
    d. All of the above.

_____ 12. The observation of some activity or the act of obtaining some type of measurement is called a(n)

    a. outcome.
    b. probability.
    c. event.
    d. experiment.

_____ 13. The particular result of an experiment is a(n)

    a. outcome.
    b. probablity.
    c. event.
    d. experiment.
    e None of the above.

_____ 14. The collection of one or more outcomes is a(n)

    a. outcome.
    b. probability.
    c. event.
    d. experiment.
    e. None of the above.

_____ 15. Which of the following is not a type of probability?

   a. Discrete
   b. Classical
   c. Subjective
   d. Relative frequency

_____ 16. For the special rule of addition the events must be

   a. continuous.
   b. mutually exclusive.
   c. independent.
   d. discrete.

_____ 17. Events are independent if

   a. event A occurs then event B cannot happen.
   b. event A occurs then the likelihood of B is altered.
   c. event A occurs then the likelihood of B is not altered.
   d. event A occurs then B must occur.
   e. None of the above.

_____ 18. The complement rules states that the probability of A *not* occurring is

   a. always greater than 1.
   b. equal to 1 minus the probability of A occurring.
   c. always twice the probability of A.
   d. always half the probability of A.

_____ 19. The likelihood of an event happening, given that another event has already occurred, is called a

   a. joint probability.
   b. probability distribution.
   c. Bayesian probability.
   d. conditional probability.

_____ 20. To apply the special rule of multiplication the events must be

   a. mutually exclusive.
   b. independent.
   c. dependent.
   d. not mutually exclusive.

PART III Problems Record your answer in the space provided. Show essential calculations.

21. The number of weeks of vacation for employees of the Lowell Label Works is summarized below.

Weeks of Vacation	Number of Employees
0	20
1	40
2	30
3	10
Total	100

Compute the following probabilities for an employee selected at random.

a. An employee has two weeks of vacation.

Answer

b. An employee has two or more weeks of vacation.

Answer

c. An employee has more than two weeks of vacation.

Answer

d. The employee has some vacation.

Answer

22. At the Quick-Gulp Restaurant 60% of the customers order some type of hamburger. Three customers have just entered the restaurant,

a. What is the probability that all three order a hamburger?

Answer

b. What is the probability at least one orders a hamburger?

Answer

63

23. William Turner, the owner of the Turner Electronics is studying the relationship between customers that buy a VCR at the regular price or the sale price and whether or not the customer purchases the extended warranty. Mr. Turner constructed the following table based on the last 400 VCR sales.

| | Extended Warranty | | |
	Purchased	Not Purchased	Total
Regular Price	90	220	310
Sale Price	50	40	90
Total	140	260	400

a. What is the probability of selecting a customer who purchased the VCR on sale or purchased the warranty?

Answer

b. What is the probability of selecting a customer who purchased the warranty given that the VCR was on sale?

Answer

c. What is the probability of selecting a customer who purchased the VCR at the regular price, given they did not purchase the warranty?

Answer

24. Robert Yelton, a management trainee at Vatter Trucking Company, drives his own car to work 70% of the time. Otherwise, he takes the bus. When he drives himself, he is late 5% of the time and when he takes a bus he is late 25% of the time. Mr. Yelton was late for work this morning. What is the probability he took the bus?

Answer

64

5

DISCRETE PROBABILITY DISTRIBUTIONS

CHAPTER GOALS

After completing this chapter, you will be able to:

1. Define the terms probability distribution and random variable.
2. Distinguish between a discrete and a continuous probability distribution.
3. Calculate the mean and standard deviation of a discrete probability distribution.
4. List the characteristics of a binomial distribution and compute probabilities.
5. List the characteristics of the hypergeometric distribution and compute probabilities.
6. List the characteristics of a Poisson distribution and compute probabilities.

Introduction

In the previous chapter we discussed the basic concepts of probability and described how the rules of addition and multiplication are used to compute probabilities. In this chapter we expand the study of probability to include the concepts of a **random variable** and a **probability distribution**.

Random Variable

What is a random variable? It is a numerical value determined by the outcome of an experiment. A random variable may have two forms: discrete or continuous. A **discrete random variable** may assume only distinct values and is usually the result of counting. For example, the number of highway deaths in Arkansas on Memorial Day weekend may be 0, 1, 2, ... Another example is the number of students earning a grade of B in your statistics class. In both instances the number of occurrences result from counting and are referred to as discrete random variables. Note that there can be 12 deaths or 15 B's but there cannot be 12.63 deaths or 15.27 B grades. Does this rule out the possibility that a discrete random variable may assume fractional values? No. A study of stock prices might reveal that 20 stocks increased by one-eighth of a point ($0.125) and that 12 increased by one-fourth of a point ($0.25). Note that the random variable itself

may assume fractional values, but there is some distance between these values. In the stock example the result is still a count—that is, 12 stocks increased by $0.25.

A **continuous random variable** may assume an infinite number of values within a given range. For example, in a high school track meet, the winning time of the mile run may be reported as 4 minutes 20 seconds, 4 minutes 20.2 seconds, or 4 minutes 20.2416 seconds, and so on, depending on the accuracy of the timing device. We will examine the continuous random variable and the continuous probability distribution in Chapter 6.

Discrete Probability Distributions

What is a **probability distribution**? It is a listing of all the possible outcomes of an experiment, and the corresponding probability associated with each outcome. As an example, the possible outcomes on the roll of a single die are ⚀ , ⚁ , ⚂ , ⚃ , ⚄ , or ⚅ . Each face should appear on about one-sixth of the rolls. Listed below are the possible outcomes and corresponding probabilities for this experiment. It is a discrete distribution because

because only certain outcomes are possible and the distribution is a result of counting the various outcomes.

| Number of Spots | Probability | |
	Fraction	Decimal
1	1/6 =	.1667
2	1/6 =	.1667
3	1/6 =	.1667
4	1/6 =	.1667
5	1/6 =	.1667
6	1/6 =	.1667
Total	6/6	1.0000

There are several important features of the discrete probability distribution: (1) The listing is exhaustive; that is, all the possible outcomes are included. (2) The total (sum) of all possible outcomes is 1.0. (3) The probability of any particular outcome is between 0 and 1 inclusive. (4) The outcomes are mutually exclusive meaning, for example, a 6 spot and a 2 spot cannot appear at the same time.

This discrete probability distribution, presented above as a table, may also be portrayed in graphic form:

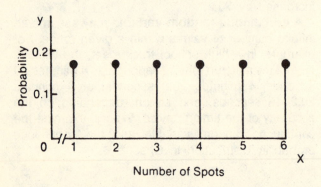

Number of Spots

By convention the probability is shown on the Y-axis (the vertical axis) and the outcomes on the X-axis (the horizonal axis).

A probability distribution can also be expressed in equation form. For example:

$P(X) = 1/6$, where X can assume the values 1, 2, 3, 4, 5, or 6.

What is the difference between a random variable and a probability distribution? A probability distribution lists all the possible outcomes as well as their corresponding probabilities. A random variable lists only the outcomes.

Mean and Variance of a Probability Distribution

In Chapters 3 the mean and variance of a frequency distribution were described. The mean is a measure of central tendency and the variance is a measure of the spread in the data. In a similar fashion, the mean (μ) and the variance (σ^2) summarize a probability distribution.

The mean, or expected value, of a probability distribution is its long-run average. It is computed by the following formula:

$$\mu = E(X) = \Sigma[XP(X)] \qquad [5\text{--}1]$$

This formula directs you to multiply each outcome (X) by its probability $P(X)$; and then add the products.

While the mean describes the center of a probability distribution, it does not tell us anything about the spread. The variance tells us about the spread or variation in the data. The variance is computed from the following formula:

$$\sigma^2 = \Sigma[(X - \mu)^2 P(X)] \qquad [5\text{--}2]$$

The steps in computing the variance using formula 5-2 are:

1. Subtract the mean (μ) from each outcome (X) and square these differences.
2. Multiply each squared difference by its probability $P(X)$.
3. Sum these products to arrive at the variance.

The Binomial Probability Distribution

One of the most widely used discrete distributions is the **binomial probability distribution**. It has the following characteristics:

1. *Each outcome is classified into one of two mutually exclusive categories.* An outcome is classified as either a "success" or a "failure." Example: It is known that 40 percent of all students attending your university are enrolled in the College of Business. There are only two possible categories—a student selected at random is either enrolled in the College of Business (designated as a success) or he/she is not enrolled (a failure).

2. *The binomial distribution results from a count of the number of successes in a fixed sample size.* Thus, in a group of five students 0, 1, 2, 3, 4, or 5 could be enrolled in the College of Business. There cannot be fractional counts, such as 3.26 students.

3. *Each sampled item is independent.* This means that if the first student selected is enrolled in the College of Business, it has no effect on the chance that the second one selected is also enrolled in Business.

4. *The probability of a success remains the same from trial to trial.* The probability of a failure also remains the same.

The number of trials, designated *n*, and the probability of success (*p*), must be known to construct a binomial distribution. The binomial probability distribution is constructed using the formula:

$$P(r) = \frac{n!}{r!\,(n-r)!}\,(p)^r\,(q)^{n-r} \qquad [5\text{--}3]$$

where *n* is the number of trials, *r* the number of successes, *p* the probability of a success and *q* is $1-p$, the probability of a failure.

Poisson Probability

Another discrete probability distribution is the **Poisson probability distribution**. It has the same four characteristics as the binomial, but in addition the probability of a success (*p*) is small, and *n*, the number of trials, is relatively large. The formula for computing the probability of a success is:

$$P(x) = \frac{\mu^x}{x!e^\mu} \qquad [5\text{--}4]$$

where *x* is the number of successes and μ is the mean number of occurrences (successes) found by $n \times p$, and e is 2.71828 which is the base of the Napierian logarithmic system.

As an example where the Poisson distribution is applicable, suppose electric utility bills are based on the actual reading of the electric meter. In 1 out of 100 cases the meter is incorrectly read ($p = .01$). Suppose the number of errors that appear in the processing of 500 customer bills approximates the Poisson distribution ($n = 500$). In this case the mean number of incorrect bills is 5, found by $\mu = np = 500\,(.01)$. The probabilities of making 1, 2, 3, ... errors can be found in Appendix C.

Hypergeometric Distribution

To qualify as a binomial distribution, the probability of a success must remain constant. What if this requirement is not met? This usually happens when the size of the population is small and samples are drawn from the population and not replaced. This causes the probability of a success to change from one trial (or sample) to the next. This means the trials are *not* independent. For example, if a class consisted of 20 students, 12 males and 8 females, what is the probability of selecting two females to serve on a committee? If Ms. Smith was selected on the first trial she cannot be selected again because she is already on the committee. Thus the outcome of the second trial depends on the outcome of the first trial. The probability of a female on the first selection is 8/20, and if a female is selected first there are 7 females out of the 19 remaining students. Hence, the probability of selecting two females for the committee is .147, found by (8/20) (7/19) .

This probability may also be calculated using the hypergeometric distribution, which is described by the formula:

$$P(r) = \frac{(_SC_r)\,(_{N-S}C_{n-r})}{_NC_n} \qquad [5\text{--}5]$$

where *N* is the size of the population, *S* is the number of successes in the population, *n* is the number sampled, and *r* is the number of successes in the sample. In the example $N = 20$, $S = 8$, $n = 2$, and $r = 2$. Therefore,

$$P(2) = \frac{(_8C_2)\,(_{20-8}C_{2-2})}{_{20}C_2}$$

$$P(2) = \frac{\left(\dfrac{8!}{2!\,6!}\right)\left(\dfrac{12!}{0!\,12!}\right)}{\left(\dfrac{20!}{2!\,18!}\right)} = .147$$

Hence, the probability of selecting two students to serve on a committee and having that committee consist of two females is .147. This is the same probability as computed above.

GLOSSARY

Probability distribution—The listing of all possible outcomes of an experiment and the probability associated with each outcome. This listing is exhaustive and the outcomes are mutually exclusive.

Discrete probability distribution—A distribution that can assume only distinct values. It is usually the result of counting the number of favorable outcomes to an experiment. Example: the number of half gallons of milk sold at the nearby Speedway convenience store yesterday.

Binomial probability distribution—A discrete probability distribution with the following characteristics: (1) The experiment consists of a sequence of n trials. (2) For each trial there are only two possible outcomes—one called a "success" the other a "failure." (3) The probability of a "success" remains the same from trial to trial. So does the probability of a failure. (4) The trials are independent.

Poisson probability distribution—A discrete probability distribution. It has the same characteristics as the binomial, but in addition, the probability of a success is usually small and the number of trials is large. The distribution is positively skewed.

Hypergeometric probability distribution—A discrete probability distribution where the outcomes of consecutive observations are not independent.

Randon variable—It is a numerical value determined by the outcome of an experiment.

CHAPTER PROBLEMS

Problem 1

Bill Russe, production manager at Ross Manufacturing, maintains detailed records on the number of times each machine breaks down and requires service during the week. Bill's records show that the Pruet grinder has required repair service according to the following distribution. Compute the mean and the variance of the number of breakdowns per week.

Number of breakdowns per week	Weeks	Probability
0	20	.333
1	20	.333
2	10	.167
3	10	.167
Total	60	1.000

Solution

The mean, or expected number of breakdowns per week for this probability distribution is computed using formula 5–1:

Number of breakdowns per week X	Probability P(X)	XP(X)
0	.333	0
1	.333	.333
2	.167	.334
3	.167	.501
	E(X) =	1.168

The mean number of times the Pruett machine breaks down per week is 1.168. The variance of the number of breakdowns is computed using formula 5–2.

Number of breakdowns per week X	Probability P(X)	$(X - \mu)$	$(X - \mu)^2 P(X)$
0	.333	0 − 1.168	(1.364) (.333) = .454212
1	.333	1 − 1.168	(0.028) (.333) = .009324
2	.167	2 − 1.168	(0.692) (.167) = .115564
3	.167	3 − 1.168	(3.356) (.167) = .560452
		Total	1.139552

The variance of the number of breakdowns per week is about 1.140. The standard deviation of the number of breakdowns per week is 1.07, found by $\sqrt{1.140}$.

Exercise 1

Check your answers against those in the ANSWER section.

The safety engineer at Ross Manufacturing reported the following probability distribution for the number of on-the-job accidents during a one-month period. Compute the mean and the variance for the distribution.

Number of Accidents	Probability
0	.60
1	.30
2	.10

Problem 2

An insurance representative has appointments with four prospective clients tomorrow. From past experience she knows that the probability of making a sale on any appointment is 1 in 5 or .20. Use the rules of probability to determine the likelihood that she will sell a policy to 3 of the 4 prospective clients.

Solution

First note that the situation described meets the requirements of the binomial probability distribution. The conditions are:

1. There are a fixed number of trials—the representative visits four customers.
2. There are only two possible outcomes for each trial—she sells a policy or she does not sell a policy.
3. The probability of a success remains constant from trial to trial—for each appointment the probability of selling a policy (a success) is .20.
4. The trials are independent—if she sells a policy to the second appointment this does not alter the likelihood of selling to the third or the fourth appointment.

If S represents the outcome of a sale and NS the outcome of no sale, one possibility is that no sale is made on the first appointment but sales are made at the last 3.

$$(NS, S, S, S)$$

These events are independent, therefore the probability of their joint occurrence is the product of the individual probabilities. Therefore, the likelihood of no sale followed by three sales is (0.8) (0.2) (0.2) (0.2) = .0064. However, the requirements of the problem do not stipulate the location of NS. It could be the result of any one of the four appointments. The following summarizes the possible outcomes.

Location of NS	Order of Occurrence	Probability of Occurrence
1	NS, S, S, S	(0.8) (0.2) (0.2) (0.2) = .0064
2	S, NS, S, S	(0.2) (0.8) (0.2) (0.2) = .0064
3	S, S, NS, S	(0.2) (0.2) (0.8) (0.2) = .0064
4	S, S, S, NS	(0.2) (0.2) (0.2) (0.8) = .0064
		.0256

The probability of exactly three sales in the four appointments is the sum of the 4 possibilities. Hence, the probability of selling insurance to 3 out of 4 appointments is .0256.

Problem 3

Now lets use formula 5–3 for the binomial distribution to compute the probability that the sales representative in **Problem 2** will sell a policy to exactly 3 out of the 4 prospective clients.

Solution

To repeat, formula 5–3 for the binomial probability distribution is:

$$P(r) = \frac{n!}{r! \, (n - r)!} \, (p)^r \, (q)^{n - r}$$

where r is the number of successes, 3 in the example.
n is the number of trials, 4 in the example.
p is the probability of a success, .20 in the example.
q is the probability of a failure, .80 in the example.

Applying the formula to find the probability of selling an insurance policy to exactly 3 out of 4 potential customers.

$$P(r) = \frac{n!}{r! \, (n - r)!} \, (p)^r \, (q)^{n - r}$$

$$= \frac{4!}{3! \, (4 - 3)!} \, (.20)^3 \, (.80)^{4 - 3} = .0256$$

Thus the probability is .0256 that the representative will be able to sell policies to exactly 3 out of the 4 clients visited. This is the same probability as computed earlier. Clearly, formula 5–3 leads to a more direct solution, and better accommodates the situation where the number of trials is large.

Exercise 2

Check your answers against those in the ANSWER section.

It is known that 60 percent of all registered voters in the 42nd Congressional District are Republicans. Three registered voters are selected at random from the district. Compute the probability that exactly 2 of the 3 selected are Republicans, using both the rules of probability and the binomial formula.

Problem 4

In **Problems 2 and 3** the probability of 3 sales resulting from 4 appointments was computed using both the rules of addition and multiplication and the binomial formula. A more convenient way of arriving at the probabilities for 0, 1, 2, 3, or 4 sales out of 4 appointments is to refer to a binomial table. We will now use the binomial table to determine the probabilities for all possible outcomes.

Solution

Refer to Appendix A, the binomial table. Find the table where n, the number of trials, is 4. Within that table find the row where $r = 0$, and move horizontally to the column headed $p = .20$. The probability of 0 sales is .410. The list for all possible outcome number of successes is:

Binomial Probability Distribution

$n = 4$ $\qquad\qquad$ $p = .20$

Number of Successes (r)	Probability
0	.410
1	.410
2	.154
3	.026
4	.002
	1.000*

$\qquad$ *Slight discrepancy due to rounding.

Problem 5

Use the information regarding the insurance representative, where $n = 4$ and $p = .20$, to compute the probability that the representative sells more than two policies. Also determine the mean and variance.

Solution

The binomial table (Appendix A) can be used to compute the probability. First, note that the solution must include the probability that exactly 3 policies are sold and exactly 4 policies are sold, but not 2. From Appendix A, $P(3) = .026$ and $P(4) = .002$. The rule of addition is then used to combine these mutually exclusive events.

$$P(\text{more than 2}) = P(3) + P(4)$$
$$= .026 + .002$$
$$= .028$$

71

Thus the probability that a representative sells more than 2 policies is .028. Suppose the question asked: "What is the probability of selling three or more policies in four trials?" Since there are no outcomes between greater than 2 and less than 3, the answer is exactly the same—.028.

To determine the mean and the variance of a binomial we use formulas 5–4 and 5–5. $\mu = np = 4(.20) = .80$. The variance is $\sigma^2 = np(1 - p) = 4(.20)(.80) = .64$. So the standard deviation is $\sqrt{.64} = .80$ policies.

Exercise 3

Check your answers against those in the ANSWER section.

Labor negotiators estimate that 30 percent of all major contract negotiations result in a strike. During the next year, 12 major contracts must be negotiated. Determine the following probabilities, using the binomial distribution in Appendix A: (a) no major strikes, (b) at least 5, and (c) between 2 and 4 (that is 2, 3, or 4).

Problem 6

Alden and Associates write weekend trip insurance at a very nominal charge. Records show that the probability a motorist will have an accident during the weekend and file a claim is quite small (.0005). Suppose Alden wrote 400 policies for the forthcoming weekend. Compute probability that exactly two claims will be filed. Depict this distribution in the form of a chart.

Solution

The Poisson distribution is appropriate for this problem because the probability of filing a claim is small ($p = .0005$), and the number of trials n is large (400).

The Poisson distribution is described by formula 5–7:

$$P(X) = \frac{\mu^x}{x!e^\mu}$$

where x is the number of successes (claims filed). In this example $X = 2$.
   μ is the expected or mean number of claims to be filed $\mu = np = (400)(.0005) = .2$
   e is a mathematical constant equal to 2.718.

The probability that exactly two claims are filed is .0164, found by

$$P(2) = \frac{\mu^x}{x!e^\mu} = \frac{(.2)^2}{2!\,(2.718)^{0.2}} = .0164$$

This indicates that the probability is somewhat small (about .0164) that exactly 2 claims will be filed.

The calculations to determine the probability .0164 were not shown above. A more convenient way to determine Poisson probabilities is to refer to Appendix C. To use this table, first find the column where $\mu = 0.20$, then go down that column to the row where $X = 2$ and read the value at the intersection. It is .0164.

72

The probabilities computed using formula 5–7 and those in Appendix C are the same. But those from the Appendix can be determined much more rapidly. The complete Poisson distribution and a graph for the case where μ = 0.20 are shown below.

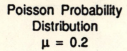
Poisson Probability
Distribution
μ = 0.2

Number of Claims	Probability
0	.8187
1	.1637
2	.0164
3	.0011
4	.0001
	1.0000

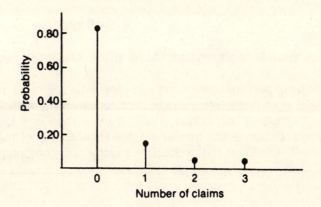

Exercise 4

Check your answers against those in the ANSWER section.

Typographical errors in a textbook follow a Poisson probability distribution. The probability of one or more typographical errors on any page is .002. If a textbook contains 1,000 pages, compute the probability (a) that there are no typos on a page and (b) that there are at least 2.

Problem 7

The government of an underdeveloped country has 8 loans payable, 5 of which are overdue. If a representative of the International Monetary Fund randomly selects 3 loans, what is the probability that exactly 2 are overdue?

Solution

Note in this problem that successive observations are not independent. That is, the outcome of one sampled item influences the next sampled item. Because the observations are not independent, the binomial distribution is not appropriate and the hypergeometric distribution is used. Formula 7–6 for the hypergeometric distribution is:

$$P(r) = \frac{(_SC_r)\ (_{N\ -\ S}C_{n\ -\ r})}{_NC_n}$$

where N is the population size, S is the number of successes in the population, n is the number sampled, and r is the number of successes in the sample. The problem asks for the probability of exactly 2 loans overdue in a sample of 3, so $r = 2$ and $n = 3$. There are 8 loans in the population, 5 of which are overdue, so $N = 8$ and $S = 5$.

The probability is computed as follows:

$$P(2) = \frac{(_5C_2)\ (_3C_1)}{_8C_3} = \frac{\left(\dfrac{5!}{2!\ 3!}\right)\ \left(\dfrac{3!}{1!\ 2!}\right)}{\left(\dfrac{8}{3!\ 5!}\right)} = \frac{30}{56} = .536$$

73

Interpreting the probability that exactly 2 of the 3 sampled loans are overdue is .536.

Exercise 5

Check your answers against those in the ANSWER section.

A retailer of personal computers just received a shipment of 30 units of a new model. The store has a quality agreement with the manufacturer which states that four of the machines are to be selected for a thorough performance check. If more than one fails a performance test the shipment is returned. Suppose the retailer did not know that 5 of the 30 incoming personal computers are defective. Compute the probability exactly two computers selected at random are defective.

CHAPTER ASSIGNMENT 5

Discrete Probability Distributions

Name _____ Section _____ Score _____

PART I **Matching** Select the correct answer and write the appropriate letter in the space provided.

_____ 1. Random variable

_____ 2. Discrete distribution

_____ 3. Continuous distribution

_____ 4. Probability distribution

_____ 5. Poisson distribution

a. usually the result of counting

b. a listing of the possible outcomes and the corresponding probability of success

c. p is usually small and n is large

d. usually the result of a measurement

e. does not include probability

PART II **Multiple Choice** Select the correct answer and write the appropriate letter in the space provided.

_____ 6. A variable that can take on different values depending on the outcome of an experiment is called a

    a. probability distribution.
    b. discrete probability distribution.
    c. random variable.
    d. cumulative frequency distribution.

_____ 7. A discrete probability distribution may assume

    a. only certain values.
    b. an infinite number of values within a range.
    c. only positive values.
    d. only fractional values.

_____ 8. The mean of a discrete probability distribution is

    a. always equal to its variance.
    b. always equal to its standard deviation.
    c. also referred to as the expected value.
    d. None of these is correct.

_____ 9. Which of the following is a requirement of the binomial probability distribution?

    a. There are only two outcomes.
    b. The trials are dependent.
    c. The probability of a success changes from trial to trial.
    d. The probability of a success is small.

_____ 10. The mean of a binomial distribution is equal to

    a. $np(1 - p)$
    b. $\sqrt{np(1 - p)}$
    c. $1/p$
    d. np

_____ 11. The Poisson distribution is

    a. negatively skewed.
    b. positively skewed.
    c. symmetrical.
    d. continuous.

_____ 12. To construct a binomial distribution, we need to know

    a. the mean and the variance.
    b. the mean only.
    c. the values of n and p.
    d. only the number of trials.

_____ 13. The binomial, the Poisson, and the hypergeometric are all examples of

    a. continuous probability distributions.
    b. discrete probability distributions.
    c. continuous random variables.
    d. symmetric distributions.

_____ 14. For any discrete distribution the

    a. sum of the probabilities of the possible outcomes must be 1.00.
    b. probability of each outcome is between 0 and 1.
    c. outcomes must be mutually exclusive.
    d. All of the above.

_____ 15. Usually a discrete random variable results from a

    a. measurement.
    b. count.
    c. small probability.
    d. small mean.

PART III Problems Record your answer in the space provided. Show essential calculations.

16. A recent study of families owning 0, 1, 2, 3, and 4 automobiles showed that 10 percent of the families did not own an automobile, 30 percent owned one, and so on. The number of automobiles owned and the corresponding probability is given in the following table.

Number of Cars X	Probability P(X)
0	.10
1	.30
2	.30
3	.20
4	.10

  a. Compute the mean number of cars per family.

Answer

  b. Compute the variance of the number of cars per family.

Answer

76

17. Big Toughie, a plastic bag manufactured by Bags Unlimited, will break open under twenty pounds of pressure 30% of the time. A sample of eight bags is selected from recent production.

a. Compute the mean and the standard deviation of the number of bags broken.

Answer

b. What is the likelihood that exactly 4 bags will break open during the test?

Answer

c. What is the likelihood that 4 or more bags will break open during the test?

Answer

18. Kankakee Clothing, a catalog mail order company that specializes in clothing for young adults, receives an average of 5 phone orders per hour.

a. What is the likelihood of receiving exactly 5 orders in a particular hour?

Answer

b. What is the likelihood of receiving less than 5 orders in a particular hour?

Answer

c. What is the likelihood of receiving at least 5 orders in an hour?

Answer

19. Suppose the Foreign Relations Committee of the U.S. Senate is comprised of eight Democrats and four Republicans. Four members of the committee are selected at random to participate in arms reduction talks. What is the likelihood that two Republicans and two Democrats are selected to participate in the arms reduction talks?

Answer

6

THE NORMAL PROBABILITY DISTRIBUTION

CHAPTER GOALS

After completing this chapter, you will be able to:

1. List the characteristics of the normal distribution.
2. Calculate the probabilities using the standard normal distribution.
3. Use the normal distribution to approximate binomial probabilities.

Introduction

The previous chapter dealt with discrete probability distributions. Recall that for a discrete distribution, the outcome can assume only a specific set of values. For example, the number of correct responses to ten true-false questions can only be the numbers 0, 1, 2, . . . , 10.

This chapter examines an important continuous probability distribution—the normal distribution. Recall that a continuous probability distribution can assume an infinite number of values within a given range. As an example, the weight of an engine block could be 54, 54.1, or 54.1437 pounds depending on the accuracy of the measuring device.

Characteristics of the Normal Distribution

The mean of a normal distribution is represented by the Greek letter μ (lower case mu), and the standard deviation by the Greek letter σ (lower case sigma). The major characteristics of the normal distribution are:

1. *The normal distribution is "bell-shaped" and the mean, median, and mode are all equal.* Exactly one-half of the observations are larger than this center value, and one-half are smaller.

2. *The distribution is symmetrical.* A vertical line drawn at the mean divides the distribution into two equal halves and these halves have exactly the same shape.

3. *It is asymptotic.* That is, the curve approaches the X-axis but never actually touches it.

4. *A normal distribution is completely described by its mean and standard deviation.* This indicates that if the mean and standard deviation are known, a normal distribution can be constructed and its curve drawn.

5. *There is a "family" of normal distributions.* There is a different normal distribution for each combination of μ and σ.

These characteristics are summarized in the following graph.

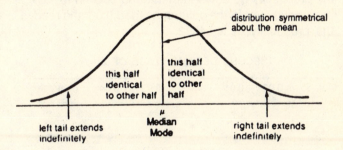

The Standard Normal Distribution

As noted in the previous discussion, there are many normal probability distributions, a different one for each pair of values for a mean and standard deviation. This principle makes the normal applicable to a wide range of real-world situations. However, since there is an infinite number of probability distributions, it would be awkward to construct tables of probabilities for so many different distributions. An efficient method for overcoming this difficulty is to standardize each normal distribution. To obtain the probability of a value falling in the interval between the variable of interest (X) and the mean (μ), first we compute the distance between the value

(*X*) and the mean (μ). Then we express that difference in units of the standard deviation by dividing (*X* − μ) by the standard deviation. This process is called **standardizing**.

The formula for a specific standardized value, called a *z* value, is:

$$z = \frac{X - \mu}{\sigma} \qquad [6\text{--}1]$$

where *X* is any observation of interest, μ is the mean of the normal distribution, σ is the standard deviation of the normal distribution, and *z* is the **standardized normal value**, usually called the **z value**.

To illustrate the probability of a value being between a selected *X* value and the mean μ, suppose the mean useful life of a car battery is 36 months, with a standard deviation of 3 months. What is the probability that such a battery will last between 36 and 40 months?

The first step is to convert the 40 months to an equivalent standard normal value, using formula 6–1. The computation is:

$$z = \frac{X - \mu}{\sigma} = \frac{40 - 36}{3} = 1.33$$

Next refer to Appendix D, a table for the normal distribution. A partial table is shown below. To find the probability go down the left-hand column to 1.3, then move over to the column headed 0.03 and read the probability. It is .4082.

SECOND DECIMAL PLACE OF Z

Z	0.00	0.01	0.02	0.03	0.04	0.05
		•	•	•	•	
		•	•	•	•	
		•	•	•	•	
1.0						
1.1		.3665	.3686	.3708	.3729	
1.2		.3869	.3888	.3907	.3925	
1.3		.4049	.4066	.4082	.4099	
1.4		.4207	.4222	.4236	.4251	

The probability that a battery will last between 36 and 40 months is .4082. Other probabilities may be calculated, such as more than 46 months, and less than 33 months. Further details are given in Problems 1 through 5.

The Normal Approximation to the Binomial

The binomial table (Appendix A) goes from a sample size of 1 to 25. What do we do when the sample size is greater than 25? A binomial probability can be estimated using the normal distribution. To apply it both *np* and *n(1 − p)* must be greater than 5. The sample size, or the number of trials, is designated by *n*, and *p* is the probability of a success. The mean and the standard deviation of the binomial are computed by:

$$\mu = np$$
$$\sigma = \sqrt{np(1 - p)}$$

To illustrate, suppose 60 percent of the applications for an exclusive credit card are approved. In a sample of 200 applications, what is the probability that more than 130 applications are approved? Since both *np* and *n(1 − p)* exceed 5 (that is, *np* = 200(0.6) = 120 and *n(1 − p)* = 200(1 − 0.60) = 80), the normal approximation to the binomial may be used.

The mean and standard deviation are computed as follows:

$$\mu = np = 200(0.60) = 120$$
$$\sigma = \sqrt{np(1 - p)} = \sqrt{200(0.6)(0.4)} = 6.93$$

This distribution is standardized by:

$$z = \frac{X - \mu}{\sigma} = \frac{130.5 - 120}{6.93} = 1.52$$

The probability of a *z* value between 0 and 1.52 is .4357. (See Appendix D.) Therefore the probability of a *z* value greater than .4357 is .0643, found by .5000 − .4357. So, the probability that more than 130 applications will be approved is .0643.

Why is 130.5 used instead of 130 in the previous example? Namely to "correct" for the fact that a continuous distribution (the normal) is used to approximate a discrete distribution (the binomial). On a continuous scale the value 130 would range from 129.5 to 130.5. On a discrete scale there would be a "gap" between 130 and 131 where there would not be any probability. The .50 is called the **correction for continuity**.

GLOSSARY

Normal distribution—A continuous probability distribution that is uniquely determined by μ and σ. Portrayed graphically, it is symmetrical and bell-shaped. The curve approaches the X-axis asymptotically as X approaches $-\infty$ or $+\infty$. For a normal distribution the mean, median, and mode are equal. Half the observations are above the mean and half below it.

Standard normal distribution—A special normal distribution where the mean is 0 and the standard deviation 1.0. A table of areas is available for computing probabilities using the standard normal distribution. The total area under the normal curve is 1.0. Thus, the area to the right of the mean μ is .5000. The area to the left of the mean is also .5000.

Normal approximation to the binomial—A binomial probability may be approximated by the normal when both np and $n(1 - p)$ are greater than 5.0.

z values—It is a unit of measure with respect to the standard normal distribution. A z value is the number of standard deviations from the mean. z may be positive or negative. A z value to the right of the mean is positive, to the left negative.

Correction for continuity—A correction factor of .5 used to improve the accuracy of the approximation of a binomial probability distribution by the normal distribution.

CHAPTER PROBLEMS

Problem 1

The mean amount of gasoline and services charged by Key Refining Company credit customers is $70 per month. The distribution of amounts spent is approximately normal with a standard deviation of $10. Compute the probability of selecting a credit card customer at random and finding the customer charged between $70 and $83 last month.

Solution

The first step is to convert the area between $70 and $83 to a z value using formula 6–1.

$$z = \frac{X - \mu}{\sigma}$$

where X is any value of the random variable ($83 in this problem), μ is the arithmetic mean of the normal distribution ($70), σ is the standard deviation ($10) of the normal distribution. Solving for z:

$$z = \frac{X - \mu}{\sigma} = \frac{\$83 - \$70}{\$10} = 1.30$$

This indicates that $83 is 1.30 standard deviations to the right of the mean of $70. Showing the problem graphically:

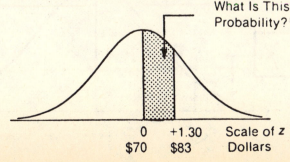

81

The probability of a z value from 0 to 1.30 is given in a table of areas of the normal curve, Appendix D. To obtain the probability, go down the left-hand column to 1.3, then move over to the column headed 0.00, and read the probability. It is .4032. To put it another way, 40.32 percent of the credit card customers charge between $70 and $83 per month.

Problem 2

Again using the Key Refinery data from **Problem 1**, compute the probability of customers charging between $57 and $83 per month.

Solution

As shown in the following graph, the probability of a customer charging between $57 and $70 per month must be combined with the probability of charging between $70 and $83 in a month to obtain the combined probability.

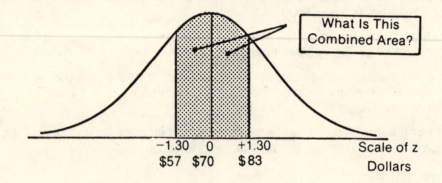

$$z = \frac{X - \mu}{\sigma} = \frac{\$57 - \$70}{\$10} = -1.30$$

The probability of between $70 and $83 was computed in Problem 1. Due to the symmetry of the normal distribution, the probability between 0 and 1.30 is the same as the probability between −1.30 and 0. It is .4032. The probability that customers will charge between $57 and $83 is .8064, found by adding .4032 and .4032.

Problem 3

Using the Key Refining data from **Problem 1**, what is the probability that a particular customer charges less than $54?

Solution

The area to be determined is shown below.

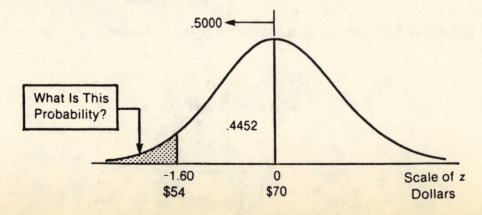

82

The z value for the area of the normal curve between $70 and $54 is –1.60, found by:

$$z = \frac{X - \mu}{\sigma} = \frac{\$54 - \$70}{\$10} = \frac{-\$16}{\$10} = -1.60$$

Referring to Appendix D, and a z of 1.60, the area of the normal curve between μ ($70) and X ($54) is .4452. Recall that for a symmetrical distribution half of the observations are above the mean, and half below it. In this problem, the probability of an observation being below $70 is, therefore, .5000. Since the probability of an observation being between $54 and $70 is .4452, it follows that .5000 – .4452 = .0548, which is the probability that an observation is below $54. To put it another way, 5.48 percent of the customers charge less than $54 per month.

Problem 4

Again using the Key Refining data from **Problem 1** compute the probability of a customer charging between $82 and $92.

Solution

The area to be determined is depicted in the following diagram.

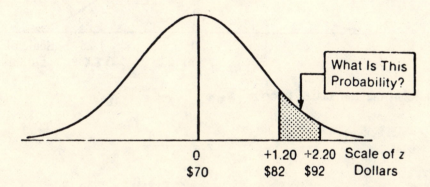

The areas of the normal curve between $70 and $82, and $70 and $92 are determined using formula 6–1.

$$z = \frac{X - \mu}{\sigma}$$

$$= \frac{\$82 - \$70}{\$10}$$

$$= 1.20$$

$$z = \frac{X - \mu}{\sigma}$$

$$= \frac{\$92 - \$70}{\$10}$$

$$= 2.20$$

The probability corresponding to a z of 1.20 is .3849 (from Appendix D).

The probability corresponding to a z of 2.20 is .4861 (from Appendix D).

The probability of a credit card customer charging between $82 and $92 a month, therefore, is the difference between these two probabilities. Thus, .4861 – .3849 = .1012. That is, 10.12 percent of the charge account customers charge between $82 and $92 monthly.

Problem 5

Key Refining (**Problem 1**) decided to send a special financing plan to charge account customers having the highest 10 percent of the money charges. What is the dividing point between the customers who receive the special plan and those who do not?

Solution

The shaded area in the following diagram represents the upper 10 percent who receive the special plan. X represents the unknown value that divides the customers into two groups—those who receive the special financing plan (the shaded area), and those who do not receive it. The area from the mean of $70 to this unknown X value is .4000, found by .5000 − .1000. From the table of areas of the normal curve (Appendix D), the closest z value corresponding to the area .4000 is 1.28. This indicates that the unknown X value is 1.28 standard deviations above the mean.

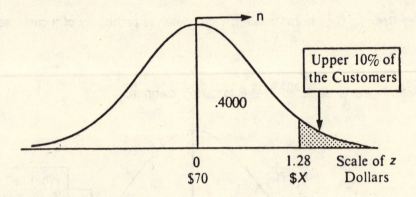

Substituting 1.28 in the formula 6–1 for z:

$$z = \frac{X - \mu}{\sigma}$$

$$1.28 = \frac{X - \$70}{\$10}$$

$$X = \$82.80$$

Key Refining should send the special financing plan to those charge account customers having a monthly charge of $82.80 and above.

Exercise 1

Check your answers against those in the ANSWER section.

A cola dispensing machine is set to dispense a mean of 2.02 liters into a container labeled 2 liters. Actual quantities dispensed vary and the amounts are normally distributed with a standard deviation of .015 liters.

a. What is the probability a container will contain less than 2 liters?
b. What is the probability a container will contain between 2.00 and 2.03 liters?
c. Two percent of the containers will contain how much cola or more?

84

Problem 6

The Key Refining Company, referred to in the earlier problems, determined that 15 percent of its customers will not pay their bill by the due date. What is the probability that for a sample of 80 customers, less than 10 will not pay their bill by the due date?

Solution

The answer could be determined by using the binomial distribution where p, the probability of a success, is 0.15, and where n, the number of trials, is 80. However, most binomial tables do not go beyond an n of 25 and the calculations by hand would be very tedious.

The probability can be accurately estimated by using the normal approximation to the binomial. The approximations are quite good when both np and $n(1 - p)$ are greater than 5. In this case, $np = (80)(0.15) = 12$, and $n(1 - p) = (80)(0.85) = 68$. Both are greater than 5.

Recall the mean and variance of a binomial distribution are computed as follows:

$$\mu = np = (80)(0.15) = 12$$
$$\sigma^2 = np(1 - p) = (80)(0.15)(0.85) = 10.2$$

The standard deviation is 3.19, found by $\sqrt{10.2}$. The area less than 9.5 is shown on the following diagram. Because we are estimating a discrete distribution using a continuous distribution, the continuity correction factor is needed. In this instance if we were actually using the binomial distribution we would add the probabilities of 0 customers not paying, one customer not paying and so on up to nine customers not paying the bill. With the discrete distribution there would be no probability of 8.6 customers not paying their bill. When we estimate binomial probabilities using the normal distribution, the area for nine corresponds to the area from 8.5 up to 9.5. In this case, we want all the area below (to the left of) 9.5. This area is depicted schematically as:

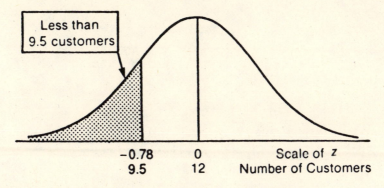

The z value associated with less than 9.5 customers is −0.78, found by

$$z = \frac{9.5 - 12.0}{3.19} = -0.78$$

The area to the left of −0.78 is .2177 found by .5000 − .2823. The probability that less than ten customers will not pay their bill is .2177. Incidentally, using the MINITAB System, the exact probability using the binomial distribution is .2211. So the approximation is in error by only .0034.

Exercise 2

Check your answers against those in the ANSWER section.

A new drug has been developed that is found to relieve nasal congestion in 90 percent of those with the condition. The new drug is administered to 300 patients with this condition. What is the probability that more than 265 will be relieved of the nasal congestion?

CHAPTER ASSIGNMENT 6

The Normal Probability Distribution

Name _____ Section _____ Score _____

PART I **Matching** Select the correct answer and write the appropriate letter in the space provided.

_____ 1. z-value

_____ 2. normal distribution

_____ 3. Continuity correction

_____ 4. Asymptotic

_____ 5. Symmetrical

a. approaches but never touches the X-axis

b. a continuous distribution

c. same shape on either side of the median

d. used when the normal is used to approximate the binomial

e. distance from the mean in units of the standard deviation

PART II **Multiple Choice** Select the correct answer and write the appropriate letter in the space provided.

_____ 6. In a normal probability distribution the mean is

a. always equal to the median.
b. always larger than the median.
c. always smaller than the median.
d. never equal to the mode.

_____ 7. The normal probability distribution is a

a. continuous distribution.
b. discrete distribution.
c. binomial distribution.
d. Poisson distribution.

_____ 8. A normal probability distribution is completely described by the

a. mean only.
b. variance only.
c. mean and the standard deviation.
d. standard deviation only.

_____ 9. The standard normal distribution

a. is a special case of the normal distribution.
b. has a mean of 0 and a standard deviation of 1.
c. measures distance from the mean in units of the standard deviation.
d. All of the above.

6

_____ 10. Any normal distribution can be converted to the standard normal distribution

    a. if np is greater than 5.
    b. by the formula $(X - \mu)/\sigma$
    c. by the formula $n(1 - p)$
    d. None of these is correct.

_____ 11. A normal distribution

    a. has at least two peaks.
    b. is symmetrical.
    c. increases as X decreases.
    d. is discrete.
    e. None of these is correct.

_____ 12. The binomial distribution can be used to approximate the normal distribution when

    a. n is greater than 30.
    b. np and $n(1 - p)$ are both greater than 5.
    c. np is larger than 25.
    d. none of the above. We approximate the binomial with the normal.

_____ 13. The area under a normal curve from a z value of –1.00 up to a z value of 2.00 is

    a. .3413
    b. .4772
    c. .8185
    d. None of the above.

_____ 14. A z value

    a. can assume both positive and negative values.
    b. can assume only negative values.
    c. is always 0.
    d. is found by np.

_____ 15. To construct a normal approximation to the binomial

    a. both n and p must be known.
    b. np and $n(1 - p)$ must be greater than 5.
    c. the binomial conditions must be met.
    d. All of the above.

PART III Problems Record your answer in the space provided. Show essential calculations.

16. The mean daily charge to a patient for medicines, nursing care, and so on at the Sunny View Medical Center is $320 with the standard deviation of the distribution of charges $25.

   a. What proportion of the patients are charged more than $350 per day?

   ![ ]

   Answer

   b. What proportion of the patients are charged more than $275 but less than $350 per day?

   ![ ]

   Answer

   c. What proportion of the patients are charged more than $275 but less than $300 per day?

   ![ ]

   Answer

   d. The president of Sunny View recently reported to the Board of Directors that the mean daily amount charged a patient was $320. He also said that a profit was only being made on the upper (largest) 30% of the charges. Above what amount does the center make a profit?

   ![ ]

   Answer

17. A study by the Quality Assurance Director at Sunny View Medical Center shows that 20% of those who are treated in their Emergency Room are subsequently admitted to the main hospital for at least one night. Last week 200 patients were treated in the Emergency Room.

a. Compute the mean and the standard deviation of the binomial distribution.

Answer

b. What is the likelihood that more than 30 patients were admitted to the main hospital after being treated in the Emergency Room?

Answer

c. What is the likelihood that exactly 30 patients were admitted to the main hospital after being treated in the Emergency Room?

Answer

d. What is the likelihood that between 45 and 50 patients were admitted to the main hospital after being treated in the Emergency Room?

Answer

7

SAMPLING METHODS AND SAMPLING DISTRIBUTIONS

CHAPTER GOALS

After completing this chapter, you will be able to:

1. Explain the various methods of selecting a sample from a population.
2. List the reasons for sampling.
3. Explain the central limit theorem and its importance to statistical inference.
4. Calculate and interpret confidence intervals for means and proportions.
5. Define and construct a sampling distribution of means.
6. Understand and apply the finite population correction factor.
7. Determine the size of a sample.

Introduction

With this chapter we begin our study of sampling. Sampling is necessary because we want to make statements about a population but we do not want to (or cannot) examine all the items in that population. Recall from Chapter 1 that a **population** refers to the entire group of objects or persons of interest. The population of interest might be all the persons in the city receiving welfare payments or all the computer chips produced during the last hour. A **sample** is a portion, a part, or a subset of the population. Fifty welfare recipients out of 4,000 receiving payments might constitute the sample, or 20 computer chips might be sampled out of 1,500 produced last hour.

Reasons for Sampling

Why is it necessary to sample? Why can't we just inspect all the items? There are several reasons.
1. *The destructive nature of certain tests*. The manufacturer of fuses cannot test all the fuses because in the testing the fuse is destroyed and none would be available for sale!
2. *The physical impossibility of checking all the items in the population*. The South Dakota Game Commission, for example, cannot check all the deer, grouse, and other wild game because they are always moving.
3. *The cost of studying all the items in the population is prohibitive*. Televisions ratings are established by analyzing the viewing habits of about

1,200 viewers. The cost of studying all the homes having television would be exorbitant.
4. *The adequacy of sample results*. If the sample results of the viewing habits of 1,200 homes revealed that only 1.1 percent of the homes watched "Mama Knows Best", no doubt the program would be replaced by another series. Checking the viewing habits of all the homes regarding "Mama Knows Best" probably would not change the percent significantly.
5. *To contact the entire population in most cases would be very time consuming*. To ask every eligible voter regarding the chances of Senator Tolson in the forthcoming election would take months. The election would probably be over before the survey was completed.

Types of Sampling

There are two basic types of sampling, probability sampling and nonprobability sampling. If all the items in the population have a chance to be included in the sample, the method is referred to as **probability sampling**. If the items included in the sample are based on the judgment of the person selecting the sample, the method is called **nonprobability sampling**.

Types of Probability Sampling

Four types of probability sampling are commonly used: simple random sampling, systematic sampling, stratified sampling, and cluster sampling.

In a **simple random sample** each item in the population has the *same* chance of being selected for inclusion in the sample.

Three ways of selecting a simple random sample are:

1. The name or identifying number of each item is recorded on a slip of paper and placed in a box. The slips of paper are shuffled and the required sample size is chosen from the box.
2. Each item is numbered and a table of random numbers, such as the one in Appendix E, is used to select the members of the sample.
3. Many computers have routines that randomly select a given number of items from the population.

In a **systematic sample** the items in the population are numbered 1, 2, 3, ... Next, a random starting point is selected—let's say 39. Every nth item thereafter, such as every 100th, is selected for the sample. This means that 39, 139, 239, 339, and so on would be a part of the sample.

In a **stratified sample** the population is divided into subgroups, or strata, and a sample is drawn from each stratum. For example, if our study involved Army personnel, we might decide to stratify the population (all Army personnel) into generals, other officers, and enlisted personnel. The number selected from each of the three strata could be proportional to the total number in the population for the corresponding strata. Each member of the population can belong to only one of the strata. That is, a military person cannot be a general and a private at the same time.

Cluster sampling is often used to reduce the cost of sampling when the population is scattered over a large geographic area. Suppose the objective is to study household waste collection in a large city. As a first step you divide the city into smaller units (perhaps precincts). Next, the precincts are numbered and several selected randomly. Finally, households within each of these precincts are randomly selected and interviewed.

Sampling Error

It is not logical to expect that the results obtained from a sample will coincide *exactly* with those from a population. For example, it is unlikely that the mean welfare payment for a sample of 50 recipients in Chicago is exactly the same as the mean for all 40,000 welfare recipients in Chicago. The difference between the actual population value (**a parameter**) and the sample value (**the statistic**) is called **sample error**. Since these errors happen by chance, they are referred to as **chance variations**.

The Sampling Distribution of the Mean

Suppose all possible samples of size *n* are selected from a specified population, and the mean of each of these samples is computed. The distribution of these sample means is called the **sampling distribution of the mean**. The sampling distribution of the mean is a probability distribution and has the following major characteristics.

1. The mean of all the sample means will be exactly equal to the population mean.
2. If the population from which the samples are drawn is normal, the distribution of sample means is also normally distributed.
3. If the population from which the samples are drawn is not normal, the sampling distribution is approximately normal, provided the samples are "sufficiently" large (usually accepted to include at least 30 observations). This phenomenon is called the **Central Limit Theorem**.

Point Estimates

A point estimate is based on the sample information. It is one value used to estimate an unknown population parameter. For example, a sample of 100 recent accounting graduates revealed a mean starting salary of $36,000. The $36,000 is a point estimate. The sample mean is our best estimate of the mean starting salary of all (population) accounting graduates.

Confidence Interval Estimates

Why is the above mentioned central limit theorem so important? It can be used to specify a range of values within which a population parameter, such as the population mean, can be expected to occur. This range of values is called the **confidence interval**. The end points of the confidence interval are called the **confidence limits**. The measure of the confidence we have that an interval estimate will include the population parameter is called the **level of confidence**. A confidence interval for the population mean is determined by:

$$\overline{X} \pm z \frac{\sigma}{\sqrt{n}} \qquad [7\text{–}3]$$

where $\bar{X}$ is the sample mean, z is the value associated with the given level of confidence, σ the population standard deviation, and n the size of the sample. If σ is not known, but the sample size is 30 or more, then s, the sample standard deviation, is used in place of σ.

The confidence interval for a population proportion is found by:

$$\bar{p} \pm z \sqrt{\frac{\bar{p}(1 - \bar{p})}{n}} \qquad [7\text{--}8]$$

where $\bar{p}$ is the sample proportion, found by X/n. X is the number of "successes" in a sample of size n. If 451 out of 2,000 voters surveyed plan to vote for the incumbent governor, $X = 451$ and $n = 2,000$. z is the z value, corresponding to the selected level of confidence. How this z value is determined will be explained in Problem 3.

Finite Correction Factor

If the sampling is done without replacement from a small population, the **finite population correction factor** is used. The usual rule is that if the sample constitutes more than 5 percent of the population, the finite correction factor is applied. Its purpose is to account for the fact that a parameter can be more accurately estimated from a small population when a large portion of that population's units are sampled. The correction factor is:

$$\sqrt{\frac{N - n}{N - 1}}$$

What is the effect of this term? If N, the number of units in the population is large relative to n, the sample size, the value of this correction factor is near 1.00. For example, if $N = 10,000$ and a sample of 40 is selected the value of the correction factor is .9980, found by $\sqrt{(10,000 - 40)/(10,000 - 1)}$. However, if N is only 500 the correction factor is .9601, found by $\sqrt{(500 - 40)/(500 - 1)}$. Logically, we can estimate a population parameter with a sample of 40 from a population of 500 more accurately, than with a sample of 40 from a population of 10,000.

The standard error of the mean or the standard error of the proportion is multiplied by the correction factor. Because the correction factor will always be less than 1.00. the effect is to reduce the standard error. Stated differently, because the sample constituted a substantial proportion of the population, the standard error is reduced. The confidence interval for the population mean, therefore, is computed as follows:

$$\bar{X} \pm z \frac{s}{\sqrt{n}} \left(\sqrt{\frac{N - n}{N - 1}} \right)$$

The confidence interval for a population proportion is:

$$\bar{p} \pm z \sqrt{\frac{\bar{p}(1 - \bar{p})}{n}} \left(\sqrt{\frac{N - n}{N - 1}} \right)$$

Required Sample Size

The size of a sample required for a particular study is based on three factors.
1. The desired level of confidence. This is expressed in terms of z.
2. The variability in the population under study (as measured by s).
3. The maximum allowable error (E).

The sample size is computed using the formula:

$$n = \left(\frac{z \cdot s}{E} \right)^2 \qquad [7\text{--}12]$$

A population with considerable variability (reflected by a large s) will require a larger sample than a population with a smaller standard deviation. E is the maximum allowable error that you, the researcher, are willing to accept. It is the amount that is added and subtracted from the mean to obtain the end points of the confidence limits.

To determine the required sample size for a proportion p, the following formula is used.

$$n = \bar{p}(1 - \bar{p}) \left(\frac{z}{E} \right)^2 \qquad [7\text{--}13]$$

where $\bar{p}$ is based on a pilot study. If no estimate of $\bar{p}$ is available then let $\bar{p} = .50$. The sample size will never be larger than that obtained when $\bar{p} = .50$.

GLOSSARY

Population—The total group of persons, or objects, of interest.

Sample—A portion, or part, of the population.

Statistical inference—Reasoning from a small group (a sample) to the large entire group (the population).

Probability sample—All the items in the population of interest have a chance to be included in the sample.

Nonprobability sample—The items included in the sample are based on the judgment of the person selecting the sample.

Simple random sample—Each item in the population has the same likelihood of being selected for the sample.

Systematic sample—The elements of the population are numbers, 1, 2, 3, 4, . . . etc. A random starting point is elected. Then every *n*th element thereafter is chosen for the sample.

Stratified random sample—The population is divided into some logical strata. Samples are drawn from each strata, either proportional to the number in each stratum, or in a nonproportional manner depending on a specified criterion.

Sampling error—The difference between the sample statistic and the population parameter.

Chance variation—Variation that is not attributable to any specific cause. It is random in nature.

Finite population correction factor—A factor used to correct the standard error of the mean, or the standard error of the proportion. It is usually applied when $n/N > .05$.

Statistic—Refers to any sample value (such as the sample mean).

Parameter—Refers to any population value (such as the population mean).

Point estimate—A single value resulting from a sample used as an estimate of a corresponding population value.

Interval estimate—The interval within which the population value such as the population mean is likely to occur.

Sampling distribution of the mean—A probability distribution of all possible sample means of a given size selected from a population.

Central Limit Theorem—The distribution of the sample means approaches the normal distribution as the sample size increases, regardless of the shape of the population.

Level of confidence—The degree of confidence the researcher has that the population value (such as the mean) will lie in a specified interval.

Cluster sample—A form of stratified sampling. The population is divided into homogeneous groups called clusters. Samples are then randomly obtained from these clusters.

CHAPTER PROBLEMS

Problem 1

Suppose that a population consists of the six families living in Brentwood Circle. You are studying the number of children in the six families. The population information is:

Family	Number of Children
Clark	1
Walston	2
Dodd	3
Marshall	5
Saner	3
White	4

94

List the possible samples of size 2 that could be selected from this population and compute the mean of each sample. Organize these sample means into a probability distribution.

Solution

There are 15 different samples. The formula for the number of combinations is used to determine the total number of samples. There are six members of the population and the sample size is two.

$$_6C_2 = \frac{6!}{2!\ 4!} = 15$$

The 15 possible samples and the sample means are:

Sample Number	Families in the Sample	Total Number of Children in Sample	Mean Number of Children Per Family in Sample
1	Clark, Walston	3	1.5 ← 3/2
2	Clark, Dodd	4	2.0
3	Clark, Marshall	6	3.0
4	Clark, Saner	4	2.0
5	Clark, White	5	2.5
6	Walston, Dodd	5	2.5
7	Walston, Marshall	7	3.5
8	Walston, Saner	5	2.5
9	Walston, White	6	3.0
10	Dodd, Marshall	8	4.0 ← 8/2
11	Dodd, Saner	6	3.0
12	Dood, White	7	3.5
13	Marshall, Saner	8	4.0
14	Marshall, White	9	4.5
15	Saner, White	7	3.5
		Total	45.0

This information is organized into the following probability distribution called the sampling distribution of the means.

Mean Number of Children	Frequency	Probability
1.5	1	.067 ← 1/15
2.0	2	.133
2.5	3	.200
3.0	3	.200 ← 3/15
3.5	3	.200
4.0	2	.133
4.5	1	.067
	15	1.000

Problem 2

Using the Brentwood Circle data in **Problem 1**, compare the mean of the sampling distribution with the mean of the population. Compare the spread of the sample means with that of the population.

Solution

The mean of the sampling distribution and the mean of the population are the same. The population mean, written μ, is found by $\mu = (1 + 2 + 3 + 5 + 3 + 4)/6 = 3.0$. The mean of the sampling distribution (written $\mu_{\bar{x}}$ because it is the mean of a group of sample means) is also 3.0, found by 45.0/15.

$\bar{X}$ Sample Means	f Frequency	$f\bar{X}$
1.5	1	1.5
2.0	2	4.0
2.5	3	7.5
3.0	3	9.0
3.5	3	10.5
4.0	2	8.0
4.5	1	4.5
	15	45.0

$$\mu_{\bar{x}} = \frac{\Sigma f\bar{X}}{\Sigma f} = \frac{45.0}{15} = 3.0$$

The population mean μ is exactly equal to the mean of the sampling distribution $\mu_{\bar{x}}$. This is always true.

Note in the following graphs, that there is less spread in the sampling distribution of the means than in the population distribution. The sample means range from 1.5 to 4.5, whereas the population values ranged from 1 to 5.

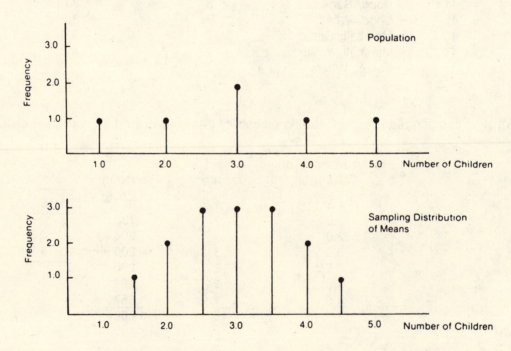

Note that the shape of the population is different than that of the sampling distribution. This phenomenon is described by the central limit theorem. Recall the central limit theorem states that regardless of the shape of the population the sampling distribution will tend toward normal as n increases.

Exercise 1

Check your answers against those in the ANSWER section.

The real estate company of Kuhlman and Associates has five sales people. Listed below is the number of homes sold last month by each of the five associates. Bruce Kuhlman, the owner, wants to estimate the population mean number of homes sold based on samples of three.

	Associate	Number of Homes Sold
A.	Sue Klaus	6
B.	John Bardo	2
C.	Jean Cannon	5
D.	A. J. Kemper	9
E.	Carol Ford	3

a. If samples of size 3 are selected, how many different samples are possible?
b. List the various samples and compute the mean of each.
c. Develop a sampling distribution of the means.
d. Draw graphs to compare the variability of the sampling distribution of the mean with that of the population. Comment.

Problem 3

Crossett Truck Rental has a large fleet of rental trucks. Many of the trucks need substantial repairs from time to time. Mr. Crossett, the owner, has requested a study of the repair costs. A random sample of 64 trucks is selected. The mean annual repair cost is $1,200, with a standard deviation of $280. Estimate the mean annual repair cost for all rental trucks. Develop the 95 percent confidence interval for the population mean.

Solution

The population parameter being estimated is the population mean—the mean annual repair cost of all Crossett rental trucks. This value is not known, but the best estimate we have of that value is the sample mean of $1,200. Hence, $1,200 is a *point estimate* of the unknown population parameter. A *confidence interval* is a range of values within which the population parameter is expected to occur. The 95 percent refers to the approximate percent of time that similarly constructed intervals would include the parameter being estimated.

The confidence interval for a mean is obtained by applying formula 7–3.

$$\overline{X} \pm z \frac{s}{\sqrt{n}}$$

How is the *z* value determined? In this problem the 95 percent level of confidence is used. This refers to the middle 95 percent of the values. The remaining 5 percent is divided equally between the two tails of curve. (See the following diagram.)

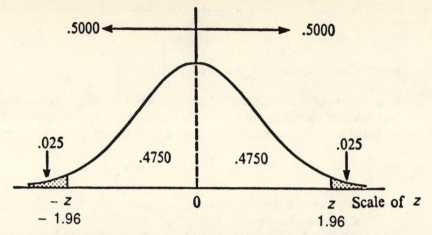

To find *z*, the standard normal distribution is used. Referring to Appendix D, the first step is to locate the value of .4750 in the body of the table, and then read the corresponding row and column values. The *z* value is 1.96.

Substitute the *z* value into the equation. The confidence interval is $1,131.40 to $1,268.60

$$\bar{X} \pm z \frac{s}{\sqrt{n}} = \$1,200 \pm 1.96 \frac{\$280}{\sqrt{64}}$$

$$= \$1,200 \pm \$68.6$$

$$= \$1,131.40 \text{ to } \$1,268.60$$

If 100 similar intervals were constructed about 95 intervals would be expected to include the population mean.

Exercise 2

Check your answers against those in the ANSWER section.

The Internal Revenue Service is studying contributions to charity. A random sample of 36 returns is selected. The mean contribution is $150 and the standard deviation of the sample is $20. Construct a 98 percent confidence interval for the population mean.

Problem 4

Refer to the information on Crossett Truck Rental in Problem 3. Suppose Crossett's fleet consists of 500 trucks. Develop a 95 percent confidence interval for the population mean.

Solution

When the sample is more than 5 percent of the population, the finite population correction factor is used. In this case the sample size is 64 and the population size is 500. Thus, *n/N* = 64/500 = .128 or 12.8 percent. The confidence interval is adjusted as follows.

$$\bar{X} \pm z \frac{s}{\sqrt{n}} \left(\sqrt{\frac{N - n}{N - 1}} \right) = \$1,200 \pm 1.96 \frac{\$280}{\sqrt{64}} \left(\sqrt{\frac{500 - 64}{500 - 1}} \right)$$

$$= \$1,200 \pm \$68.6(.9347)$$

$$= \$1,200 \pm \$64.12$$

$$= \$1,135.88 \text{ to } \$1,264.12$$

Notice that when the correction factor is included the confidence interval becomes smaller. This is logical because the number of items sampled is large relative to the population.

Exercise 3

Check your answers against those in the ANSWER section.

Refer to Exercise 2. Compute the 98 percent confidence interval, if the population consists of 200 tax returns.

Problem 5

The Independent Department Store wants to determine the proportion of their charge accounts having an unpaid balance of $500 or more. A sample of 250 accounts revealed that 100 of them had an unpaid balance of $500 or over. What is the 99 percent confidence interval for the population proportion?

Solution

In the sample of 250 charge accounts, there were 100 with balances of over $500. The point estimate of the proportion of charge customers with balances of more than $500 is .40, found by 100/250. The z value corresponding to a 99 percent level of confidence is 2.58 (from Appendix D). The formula for the confidence interval of a proportion is: (See formula 7–5.)

$$\bar{p} \pm z \sqrt{\frac{\bar{p}(1 - \bar{p})}{n}} = .40 \pm 2.58 \sqrt{\frac{(.40)(1 - .40)}{250}}$$

$$= .40 \pm (2.58) \sqrt{.00096}$$

$$= .40 \pm .08 = .32 \text{ and } .48$$

The confidence interval is .32 to .48. This means that about 99 percent of the similarly constructed intervals would include the population proportion.

Exercise 4

Check your answers against those in the ANSWER section.

A random sample of 100 light bulbs is selected. Sixty were found to burn for more than 1,000 hours. Develop a 90 percent confidence interval for the proportion of bulbs that will burn more than 1,000 hours.

Problem 6

Refer to the charge account data of Independent Department Stores in **Problem 5**. Recall that 250 accounts were sampled. Suppose there is a total of 900 charge customers. Develop a 99 percent confidence interval for the proportion of charge customers with an account balance of over $500.

Solution

The finite population correction factor should be used because the sample is 28 percent of the population, found by 250/900. (Note that 28 percent is more than 5% of the population.)

$$\overline{p} \pm z \sqrt{\frac{\overline{p}(1 - \overline{p})}{n}} \sqrt{\frac{N - n}{N - 1}} = .40 \pm 2.58 \sqrt{\frac{.40(1 - .40)}{250}} \left(\sqrt{\frac{900 - 250}{900 - 1}} \right)$$

$$= .40 \pm .08(.8503)$$

$$= .40 \pm .068 = .332 \text{ and } .456$$

Using the correction factor the interval is reduced from $.40 \pm .08$ to $.40 \pm .068$. Again, this is because Independent Stores has sampled a large proportion (28 percent of its customers).

Problem 7

The manager of the A&B Supermarket wants to estimate the mean time a customer spends in the store. A 95 percent level of confidence is to be used. The standard deviation of the population based on a pilot survey is estimated to be 3.0 minutes. The manager requires the estimate to be within plus or minus 1.00 minute of the population value. What sample size is needed?

Solution

The size of the sample is dependent on three factors.

1. The allowable error (E).
2. The level of confidence. (z)
3. The estimated variation in the population, usually measured by s, the sample standard deviation.

In this problem, the store manager has indicated that the estimate must be within 1.0 minute of the population parameter. The level of confidence is .95 and the population standard deviation is estimated to be 3.0 minutes. The formula (7–11) for determining the size of the sample is:

$$n = \left(\frac{z \cdot s}{E} \right)^2$$

where z refers to the level of confidence, s is the estimated population standard deviation, and E the allowable error.

$$z = \left(\frac{(1.96)(3.0)}{1.0} \right)^2 = (5.88)^2 = 34.57 = 35$$

Hence, the manager should randomly select 35 customers and determine the amount of time they spend in the store.

Exercise 5

Check your answers against those in the ANSWER section.

A health maintenance organization (HMO) wants to estimate the mean length of a hospital stay. How large a sample of patient records is necessary if the HMO wants to be 99 percent confident of the estimate, and wants the estimate to be within plus or minus .2 days? An earlier study showed the standard deviation of the length of stay to be .25 days.

Problem 8

The Ohio Unemployment Commission wants to estimate the propoprtion of the labor force that was unemployed during last year in a certain depressed region. The Commission wants to be 95 percent confident that their estimate is within 5 percentage points (written .05) of the population proportion. If the population proportion has been estimated to be .15, how large a sample is required? If no estimate of p was available, how large a sample would be required?

Solution

Note that the estimate of the population proportion $(\bar{p})$ is .15. The allowable error (E) is .05. Using the 95 percent level of confidence the z value is 1.96. Applying formula 7–12 to determine the sample size:

$$n = \bar{p}(1 - \bar{p}) \left(\frac{z}{E}\right)^2 = .15(1 - .15) \left(\frac{1.96}{.05}\right)^2 = 196$$

The required sample size is 196.

When no estimate of $\bar{p}$ is available, .50 is used. The size of the sample will never be larger than that obtained when $\bar{p} = .50$. The calculations for the sample size when $\bar{p} = .50$ are:

$$n = \bar{p}(1 - \bar{p}) \left(\frac{z}{E}\right)^2 = .5(1 - .5) \left(\frac{1.96}{.05}\right)^2 = 385$$

Note that the required sample size is considerably larger (385 versus 196) when $\bar{p}$ is set at .50.

Exercise 6

Check your answers against those in the ANSWER section.

A large bank believes that one-third of its checking customers have used at least one of the bank's other services during the past year. How large a sample is required to estimate the actual proportion within a plus and minus .04? Use the 98 percent level of confidence.

101

CHAPTER ASSIGNMENT 7

Sampling Methods and Sampling Distributions

Name _____ Section _____ Score _____

PART I Matching Select the correct answer and write the appropriate letter in the space provided.

_____ 1. Probability sampling

_____ 2. Systematic sample

_____ 3. Random sample

_____ 4. Point estimate

_____ 5. Central limit theorem

_____ 6. Correction factor

_____ 7. Nonprobability sampling

_____ 8. Sampling error

_____ 9. Sampling distribution of the mean

_____ 10 Confidence interval

a. estimate of the population parameter

b. Each item in the population has the *same* chance of selection

c. Each item in the population has a chance of being included in the sample

d. difference between sample statistic and population parameter

e. A probability distribution

f. Every nth element selected for the sample

g. sample means approach normal

h. Sampling based on personal judgement

i. A range of values

j. used in n/N is greater than .05

PART II Multiple Choice Select the correct answer and write the appropriate letter in the space provided.

_____ 11. In a probability sample each item in the population has

a. a 50 percent chance of being selected for the sample.
b. no chance of being selected for the sample.
c. a chance of being selected for the sample.
d. a 50% chance of being selected for the sample.

_____ 12. In a simple random sample each item in the population has

a. the same chance of being selected for the sample.
b. no chance of being selected for the sample.
c. a chance of being selected for the sample.
d. a 50% chance of being selected for the sample.

_____ 13. The sampling error is

a. always positive.
b. the difference between the sample statistic and the population parameter.
c. equal to the population parameter.
d. equal to the sample statistic.

_____ 14. The population mean is an example of a(n)

a. statistic.
b. parameter.
c. interval estimate.
d. sample.

_____ 15. A population is positively skewed. According to the Central Limit Theorem the sampling distribution of means will

   a. be negatively skewed.
   b. become even more positively skewed.
   c. form a binomial.
   d. approach a normal distribution.

_____ 16. Suppose we select every tenth item in a file. This is an example of a

   a. simple random sample.
   b. cluster sample.
   c. systematic sample.
   d. stratified sample.

_____ 17. If the level of confidence is increased from 95% to 99%, the width of the confidence interval will

   a. be increased.
   b. stay the same.
   c. depend on any change we make in σ^2.
   d. be decreased.

_____ 18. The six employees in the Murnen Machine Shop are the population. The number of possible random samples of size three which are possible is

   a. 6
   b. 20
   c. 120
   d. Cannot be determined.

_____ 19. A random sample of 5 observations is selected from a population of 2,000 observations. The following values were obtained.

   12   11   10   9   8

   A point estimate of the population mean is

   a. 12
   b. 10
   c. 5
   d. 50

_____ 20. A 95% confidence interval means that about 95 out of 100 similarly constructed intervals will include the

   a. sampling error.
   b. z value.
   c. parameter being estimated.
   d. significance level.

21. Ralph's Supermarket has six 5-pound bags of apples. Ralph counts the number of apples in each bag, with the following results.

Bag #	Number of Apples
1	8
2	10
3	10
4	12
5	12
6	12

   a. If all possible samples of size two are selected, how many different samples are possible?

   b. List the various samples of size 2 and compute the mean of each sample.

   c. Develop a sampling distribution of the means and compute the mean of the sampling distribution.

   d. Compute the population mean and compare it to the mean of the sample means.

22. The management of Clark Cable Vision want to estimate the mean number of hours per day that subscribers watch TV. A random sample of 40 homes revealed the mean number of hours subscribers watched is 5.67 hours per day. The standard deviation of the sample is 1.56 hours. Determine a 90% confidence interval for the mean number of hours of TV watched.

23. Bank II, a large financial institution in the southwest, is studying the use of safe deposit boxes among senior citizen customers.

   a. A sample of 200 senior citizen customers showed that 80 had a safe deposit box. Determine a 95% confidence interval for the proportion of senior citizen customers at Bank II with a safe deposit box.

   b. Bank II has 1,000 senior citizen customers. Determine the 95% confidence interval for the proportion of customers with a safe deposit box.

24. A customer relations department of an airline wants to estimate the proportion of customers on their Los Angeles to San Francisco flights that carry only hand luggage. The estimate needs to be within .04 of the true proportion, with a 95% level of confidence. No estimate of the population proportion is available. How large of a sample is required?

Answer

25. The Executive, a magazine designed for top management of large corporations, would like to report the mean salaries of its subscribers in its expanded year-end issue. How large of a sample is required if the 96% level of confidence is used and the estimate is within $3,000. The standard deviation is estimated to be $15,000.

Answer

8

TESTS OF HYPOTHESES: LARGE SAMPLES

CHAPTER GOALS

After completing this chapter, you will be able to:

1. Describe and employ the five step hypothesis testing procedure.
2. Distinguish between one and two-tailed statistical tests.
3. Determine p-values.
4. Identify possible statistical errors in hypothesis testing.
5. Conduct a test of hypothesis about a population mean or a population proportion.
6. Conduct a hypothesis test about two population means or two population proportions.

Introduction

In the previous chapter we used the normal probability distribution to describe a sampling distribution of means. In this chapter we will extend this knowledge to use *sample* information to draw conclusions regarding the value of the *population parameter*. Recall that a sample is a part or subset of the population, while a parameter is a value calculated from the entire population. Two statements called **hypotheses** are made regarding the possible values of population parameters. What is **statistical hypothesis testing**? *It is a method for choosing between statements or courses of action.*

For example, one statement about the performance of a new model car is that the mean miles per gallon is 30. The other statement is that the mean miles per gallon is not 30. Only one of these statements is correct.

Steps in Hypothesis Testing

Statistical hypothesis testing is a five-step procedure. These steps are:

1. State the null hypothesis and the alternate hypothesis.
2. Select a level of significance.
3. Select an appropriate test statistic.
4. Formulate a decision rule based on the selected test statistic and level of significance.
5. Take a sample and make a decision whether or not to reject the null hypothesis.

(Each step will be discussed in detail shortly.)

When conducting hypothesis tests we actually employ a strategy of "proof by contradiction." That is, generally we hope to accept a statement to be true by rejecting or ruling out another statement. The steps involved in hypothesis testing will now be described in more detail.

Step 1. State the null hypothesis and the alternate hypothesis.

The **null hypothesis** is a claim about the value of a population parameter. For example, a recent newspaper report made the claim that the mean length of a hospital stay was 3.3 days. You think that the true length of stay is some value other than 3.3 days. The null hypothesis is written H_0: $\mu = 3.3$, where H_0 is an abbreviation of the null hypothesis. It is the statement about the value of the population parameter—in this case the population mean. The null hypothesis is established for the purpose of testing. On the basis of the sample evidence, it is either rejected or not rejected.

The **alternate hypothesis,** written H_1, is the claim that is accepted if the null hypothesis is rejected. The alternate hypothesis is a statement that the mean length of stay is not 3.3 days. It is written H_1: $\mu \neq 3.3$ ($\neq$ is read "not equal to"). H_1 is accepted only if H_0 is rejected. When the "$\neq$" sign appears in the alternate hypothesis, the test is called a **two-tailed** test.

There are two other formats for writing the null and alternate hypotheses. Suppose you think that the mean length of stay is *greater than* 3.3 days.

The null and alternate hypotheses would be written as follows: (> is the sign for "greater than").

$$H_0: \mu = 3.3$$
$$H_1: \mu > 3.3$$

Notice that in this case the null hypothesis indicates "no change" in the mean length of hospital stay. The alternate hypothesis states that the mean length of stay is greater than 3.3 days. Acceptance of the alternate hypothesis would allow us to conclude that the mean length of stay is greater than 3.3 days.

What if you think that the mean length of stay is less than 3.3 days? The null and alternate hypotheses would be written as:

$$H_0: \mu = 3.3$$
$$H_1: \mu < 3.3$$

Acceptance of the alternate hypothesis in this instance would allow you to conclude the mean length of stay is less than 3.3 days. When a direction is expressed in the alternate, such as > or <, the test is called **one-tailed**.

Step 2. Select the level of significance

The **level of significance** is the probability that the null hypothesis is rejected when it is true. It will indicate when the sample mean is too far away from the hypothesized mean for the null hypothesis to be true. Usually the significance level is set at either .01 or .05, although other values may be chosen. Testing a null hypothesis at the .05 significance level, for example, indicates that the probability of rejecting the null hypothesis, even though it is true, is .05. When a true hypothesis is rejected it is referred to as a **Type I error**. The decision whether to use the .01 or the .05 significance level, or some other value, depends on the consequences of making a Type I error. The significance level is chosen *before* the sample is selected.

A **Type II error** is accepting a false null hypothesis. That is, the null hypothesis is not true, but our sample results indicate that it is. For example, if H_0 asserts that the mean length of a hospital stay is 3.3 days and we accept this hypothesis when, in fact, the mean length of stay is 4.0 days, then a Type II error is committed.

Step 3. Identify a test statistic

A **test statistic** is a quantity calculated from the sample information and is used as the basis for deciding whether or not to reject the null hypothesis. Exactly which test statistic to employ is determined by factors such as whether the samples are independent, whether the population standard deviation is known, and the size of the sample. The standard normal distribution, the z statistic, is the test statistic used in this chapter.

Step 4. Formulate a decision rule

A decision rule is based on H_0 and H_1, the level of significance, and the test statistic. The **decision rule** is a statement of the conditions under which the null hypothesis is rejected. If we are applying a one-tailed test, the dividing point between the condition under which the null hypothesis is rejected and under which it is not rejected is called the **critical value**. If we are applying a two-tailed test, there are two critical values. The following diagram shows the conditions under which the null hypothesis is rejected, using the .05 significance level, a one-tailed test, and the standard normal distribution—the test statistic used in this chapter.

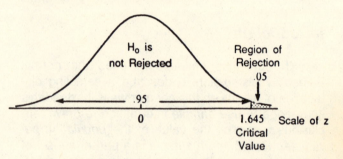

When is the standard normal distribution used? It is appropriate when the population standard deviation is known or when it is estimated from a large sample (one with more than 30 values). If the computed value of z is greater than 1.645, the null hypothesis is rejected. If the computed value of z is smaller than 1.645, the null hypothesis is not rejected.

Step 5. Select the sample and make a decision.

The final step is to select the sample and compute the value of the test statistic. This value is compared to the critical value, or values, and a decision is made whether to accept or reject the null hypothesis. These results are then interpreted.

A **p-value** is the probability that the test statistic is as extreme or more extreme than that actually observed, when the null hypothesis is true. The p-value for a given test depends on three factors: (1) whether the alternate hypothesis is one-tailed or two-tailed, (2) the particular test statistic that is used, and (3) the computed value of the test statistic.

A p-value is frequently compared to the significance level to evaluate the decision regarding the null hypothesis. If the p-value is greater than the significance level, then H_0 is not rejected. If it is less than the significance level, then H_0 is rejected. For example, if $\alpha = .05$ and the p-value is .0025, H_0 is rejected and there is only a .0025 likelihood that H_0 is true.

Tests for Means

Suppose, we are concerned with a single population mean. We test to determine if the sample mean could have been obtained from a population with a hypothesized mean. For example, we may be interested in testing whether the mean starting salary of recent marketing graduates is equal to $23,000 per year. It is assumed that (1) the population is normal and (2) the population standard deviation is known. If σ is not known, the sample standard deviation is substituted for the population standard deviation provided the sample size is 30 or more.

Under these conditions the test statistic is the standard normal distribution and is given by formula 8–1:

$$z = \frac{\overline{X} - \mu}{\sigma / \sqrt{n}} \qquad [8\text{--}1]$$

where $\overline{X}$ is the sample mean, μ is the population mean, σ is the population standard deviation. As noted above, the sample standard s is substituted for σ providing that the sample size is 30 or more. n is the sample size, and z the value of the test statistic.

The formula is written as follows.

$$z = \frac{\overline{X} - \mu}{s / \sqrt{n}} \qquad [8\text{--}2]$$

If there are two populations, we can compare two sample means to determine if they came from populations with the same or equal means. For example, a purchasing agent is considering two brands of tires for use on the company's fleet of cars. A sample of 60 Rossford tires indicates that the mean useful life to be 45,000 miles. A sample of 50 Maumee tires revealed the useful life to be 48,000 miles. Could the difference between the two sample means be due to chance? The assumption is that for both populations (Rossford and Maumee) the standard deviations are either known or have been computed from samples *greater than* 30. The test statistic used is the standard normal distribution and its value is computed from the following formula:

$$z = \frac{\overline{X}_1 - \overline{X}_2}{\sqrt{\dfrac{s_1^2}{n_1} + \dfrac{s_2^2}{n_2}}} \qquad [8\text{--}3]$$

where $\overline{X}_1$ and $\overline{X}_2$ refer to the two sample means, s_1^2 and s_2^2 are the two sample variances, and n_1 and n_2 to the two sample sizes.

Tests for Proportions

A **proportion** is a fraction, or a percent, that indicates what part of the sample or population has a particular trait. For example, we want to estimate the proportion of all home sales made to first time buyers. A random sample of 200 recent transactions showed that 40 were first time buyers. Therefore, we estimate that .20, or 20 percent, of all sales are made to first time buyers, found by 40/200.

To conduct the test of hypothesis for proportions, the same assumptions required for the binomial distribution must be met. Recall from Chapter 5 that those assumptions are:

1. Each outcome is classified into one of two categories—buyers were either first time home buyers or they were not.
2. The number of trials is fixed. In this case it is 200.
3. Each trial is independent, meaning that the outcome of one trial has no bearing on the outcome of any other. Whether the 20th sampled person was a first time buyer does not affect the outcome of any other trial.
4. The probability of a success is fixed—the probability is .20 for all 200 buyers in the sample.

Recall from Chapter 6 that the normal distribution is a good approximation of the binomial distribution when np and $n(1 - p)$ are both greater than 5. In this instance n refers to the sample size and p to the probability of a success. The test statistic that is employed for testing hypotheses about proportions is the standard normal distribution.

There are three formats for testing a hypothesis about a proportion. For a one-tailed test there are two possibilities, depending on the intent of the researcher. For example, if we wanted to determine whether more than 25 percent of the sales of homes were to be first time buyers, the hypotheses would be given as follows:

$$H_0\text{: } p = .25$$
$$H_1\text{: } p > .25$$

If we wanted to find out whether fewer than 25 percent of the homes were sold to first time buyers, the hypotheses would be given as follows:

$$H_0\text{: } p = .25$$
$$H_1\text{: } p < .25$$

For a two-tailed test the null and alternate hypotheses are written:

$$H_0: p = .25$$
$$H_1: p \neq .25$$

where $\neq$ means "not equal to." Rejection of H_0 and acceptance of H_1 allows us to conclude only that the population proportion is "different from" or "not equal to" the population value. It does not allow us to make any statement about the direction of the difference.

Two tests are considered about proportions. The first is for a *single population*. In the illustration a sample was drawn and the results tested against a hypothesized population proportion. The test statistic is z and it is found by the formula:

$$z = \frac{\bar{p} - p}{\sqrt{\dfrac{p(1 - p)}{n}}} \qquad [8\text{--}6]$$

where $\bar{p}$ is the proportion of "successes" in the sample of size n and p is the hypothesized population proportion.

The second test of population compares the proportions of *two populations*. For example, we might want to compare the proportion of rural voters planning to vote for the incumbent governor, with the proportion of urban voters. The test statistic is:

$$z = \frac{\bar{p}_1 - \bar{p}_2}{\sqrt{\dfrac{\bar{p}_c(1 - \bar{p}_c)}{n_1} + \dfrac{\bar{p}_c(1 - \bar{p}_c)}{n_2}}} \qquad [8\text{--}7]$$

If we let X_1 be the number in the first sample possessing the trait of interest, X_2 the number in the second sample possessing the trait, and n_1 and n_2 the respective sample sizes, then $\bar{p}_1 = X_1/n_1$ and $\bar{p}_2 = X_2/n_2$. The value $\bar{p}_c$ refers to a combined or **pooled estimate** of the population proportion and is found by applying formula 8–8.

$$\bar{p}_c = \frac{\text{total number of successes}}{\text{total number of items}} = \frac{X_1 + X_2}{n_1 + n_2}$$

GLOSSARY

Statistical inference—It involves drawing a conclusion about a population parameter based on sample information.

Hypothesis testing—A procedure for choosing between alternative statements or courses of action.

Null hypothesis—A claim about the value of a population parameter. It is designated H_0. Based on sample information, a decision is made to reject or not to reject the null hypothesis.

Alternate hypothesis—The claim that is accepted if the null hypothesis is rejected. It is denoted H_1. If the null hypothesis is rejected, the alternate hypothesis is accepted.

Level of significance—It is selected by the researcher, and defined as the probability that the null hypothesis will be rejected when it is actually true. It is referred to as the Type I error.

Type II error—Accepting a false null hypothesis.

Test statistic—A random variable used as a basis for making a decision to reject or not to reject the null hypothesis.

Decision rule—A statement of the condition or conditions under which the null hypothesis is rejected and the conditions under which it is not rejected.

Rejection region—It is a region of values for a particular test statistic. When the computed value of z (or any other value computed in the forthcoming chapters) falls in this region, the null hypothesis is rejected.

Critical value—A value, or values, that separates the rejection region from the region where the null hypothesis is not rejected.

p-value—The probability that the test statistic is as extreme or more extreme than that actually observed, when the null hypothesis is actually true.

Proportion—A fraction or a percent indicating what part of the sample or population has a particular trait of interest.

Standard error of the proportion—A measurement of sampling error. The standard deviation of the distribution of sample proportions.

CHAPTER PROBLEMS

Problem 1

The manufacturer of subcompact automobiles claims its new Clipper averages 40 miles per gallon in highway driving. An independent testing agency road-tested 64 of the Clippers. The sample mean was 38.9 miles per gallon (mpg), with a sample standard deviation of 4.0 miles per gallon. Using the .01 level of significance and the five-step hypothesis testing procedure, determine if there is reason to reject the manufacturer's claim. Determine the p-value. Can we conclude that the mean mileage for the clipper is less than 40?

Solution

The first step is to state the null and alternate hypotheses. The null hypothesis refers to the "no change" situation. That is, there has been no change in the Clipper's mileage, it is 40 mpg. This written $H_0: \mu = 40$ and is read that the population mean is 40. The alternate hypothesis is that the population mean is less than 40. It is written $H_1: \mu < 40$. If the null hypothesis is rejected, then the alternate is accepted. It would be concluded that the Clipper's mileage is less than 40 mpg.

The second step is to select the level of significance. We decide on the .01 significance level. This is the probability that the null hypothesis will be rejected, when in fact it is true.

The third step is to decide on a test statistic. The use of the standard normal distribution requires that the population standard deviation σ be known. When it is not known, as in this problem, the sample standard deviation designated by s, is used as an estimate of σ. When the sample standard deviation is based on a large sample, the standard normal distribution is still an appropriate test statistic. "Large" is usually defined as being 30 or more.

To determine z we use formula 8–2.

$$z = \frac{\overline{X} - \mu}{s/\sqrt{n}}$$

where $\overline{X}$ is the sample mean, μ is the population mean, s is the standard deviation computed from the sample, and n is the sample size.

The fourth step is to develop the decision rule. The decision rule is a statement of the conditions under which the null hypothesis is rejected. The decision rule is shown in the following diagram. If the computed value of z is to the left of −2.33 the null hypothesis is rejected. The −2.33 is the critical value. How is it determined? Remember that the significance level stated in the problem is .01. This indicates that the area to the left of the critical value under the normal curve is .01. For the standard normal distribution the total area to the left of 0 is .5000. Therefore, the area between the critical value and 0 is .4900, found by .5000 − .0100. Now refer to Appendix D, and search the body of the table for a value close to .4900. The closest value is .4901. Read 2.3 in the left margin and .03 in the column containing .4901. Thus the z value corresponding to .4901 is 2.33.

Recall from Step 1 that the alternate hypothesis is H_1: $\mu < 40$. The inequality sign points in the negative direction. Thus the critical value is −2.33 and the rejection region is all in the lower left tail.

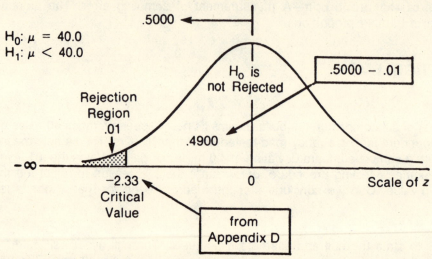

H_0: $\mu = 40.0$
H_1: $\mu < 40.0$

.5000

.5000 − .01

H_0 is not Rejected

Rejection Region .01

.4900

−∞

−2.33
Critical Value

0

Scale of z

from Appendix D

The fifth step is to compute the value of the test statistic, make a decision regarding the null hypothesis, and interpret the results. Since the standard deviation of the population is not known, the sample standard deviation is used as its estimate. Repeating the formula for z:

$$z = \frac{\overline{X} - \mu}{s/\sqrt{n}}$$

Recall that the manufacturer claims 40 mpg and the mean of the sample is 38.9 mpg.

Solving for z: $\quad z = \dfrac{38.9 - 40.0}{4.0/\sqrt{64}} = \dfrac{-1.1}{0.5} = -2.20$

The computed value of −2.20 is to the right of −2.33, so the null hypothesis is not rejected. We do not reject claim of the manufacturer that the Clipper gets 40.0 miles per gallon. It is reasonable that the 1.1 miles per gallon (40.0 and 38.9) could be due to chance.

We do observe that −2.20 is fairly close to the critical value of −2.33. What is the likelihood of a z value to the left of −2.20? It is .0139, found by .5000 − .4861, where .4861 is the likelihood of a z value between 0 and 2.20. The .0139 is referred to as the p-value. It is the probability of getting a value of the test statistic (z in this case) more extreme than that actually observed, if the null hypothesis is true. Had the significance level been set at .02 instead of .01, the null hypothesis would have been rejected. By reporting the p-value we give information on the strength of decision on the null hypothesis.

Exercise 1

Check your answers against those in the ANSWER section.

Last year the records of Ski and Golf, Inc., a sporting goods chain, showed the mean amount spent by a customer was $30. A sample of 40 transactions this month revealed the mean amount spent was $33 with a standard deviation of $12. At the .05 significance level can we conclude that the mean amount spent has increased? What is the p-value?

Problem 2

Two manufacturers of sinus relief tablets, SINUS and ANTIDRIP, have made conflicting claims regarding the effectiveness of their tablets. A private testing organization was hired to evaluate the two tablets. The testing company tried SINUS on 100 sinus sufferers and found the mean time to relief was 85.0 minutes with a sample standard deviation of 6.0 minutes. A sample of 81 sinus sufferers used ANTIDRIP. The mean time relief was 86.2 minutes, the sample standard deviation 6.8 minutes. Does the evidence suggest a difference in the amount of time required to obtain relief? Use the .05 significance level and the five-step procedure. What is the p-value?

Solution

Note that the testing company is attempting to show only that there is a *difference* in the time required to affect relief. There is no attempt to show one tablet is "better than" or "worse than" the other. Thus, a two-tailed test is applied.

$$H_0: \mu_1 = \mu_2$$
$$H_1: \mu_1 \neq \mu_2$$

Let μ_1 refer to the mean time to obtain relief using SINUS and μ_2 to the mean time to obtain relief using ANTIDRIP.

The .05 significance level is to be used. Because both samples are large (greater than 30) the standard normal distribution is used as the test statistic. Because the alternate hypothesis does not state a direction this is a two-tailed test. The .05 significance level is divided equally into two tails of the standard normal distribution. Hence the area in the left tail is .0250 and .0250 in the right tail.

The critical values which separate the two rejection regions from the region of acceptance are −1.96 and +1.96. To explain: if the area in a rejection region is .0250, the acceptance area is .4750, found by .5000 − .0250. The z value corresponding to an area of .4750 is obtained by referring to the table of areas of the normal curve (Appendix D). Search the body of the table for a value as close to .4750 as possible and read the corresponding row and column values. The area of .4750 is found in the row 1.9 and the column .06. Hence, the critical values are ± 1.96. This is shown on the following diagram.

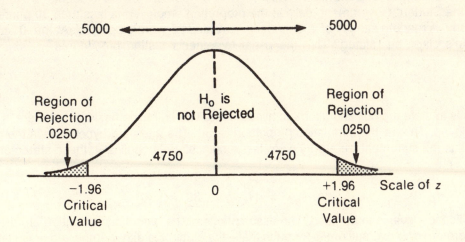

113

The computed value of z is -1.24, found by using formula 8–3.

$$z = \frac{\overline{X}_1 - \overline{X}_2}{\sqrt{\frac{s_1^2}{n_1} + \frac{s_2^2}{n_2}}} = \frac{85.0 - 86.2}{\sqrt{\frac{(6.0)^2}{100} + \frac{(6.8)^2}{81}}} = -1.24$$

The computed value of z falls in the acceptance region which is between -1.96 and $+1.96$. The null hypothesis is, therefore, not rejected at the .05 level. This indicates that there is no difference in the mean time it takes SINUS and ANTIDRIP to bring relief. The difference of 1.2 minutes ($85.0 - 86.2$) can be attributed to sampling error (chance).

To determine the p-value we need to find the area to the left of -1.24 and add to it the area to the right of 1.24. Why are we concerned with both tails? Because H_1 was two-tailed. The p-value is .2150, found by $2(.5000 - .3925)$.

Exercise 2

Check your answers against those in the ANSWER section.

The county commissioners received a number of complaints from county residents that the Youngsville Fire Department takes longer to respond to fires than the Claredon Fire Department. To check the validity of these complaints, a random sample of 60 fires handled by the Youngsville Fire Department was selected. It was found that the mean response time was 6.9 minutes and the standard deviation of the sample 3.8 minutes. A sample of 70 fires handled by the Claredon Fire Department found the mean response time was 4.9 minutes with a sample standard deviation of 3.0 minutes. Does the data suggest that it takes longer for the Youngsville Department to respond? Use the .05 significance level.

Problem 3

The Dean of Students at Scandia Tech believes that 30 percent of the students are employed. You, as President of the Student Government, believe the proportion employed is less than 30 percent and decide to conduct a study. A random sample of 100 students revealed 25 were employed. At the .01 significance levels can the Dean's claim be refuted? Use the usual hypothesis testing procedures.

Solution

The first step is to state the null and alternate hypotheses. The null hypothesis is that there is no change in the percent employed. That is, the population proportion is .30. The alternate hypothesis is the proportion is less than .30. This is the statement we are trying to test empirically. Symbolically, these statements are written as follows:

$$H_0: p = .30$$
$$H_1: p < .30$$

The .01 significance level is to be used. The assumptions of the binomial distribution are met in the problem. That is (1) there are only two outcomes for each trial—the student is either employed or isn't employed; (2) the number of trials is fixed—100 students; (3) each trial is independent, meaning that the employment of one student selected does not affect another; (4) the probability that any randomly selected student is employed is .30.

Note that the problem also allows us to use the normal approximation to the binomial because both np and $n(1 - p)$ exceeds 5. ($np = 100(.30) = 30$ and $n(1 - p) = 100(.70) = 70$).

114

Since the normal distribution is used, z is the test statistic. To formulate a decision rule, we need the critical value of z. It is obtained from Appendix D. The significance level, stated earlier, is .01. This means the area between 0 and the critical value is .4900, found by .5000 − .0100.

Search the body of Appendix D for a value as close to .4900 as possible. It is .4901. The value associated with .4901 is 2.33. The alternate hypothesis points in the negative direction, hence the rejection region is in the left tail and the critical value of z is −2.33.

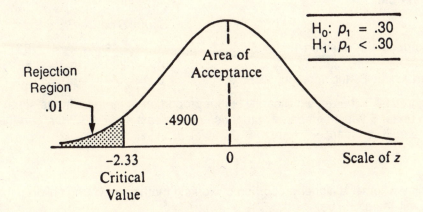

$$H_0: p_1 = .30$$
$$H_1: p_1 < .30$$

The decision rule is to reject the null hypothesis if the computed value of the test statistic lies in the rejection region to the left of −2.33.

Recall that the sample of 100 Scandia Tech students revealed that 25 were employed. The question is whether the sample proportion of .25, found by 25/100, is significantly less than .30.

$$z = \frac{\bar{p} - p}{\sqrt{\dfrac{p(1 - p)}{n}}} = \frac{.25 - .30}{\sqrt{\dfrac{(.30)(1 - .30)}{100}}} = -1.09$$

The computed value of z falls in the region between 0 and −2.33. H_0 is not rejected. There is a difference between the Dean's hypothesized proportion (.30) and the sample proportion (.25), but this difference of .05 is not sufficient to reject the null hypothesis. The .05 can be attributed to sampling (chance). The Dean's claim cannot be refuted.

The p-value is the probability of a z value to the left of −1.09. It is .1379, found by .5000 − .3621. The p-value is larger than the significance level of .01, which is consistent with our decision not to reject the null hypothesis.

Exercise 3

Check your answers against those in the ANSWER section.

The producer of a TV special expected about 40 percent of the viewing audience to watch a rerun of a 1965 Beatles Concert. A sample of 200 homes revealed 60 to be watching the concert. At the .10 significance level, does the evidence suggest that less than 40 percent were watching? Use the usual hypothesis testing format. What is the p-value?

Problem 4

Two different sites are being considered for a day-care center. One is on the south side of the city and the other is on the east side. The decision where to locate the day-care center depends in part on how many mothers work and have children under 5 years old.

A sample of 200 family units on the south side revealed that 88 working mothers have children under 5 years. A sample of 150 family units on the east side revealed that 57 have children under 5 years and the mother worked. Summarizing the data:

	South Side	East Side
Number of working mothers with children under 5	$X_1 = 88$	$X_2 = 57$
Number in sample	$n_1 = 200$	$n_2 = 150$
Proportion with children under 5 and mothers work	$p_1 = .44$	$p_2 = .38$

The question to be explored is: Is there a significantly higher proportion of mothers in the south side (.44) who work and have children under 5 years compared with those on the east side (.38)? Or, can the difference be attributed to sampling variation (chance)? Use the .05 level of significance.

Solution

The problem is to examine whether a higher proportion of working mothers of young children live on the south side. The hypotheses will therefore be:

$$H_0: p_1 = p_2$$
$$H_1: p_1 > p_2$$

The standard normal distribution is the test statistic to be used. The significance level decided on above is .05. The critical value is 1.645 obtained from Appendix D. The area in the upper tail of the curve is .05, therefore the area between $z = 0$ and the critical value is .4500, found by .5000 − .0500. Search the body of the table for a value close to .4500. Since 1.64 is equal to .4495 and 1.65 is equal to .4505, a value between 1.64 and 1.65 or (1.645) is used as the critical value. The null hypothesis is rejected if the calculated value is greater than 1.645. This information is shown in the following diagram.

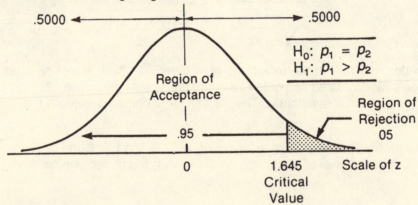

Formula 8–7 for z is repeated below.

$$z = \frac{\bar{p}_1 - \bar{p}_2}{\sqrt{\dfrac{\bar{p}_c(1 - \bar{p}_c)}{n_1} + \dfrac{\bar{p}_c(1 - \bar{p}_c)}{n_2}}}$$

where $\bar{p}_c$ is a pooled estimate of the population proportion and is computed using 8–8.

$$\bar{p}_c = \frac{X_1 + X_2}{n_1 + n_2}$$

116

In this problem X_1 and X_2 refer to the number of "successes" in each sample (number of working mothers with children under 5 years). n_1 and n_2 refer to the number of housing units sampled in the south side and east side, respectively.

The pooled estimate of the population proportion is .4143, found as follows:

$$\bar{p}_c = \frac{X_1 + X_2}{n_1 + n_2} = \frac{88 + 57}{200 + 150} = .4143$$

Inserting the pooled estimate of .4143 in the formula and solving for z in formula 8–8 gives 1.13.

$$z = \frac{\bar{p}_1 - \bar{p}_2}{\sqrt{\dfrac{\bar{p}_c(1 - \bar{p}_c)}{n_1} + \dfrac{\bar{p}_c(1 - \bar{p}_c)}{n_2}}}$$

$$= \frac{.44 - .38}{\sqrt{\dfrac{(.4143)(1 - .4143)}{200} + \dfrac{(.4143)(1 - .4143)}{150}}} = 0.73$$

The computed value of z (0.73) is less than the critical value of 1.645 so the null hypothesis is not rejected. The two proportions in the population are equal. The difference of .06 can be attributed to sampling error (chance). To put it another way, the proportion of mothers who work and have children under 5 on the south side and east side is not significantly different. The p-value is .2327, found by .5000 − .2673.

Exercise 4

Check your answers against those in the ANSWER section.

A recent study was designed to compare smoking habits of young women with those of young men. A random sample of 150 women revealed that 45 smoked. A random sample of 100 men indicated that 25 smoked. At the .05 significance level does the evidence show that a higher proportion of women smoke? Compute the p-value.

117

CHAPTER ASSIGNMENT 8

Tests of Hypothesis: Large Sample Methods

Name _____ Section _____ Score _____

PART I **Matching** Select the correct answer and write the appropriate letter in the space provided.

_____ 1. p-value

_____ 2. Type I error

_____ 3. Type II error

_____ 4. Null hypothesis

_____ 5. Critical value

_____ 6. Test statistic

_____ 7. Decision rule

_____ 8. Alternate hypothesis

_____ 9. Significance level

_____ 10 Proportion

a. conditions to reject H_o

b. accepted if H_o is rejected

c. probability of a Type I error

d. accepting a false H_o

e. probability H_o is true

f. separates region where H_o is rejected from where it is not rejected

g. statememt about a population parameter used for testing

h. rejecting a true H_o

i. quantity calculated from sample information

j. faction of sample having the trait

PART II **Multiple Choice** Select the correct answer and write the appropriate letter in the space provided.

_____ 11. The null hypothesis is a claim about the value of

    a. a sample statistic.
    b. the sampling error.
    c. sample size.
    d. population parameter.

_____ 12. If the null hypothesis is rejected

    a. the alternate hypothesis is not rejected.
    b. the alternate hypothesis is accepted.
    c. the alternate hypothesis is therefore false.
    d. then the null hypothesis must be true.

_____ 13. The level of significance is the probability of

    a. making a Type I error.
    b. making a Type II error
    c. a p-value.
    d. accepting H_o.

_____ 14. The condition or conditions under which the null hypothesis is rejected is called

    a. the test statistic.
    b. the decision rule.
    c. a Type II error.
    d. a Type I error.

_____ 15. If the p-value is larger than the significance level

    a. the null hypothesis is not rejected.
    b. the null hypothesis is rejected.
    c. a Type II error is committed.
    d. the critical value is reached.

_____ 16. A Type II error is

    a. rejecting a true H_0.
    b. not rejecting a false H_0.
    c. rejecting a true H_1.
    d. not rejecting a false H_1.

_____ 17. A population is normal, but σ is not known. In a test for means the sample standard deviation, s, is substituted for σ in the test statistic if

    a. μ is greater than 5.
    b. μ is greater than 30.
    c. n is less than 30.
    d. n is at least 30.

_____ 18. The critical value

    a. is the same as Type II error.
    b. separates the region where H_0 is rejected from the region where H_0 is not rejected.
    c. always appears in the alternate hypothesis.
    d. depends on the sample size.

_____ 19. If H_0 is rejected at the .05 significance level

    a. it would also be rejected at the .10 level.
    b. it would also be rejected at the .01 level.
    c. the p-value is greater than .05.
    d. a Type II error is committed.

_____ 20. Tests of proportions require

    a. only the nominal scale of measurement.
    b. at least the ordinal scale of measurement.
    c. at least the interval scale of measurement.
    d. at least the ratio scale of measurement.

_____ 21. A proportion

    a. always refers to a sample.
    b. always refers to a population.
    c. is the fraction of a sample or population that has a particular trait.
    d. is a z value.
    e. None of these is correct.

_____ 22. To conduct a test of proportions

    a. np and $n(1 - p)$ must both be at least 30.
    b. np and $n(1 - p)$ must both be at least 5.
    c. p must be greater than .50.
    d. n must be less than 10.

_____ 23. To conduct a test of proportions

   a. the population must be normal.
   b. the population must be skewed.
   c. the binomial assumption must be met.
   d. the data must be interval scale.
   e. None of these is correct.

_____ 24. When conducting a one-tailed or a two-tailed test of proportions the appropriate test statistic is

   a. the standard normal distribution.
   b. any normal distribution.
   c. the Poisson distribution.
   d. the binomial distribution.

_____ 25. The standard error of the proportion is

   a. an estimate of the population proportion.
   b. always negative.
   c. the same as the pooled proportion $\bar{p}_c$.
   d. the standard deviation of the distribution of the sample proportions.

PART III Problems Record your answer in the space provided. Show essential calculations.

26. FM-105, the local rock station, claims that there is "at least 50 minutes of music each hour." A random sample of 36 hours revealed that the mean number of minutes of music is 48.2 minutes, with a standard deviation of 4.2 minutes. At the .01 significance level can we conclude that the claim is false and that the mean number of minutes of music is less than 50 minutes per hour?

   a. State the null hypothesis and the alternate hypothesis.

   H_0: _____

   H_1: _____

   b. State the decision rule.

   _____

   c. Compute the value of the test statistic.

   ┌─────────────┐
   │   │
   └─────────────┘
   Answer

   d. State your decision regarding H_0. Interpret your result.

   _____

   _____

121

27. At the time of last survey 30% of those watching TV during the early evening news hour in the Buffalo area watch the news on TV-13. In an effort to increase the ratings, more local news was included. A phone survey yesterday revealed 70 out of 200 persons contacted who were watching TV during the early evening news hour were watching TV-13. Can management conclude that the proportion watching TV-13 news has increased? Use the .05 significance level.

a. State the null hypothesis and the alternate hypothesis.

H_0: _____

H_1: _____

b. State the decision rule.

_____

c. Compute the value of the test statistic.

Answer

d. State your decision regarding H_0. Interpret your result.

_____

_____

e. Determine the p-value.

Answer

28. The Metgzer's Department Store is studying the amounts owed by their credit card customers at the end of the month. A random sample of 40 customers over 50 years of age revealed that the mean amount owed to be $545 with a standard deviation of $56. A sample of 35 customers under 30 years of age showed the mean amount owed is $590 with a standard deviation of $75. At the .05 significance level, can Metgzer's conclude that the mean amount owed by the younger customers is larger?

a. State the null hypothesis and the alternate hypothesis.

H_0: _____

H_1: _____

b. State the decision rule.

_____

c. Compute the value of the test statistic.

```
┌─────────────┐
│             │
└─────────────┘
    Answer
```

d. State your decision regarding H_0. Interpret your result.

_____

_____

e. Determine the p-value.

```
┌─────────────┐
│             │
└─────────────┘
    Answer
```

29. The Human Relations Director for a large company is studying absenteeism among hourly workers. A sample of 120 day shift employees showed that 15 were absent more than five days last year due to illness. A sample of 80 afternoon shift employees showed that 18 were absent more than five days due to illness during the same period. At the .01 significance level can we conclude that there is more absenteeism among afternoon shift employees?

a. State the null hypothesis and the alternate hypothesis.

H_0: _____

H_1: _____

b. State the decision rule.

_____

c. Compute the value of the test statistic.

Answer

d. State your decision regarding H_0. Interpret your results.

_____

_____

e. Determine the p-value.

Answer

124

9

STUDENT'S *t* TEST: SMALL SAMPLES

CHAPTER GOALS

After completing this chapter, you will be able to:

1. Describe the characteristics of the *t* distribution.
2. Conduct a hypothesis test for a population mean when the population standard deviation is not known and the sample size is less than 30.
3. Conduct a hypothesis test for the difference between two population means when the population standard deviations are not known and both sample sizes are less than 30.
4. Conduct a hypothesis test for the difference between paired observations when the sample size is less than 30.

Introduction

In this chapter we continue our study of hypothesis testing. Recall that in Chapter 8 we considered hypothesis tests for means where the population standard deviation was known. If it was not known but we have a sample of more than 30 observations, then the sample standard deviation was substituted for the population standard deviation. The standard normal distribution was used as the test statistic.

What if the standard deviation of the population is not known and the sample size is less than 30? Under these conditions the standard normal distribution is *not* the appropriate test statistic. The appropriate test statistic is the **Student *t*** distribution. This distribution was first described by William S. Gosset, who wrote under the name "Student," in the early 1900s.

Characteristics of the t Distribution

The Student *t* distribution is similar to the standard normal distribution in some ways, but quite different in others. It has the following major characteristics:

1. It is a continuous distribution, like the standard normal distribution described in Chapter 6.
2. It is bell shaped and symmetrical, again similar to the standard normal distribution.
3. There is a "family" of *t* distributions. That is, each time the size of the sample changes, a new *t* distribution is created.
4. The *t* distribution is more spread out (that is "flatter") at the center than the standard normal distribution.

The *t* distribution has a greater spread than the standard normal distribution. Thus, with a stated level of significance, the critical values for *t* are further removed from 0 than they are in the standard normal distribution. For a one-tailed test with a .05 significance level, the following graphs show that values of *t* are larger than those of *z*. Exactly how these values are obtained will be explained shortly. Note that when *t* is used as the test statistic instead of the standard normal: (1) the acceptance region will be wider, and (2) a larger value of *t* will be required to reject the null hypothesis. A further requirement is that the population from which the sample is selected should be normal or approximately normal.

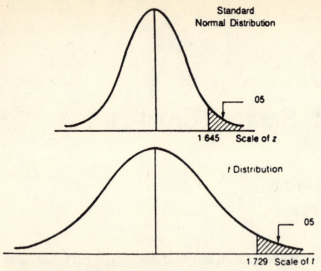

Standard Normal Distribution

.05

1.645   Scale of z

t Distribution

.05

1.729   Scale of t

Degrees of Freedom

To locate the critical value of t, we need to know the number of **degrees of freedom**. For one sample tests, the number of degrees of freedom is found by the number of sample observations minus one $(n - 1)$. Thus for a sample of three observations there are two degrees of freedom, $3 - 1 = 2$. Why is this so? Suppose the values of the three sample observations are 5, 7, and 9. The mean of the sample is 7. If any two of these values are changed, then the third is automatically fixed so the mean can remain 7. Suppose the first two are changed to 4 and 5, then the last must be changed to 12 for the three values to have a mean of 7, that is $(4 + 5 + 12)/3 = 7$. Hence, only two of the three values are free to vary and we say there are two degrees of freedom. For a sample of size 15, there are 14 degrees of freedom, found by $n - 1 = 15 - 1 = 14$.

The decision rule involving the t distribution is formulated from Appendix F. This table can be used for both one-tailed and two-tailed tests. To show how the table is used, suppose we have a sample of six, a one-tailed test, and the .05 significance level is to be used. First, determine the number of degrees of freedom. There are 5, found by $n - 1 = 6 - 1 = 5$. Next go down the left-hand column in Appendix F, labeled "df" to the row of 5. Find the column for a one-tailed test and the .05 significance level. The critical value is 2.015. These results are summarized in the following chart.

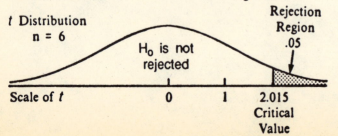

t Distribution
$n = 6$

H_0 is not rejected

Rejection Region
.05

Scale of t 0   1   2.015
Critical Value

One Sample Test for Means

In this chapter the t distribution is used as a test statistic for three tests: (1) for a single population mean, (2) for two population means, and (3) to test for the difference between paired observations.

The value of the t statistic for a one-sample test of means is computed by the formula 9–1, which is:

$$t = \frac{\overline{X} - \mu}{s/\sqrt{n}} \qquad [9\text{–}1]$$

where $\overline{X}$ is the sample mean, s the sample standard deviation, n the sample size, and μ the population mean. This formula is the same as the one presented in Chapter 8 for the standard normal distribution, except s is substituted for σ and the Student t distribution is used to locate the critical value.

Two Sample Test of Means

The t distribution may be employed as the test statistic for a test of hypothesis for the *difference* between two population means. The required assumptions are:

1. The observations in the two samples are unrelated—that is, independent.
2. The populations from which the samples were obtained are approximately normal.
3. The two populations have approximately equal variances.

To conduct the two-sample test, the first step is to pool the sample variances. This is accomplished by using the following formula.

$$s_p^2 = \frac{(n_1 - 1)s_1^2 + (n_2 - 1)s_2^2}{n_1 + n_2 - 2} \qquad [9\text{–}2]$$

where s_1^2 and s_2^2 are the sample variances and n_1 and n_2 are the sample sizes. The value of t is then computed using formula 9–3.

$$t = \frac{\overline{X}_1 - \overline{X}_2}{\sqrt{s_p^2\left(\dfrac{1}{n_1} + \dfrac{1}{n_2}\right)}} \qquad [9\text{–}3]$$

$\overline{X}_1$ and $\overline{X}_2$ refer to the sample means. The degrees of freedom for a two-sample test is found by $n_1 + n_2 - 2$.

The Test for Paired Differences

A third hypothesis testing situation occurs when we are concerned with the difference *related* observations. Typically, this is a before-and-after situation, where we want to measure the improvement. To illustrate, suppose we administer a reading test to a sample of ten students. Then we have them take a course in speed reading. Thus the test focuses on the reading improvements of each of the ten students. The distribution of the population of differences is assumed to be approximately normal. The test statistic is *t*, and the formula is:

$$t = \frac{\bar{d}}{s_d/\sqrt{n}} \qquad [9\text{-}4]$$

where

d is the mean of the differences between paired observations.

s_d is the standard deviation of the differences in the paired observations.

n is the number of paired observations.

For a paired difference test there are $n - 1$ degrees of freedom.

GLOSSARY

Student's *t* distribution—A continuous symmetric probability distribution with a mean of 0. The distribution of *t* differs for each sample size, *n*. It is flatter and more spread out than the standard normal distribution, *z*.

Degrees of freedom—It is the number of observations in the samples that are free to vary. For a test of hypothesis involving one population mean it is found by $n - 1$, for two means $n_1 + n_2 - 2$, and for a paired difference test $n - 1$.

CHAPTER PROBLEMS

Problem 1

Suppose you drive your car to work. The mean driving time is 30 minutes. A fellow worker suggests a different, faster route. As an experiment you recorded these times: 29, 27, 30, 26, and 28 minutes, along the suggested route. You want to use the .05 significance level, to decide if the new route takes less driving time.

Solution

The null hypothesis is that the population mean is 30 minutes. The alternate hypothesis is that the mean driving time is less than 30 minutes. These hypotheses are written symbolically:

$$H_0: \mu = 30$$
$$H_1: \mu < 30$$

To determine the decision rule, we must first assume that the population is normally distributed. Since the population standard deviation is not known, and the sample size is small, the *t* distribution is used as the test statistic.

The value that will determine whether we should reject the null hypothesis is obtained from Appendix F. Note that in this problem there are 4 degrees of freedom ($n - 1 = 5 - 1 = 4$). We stipulated a .05 significance level and a one-tailed test. To find the critical value of *t*, move down the left-hand column of Appendix F to 4 degrees of freedom. Move across that row to the column headed by .05 and a one-tailed test. The value given is 2.132. Since the direction of the alternate hypothesis is negative, the critical value is −2.132. The null hypothesis is rejected if the computed *t* is to the left of −2.132; otherwise, it is not rejected. The decision rule is shown in the following diagram:

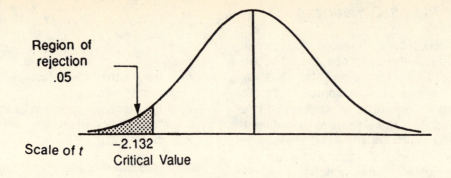

Region of
rejection
.05

Scale of t −2.132
Critical Value

Next the value of the test statistic is computed. Since the mean and standard deviation of the sample are not given they must be computed from the sample information. The sample mean is computed using formula 3–1, and the standard deviation by taking the square root of formula 3–15. (Formula 3–15 determines the sample variance.)

Sample Times

X	X²
29	841
27	729
30	900
26	676
28	784
140	3,930

$$\bar{X} = \frac{\Sigma X}{n} = \frac{140}{5} = 28.0$$

$$s = \sqrt{\frac{\Sigma X^2 - \frac{(\Sigma X)^2}{n}}{n - 1}} = \sqrt{\frac{3,930 - \frac{(140)^2}{5}}{5 - 1}} = 1.58$$

These values are inserted into formula 9–1 and the value of the test statistic is computed.

$$t = \frac{\bar{X} - \mu}{s/\sqrt{n}} = \frac{28 - 30}{1.58/\sqrt{5}} = -2.83$$

Since the computed value of −2.83 is to the left of −2.132, the null hypothesis is rejected and the alternate accepted. The route suggested by your fellow worker is faster.

How can we determine the p-value for this test? We cannot get the exact p-value as we did in the previous chapters when the standard normal distribution was the test statistic. However, with Appendix F we can estimate the p-value. Go to Appendix F and find the row with 4 degrees of freedom (there were four degrees of freedom in this problem), and use the levels of significance for one-tailed tests (this test was one-tailed). Locate a value as close to 2.83, the value of the test statistic, as possible. At the .025 significance level the t value is 2.776 and at the .01 significance level it is 3.747. So the p-value is between .025 and .010.

Exercise 1

Check your answers against those in the ANSWER section.

A supervisor believes employees are taking longer than ten minutes for their breaks. A sample of six employees revealed the following times (in minutes) spent on a break: 9, 12, 14, 15, 10, and 12. At the .01 significance level, can it be concluded that employees are taking too long for their breaks? Estimate the p-value.

Problem 2

A study of recent graduates from your school revealed that for a sample of ten accounting majors the mean salary was $30,000 per year with a sample standard deviation of $2,000. A sample of eight general business majors revealed a mean salary of $29,000 per year with a standard deviation of $1,500. At the .05 significance level can we conclude accounting majors earn more?

Solution

The null hypothesis is that there is no difference in the mean salary of the two groups. The alternate hypothesis is that accounting graduates earn more. They are written as follows:

$$H_0: \mu_1 = \mu_2$$
$$H_1: \mu_1 > \mu_2$$

where μ_1 refers to accounting graduates and μ_2 general business graduates.

Assuming the two populations to be normally distributed and their population variances to be equal, the t distribution is the test statistic. There are a total of 16 degrees of freedom, found by $n_1 + n_2 - 2 = 10 + 8 - 2 = 16$. The alternate hypothesis is a one-tailed test with the rejection region in the upper tail. From Appendix F, the critical value is 1.746. Hence, H_0 is rejected if the computed value of the test statistic exceeds 1.746.

The first step is to pool the variances, using formula 9–2.

$$s_p^2 = \frac{(n_1 - 1)(s_1^2) + (n_2 - 1)(s_2^2)}{n_1 + n_2 - 2} = \frac{(10 - 1)(2,000)^2 + (8 - 1)(1,500)^2}{10 + 8 - 2} = 3,234,375$$

Next, the value of t is computed, using formula 9–3.

$$t = \frac{\$1,000}{\sqrt{(3,234,375)\left(\frac{1}{10} + \frac{1}{8}\right)}} = 1.17$$

Because the computed value of t (1.17) is less than the critical value of 1.746, H_0 is not rejected. The sample evidence does not suggest a difference in the mean salaries of the two groups. The p-value, from Appendix F, is greater than .10.

Exercise 2

Check your answers against those in the ANSWER section.

A large department store hired a researcher to compare the average purchase amounts for the downtown store with that of its mall store. The following information was obtained:

	Downtown Store	Mall Store
Mean amount purchased	$36.00	$40.00
Sample standard deviation	$10.00	$12.00
Sample size	10	10

At the .01 significance level can it be concluded that the mean amount spent at the mall store is larger? Estimate the p-value.

Problem 3

The dean of the College of Business at Kingsport University wants to determine if the Grade Point Average (GPA) of business college students decreases during the last semester of their senior year. A sample of six students is selected. Their GPAs for the fall and spring semesters of their senior year are:

Student	Fall Semester	Spring Semester
A	2.7	3.1
B	3.4	3.3
C	3.5	3.3
D	3.0	2.9
E	2.1	1.8
F	2.7	2.4

At the .05 significance level, can the dean conclude that the GPA of graduating seniors declined during their last semester?

Solution

Let μ_d be the mean difference between the fall and spring semester grades for all business students at Kingsport U. in their senior year. Since we want to explore whether grades decrease, a one-tailed test is appropriate.

$$H_0: \mu d = 0$$
$$H_1: \mu d > 0$$

There are six paired observations; therefore, there are $n - 1 = 6 - 1 = 5$ degrees of freedom. Using Appendix F with 5 degrees of freedom, the .05 significance level and a one-tailed test, the critical value of t is 2.015. H_0 is rejected if the computed value of the test statistic exceeds 2.015.

The value of the test statistic is determined from formula 9–4 below.

$$t = \frac{\bar{d}}{s_d/\sqrt{n}}$$

where $\bar{d}$ is the mean of the differences between fall and spring GPAs, s_d is the standard deviation of those differences, and n is the number of paired observations. First, subtract spring semester grades from fall semester grades. If this difference is *positive* then a decline has occurred.

The sample data is shown below and the values of $\bar{d}$ and s_d computed:

Student	Fall	Spring	d	d²
A	2.7	3.1	−.4	.16
B	3.4	3.3	.1	.01
C	3.5	3.3	.2	.04
D	3.0	2.9	.1	.01
E	2.1	1.8	.3	.09
F	2.7	2.4	.3	.09
			.6	.40

$$\bar{d} = \frac{\Sigma d}{n} = \frac{.6}{6} = .10$$

$$s_d = \sqrt{\frac{\Sigma d^2 - \frac{(\Sigma d)^2}{n}}{n - 1}} = \sqrt{\frac{.40 - \frac{(.6)^2}{6}}{6 - 1}} = .2608$$

130

The *t* statistic is computed by:

$$t = \frac{\overline{d}}{s_d/\sqrt{n}} = \frac{.10}{.2608/\sqrt{6}} = \frac{.10}{.1065} = 0.94$$

Since the computed value of *t* (.94) is less than the critical value of 2.015, H_o is not rejected. The evidence does not suggest a reduction in grades from the fall to the spring semester. The decrease in GPA's can be attributed to chance. The p-value is greater than .100.

Exercise 3

Check your answers against those in the ANSWER section.

An independent government agency is interested in comparing the heating cost of all-electric homes and those of homes heated with natural gas. A sample of eight all-electric homes is matched with eight homes of similar size and other features that use natural gas. The heating costs for last January are obtained for each home.

Matched Pair	Electric Heat	Gas Heat
1	265	260
2	271	270
3	260	250
4	250	255
5	248	250
6	280	275
7	257	260
8	262	260

At the .05 significance level is there reason to believe there is a difference in heating costs?

CHAPTER ASSIGNMENT 9

Student's *t* Test: Small Sample Methods

Name _____ Section _____ Score _____

PART I **Matching** Select the correct answer and write the appropriate letter in the space provided.

_____ 1. Degrees of freedom

_____ 2. Student's *t*

_____ 3. Paired paired samples

_____ 4. Independent samples

_____ 5. Pooled variance

    a. unrelated samples

    b. estimated of common population variance

    c. used for related samples

    d. observations free to vary

    e. continuous distribution

PART II **Multiple Choice** Select the correct answer and write the appropriate letter in the space provided.

_____ 6. Student's *t* distribution is an example of a

    a. continuous distribution.
    b. discrete distribution.
    c. binomial distribution.
    d. None of these is correct.

_____ 7. Which of the following statements is correct regarding the *t* and *z* distributions?

    a. The *t* distribution is postivitely skewed.
    b. The *t* distribution is discrete.
    c. The *z* distribution approaches *t* as σ increases.
    d. Both have means equal to zero.

_____ 8. As the degrees of freedom increase the *t* distribution

    a. approaches the normal.
    b. moves away from the normal.
    c. becomes flatter.
    d. becomes continuous.

_____ 9. In a one sample test of means with a sample size of 10 and σ unknown, there are

    a. 9 degrees of freedom.
    b. 10 degrees of freedom.
    c. 11 degrees of freedom.
    d. 8 degrees of freedom.

For questions 10 through 13 use the following information.

$$H_0: \mu = 20 \qquad n = 12 \qquad \alpha = .01$$
$$H_1: \mu > 20 \qquad s = 2$$

_____ 10. Which of the following statements is (are) correct?

    a. This is a test of means.
    b. This is a one-tailed test.
    c. The *t* distribution is the appropriate test statistic.
    d. All of the above.

_____ 11. The decision rule is

    a. reject H_0 if $t > 2.718$.
    b. reject H_0 if $t < -3.106$.
    c. reject H_0 if $t < -2.718$ or $t > 2.718$.
    d. reject H_0 if $t > 1.796$.

_____ 12. If $\overline{X}$ is determined to be 22, the computed value of t is

    a. 1.00
    b. 2.718
    c. 3.464
    d. None of the above.

_____ 13. Assuming $\overline{X} = 22$, the p-value is estimated to be

    a. greater than .100.
    b. between .05 and .025.
    c. between .010 and .001.
    d. between .005 and .0005.
    e. Cannot estimate the p-value.

_____ 14. The paired t test assumes that the differences between the paired or related observations are

    a. all equal to 0.
    b. approximately normally distributed.
    c. ordinal scale.
    d. None of the above.

_____ 15. For a particular level of significance

    a. the value of t is smaller than the value of z for a given sample size.
    b. the value of z is smaller than the value of t for a given sample size.
    c. the values of t and z are always equal.
    d. the value of z is twice that of t.

PART III Problems Record your answer in the space provided. Show essential calculations.

16. Southern Airlines is studying the weight of luggage of its passengers. A sample of eight passengers revealed that the total weight of their luggage (in pounds) was:

        60 44 58 52 47 52 62 63

At the .05 significance level can the airlines conclude that the mean weight of the luggage exceeds 50 pounds?

a. State the null hypothesis and the alternate hypothesis.

H_0: _____

H_1: _____

b. State the decision rule.

_____

c. Compute the value of the test statistic.

Answer

d. State your conclusion regarding H_0. Interpret your result.

_____

_____

e. Estimate the p-value.

Answer

17. The state insurance commissioner in Kentucky is comparing the premiums for homeowners insurance in Kentucky with those in Georgia. A sample of 14 home owners in Kentucky paid a mean of $380 per year with a standard deviation of $41 per year for insurance. In Georgia a sample of 10 home owners paid a mean of $435 per year with a standard deviation of $35 per year. At the .01 significance level, can the commissioner conclude that home owners in Kentucky pay less?

a. State the null hypothesis and the alternate hypothesis.

H_0: _____

H_1: _____

b. State the decision rule.

_____

c. Compute the value of the test statistic.

Answer

d. State your conclusion regarding the null H_0. Interpret your result.

_____

_____

135

18. The G. G. Greene Manufacturing Co. has just settled a bitter labor dispute. Glen Greene, the owner, would like to compare the weekly production of workers before and after the strike. A random sample of twelve workers is selected and the weekly production information determined. At the .05 significance level, is there a difference in production since the strike?

Worker	Production Before Strike	Production After Strike
Balazy	30	28
Bauer	28	29
Connolly	27	26
Dennis	28	32
Devlin	33	33
Elliot	27	33
Gregory	30	36
Pardoe	31	29
Hayson	29	34
Sofo	32	25
Buttler	33	25
Whitfield	30	25

a. State the null hypothesis and the alternate hypothesis.

H_0: _____

H_1: _____

b. State the decision rule.

_____

c. Compute the value of the test statistic.

Answer

d. State your decision regarding H_0. Interpret your result.

_____

_____

10

TESTING FOR DIFFERENCES IN VARIANCES

CHAPTER GOALS

After completing this chapter, you will be able to:

1. List the characteristics of the *F* distribution.
2. Conduct a test of hypothesis to determine if two population variances are equal.
3. Set up an analysis of variance table.
4. Conduct a test for a difference among three or more treatment means.

Introduction

In Chapter 9 a method was developed for determining whether there was a difference between two population means, when the sample sizes are less than 30. What if we wanted to compare more than two populations? The two sample *t* test used in Chapter 9 requires that the populations be compared two at a time. This would be very time consuming, offers the possibility of errors in calculations, but most seriously there would be a build-up of TYPE I errors. That is, the total value of α would become large as the number of comparisons increased. In this chapter we will describe a technique that is efficient when simultaneously comparing more than two population means. This technique is known as **analysis of variance (ANOVA)**.

A second test compares two sample variances to determine if they were obtained from the same or equal populations. This test is particularly useful in validating the requirement of the two sample *t* test that both populations have the same standard deviations.

The F Distribution

The test statistic used to compare the sample variances and to conduct the ANOVA test is the *F distribution*. The major characteristics of the *F* distribution are:

1. The value of *F* is at least zero. That is, *F* cannot be negative.
2. The *F* distribution is continuous, is positively skewed, and its values may range from 0 to plus infinity.
3. The *F* distribution is based on two sets of degrees of freedom. One set is for the numerator and the other for the denominator.
4. There is a family of *F* distributions. Each time the number of degrees of freedom in either the numerator or the denominator change, a new *F* distribution is created.

Assumptions of ANOVA

To employ ANOVA, four conditions must be met:

1. The data must be at least of interval scale.
2. The populations being studied must be approximately normally distributed.
3. The populations should have approximately equal standard deviations.
4. The samples should be randomly selected and the populations independent.

The ANOVA Test

The same hypothesis-testing procedure used with the standard normal distribution (*z*) and Student's *t* is also employed with analysis of variance. The test statistic is the *F* distribution.

Step 1. The null hypothesis and the alternate hypothesis are stated.

When three populations means are compared, the null and alternate hypotheses are written:

H_0: $\mu_1 = \mu_2 = \mu_3$
H_1: not all means are equal

Note that rejection of the null hypothesis does not identify which populations differ significantly. It merely indicates that *a difference between at least one pair of means exists.*

Step 2. The level of significance is selected.

The most common values selected are .01 or .05.

Step 3. An appropriate test statistic is selected.

For an analysis of variance problem the appropriate test statistic is F. The F statistic is the ratio of two variance estimates and is computed by the formula:

$$F = \frac{\text{estimated population variance based on variance among the sample means}}{\text{estimated population variance based on variation within samples}}$$

There are $k - 1$ degrees of freedom associated with the numerator of the formula for F, and $N - k$ degrees of freedom with the denominator, where k is the number of populations and N is the total number of sample observations.

Step 4. Formulate the Decision Rule.

The critical value is determined from the F table found in Appendix G.

To illustrate how the decision rule is established, suppose a package delivery company purchased 14 trucks at the same time. Five trucks were purchased from Ford, four from General Motors, and five from Chrysler. All the trucks were used to deliver packages. The cost of maintaining the trucks for the first year is shown below. Is there a significant difference in the mean maintenance cost of the three manufacturers?

Maintenance Cost, By Manufacturer

Ford	General Motors	Chrysler
$ 914	$933	$1,004
1,000	874	1,114
1,127	927	1,044
988	983	1,100
947		1,139

The three different manufacturers are called **treatments**. A treatment is a specific source, or cause, of variation in a set of data. The term is borrowed from agricultural research, where much of the early development of the ANOVA technique took place. Crop yields were compared after different fertilizers (that is, treatments) had been applied to various plots of land.

In the study comparing truck manufacturers there are three treatments. Therefore there are two degrees of freedom in the numerator, found by $k - 1 = 3 - 1 = 2$. How is the number of degrees of freedom for the denominator determined? Note that in the three samples there is a total of 14 observations. Thus the total number of observations, designated by N, is 14. The number of degrees of freedom in the denominator is 11, found by $N - k = 14 - 3$.

The critical value of F can be found in Appendix G at the back of the study guide. There are tables for both the .01 and the .05 significance levels. Using the .05 significance level, note that the degrees of freedom for the numerator are at the top of the table and for the denominator in the left margin. To locate the critical value, move horizontally at the top of the table to 2 degrees of freedom in the numerator, then down that column to the number opposite 11 degrees of freedom in the left margin (denominator). That number is 3.98, which is the critical value of F.

The decision rule is to reject the null hypothesis if the computed value of F exceeds 3.98, otherwise it is not rejected. To reject the null hypothesis and accept the alternate hypothesis allows us to conclude that there is a significant difference between at least one pair of means. If the null hypothesis is not rejected this implies the differences between the sample means could have occurred by chance.

Portrayed graphically, the decision rule is:

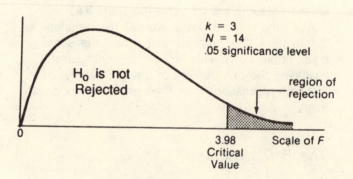

Step 5. Compute F and make a decision.

The value of F is computed from the sample information and a decision is made regarding the null hypothesis. If the computed value of F is 1.98, for example, the null hypothesis is not rejected. If it is greater than 3.98, say 4.26, then the null hypothesis is rejected and the alternate accepted.

The ANOVA Table

A convenient way of organizing the calculations for F is to put them in a table referred to as an ANOVA table. The meaning of SSTotal, SSE, SST, k, and N are explained in Problem 1.

ANOVA Table

Source of Variation	Sum of Squares	Degrees of Freedom	Mean Square
Treatments	SST	$k - 1$	$SST/(k - 1)$
Within	SSE	$N - k$	$SSE/(N - k)$
Total	SS Total		

The formula for computing F is:

$$F = \frac{SST/(k - 1)}{SSE/(N - k)} \qquad 10\text{--}5$$

Comparing Two Population Variances

The F distribution can be used to determine if the sample variance from one normal population is the same as the variance obtained from another normal population. For example, if you were comparing the mean starting salaries for this year's marketing graduates to this year's computer science graduates, an assumption required of the two-sample t test is that both populations have the same standard deviation. Therefore, before conducting the test for means, it is essential to show that the two population standard deviations are equal.

The idea behind the test for standard deviations is that if the null hypothesis is true that the two sample variances are equal, then their ratio will be approximately 1.00. If the null hypothesis is false, then the ratio will be much larger than 1.00. The F distribution provides a decision rule to let us know when the departure from 1.00 is too large to have happened by chance.

GLOSSARY

Analysis of variance (ANOVA)—A statistical technique for determining whether more than two populations have the same mean. This is accomplished by comparing the sample variances.

F distribution—A continuous probability distribution where F is always 0 or positive. The distribution is positively skewed. It is based on two parameters, the number of degrees of freedom in the numerator and the number of degrees of freedom in the denominator.

Treatment—A treatment is a specific source, cr cause, of variation in the set of data.

CHAPTER PROBLEMS

Problem 1

The BonTon Store accepts three types of credit cards—MasterCard, Visa, and their own store card. The sales manager is interested in finding out whether there is a difference in the mean amounts charged by customers on the three cards. A random sample of 18 credit card purchases (rounded to the nearest dollar) revealed these credit card amounts.

MasterCard	Visa	Store
$61	$85	$61
28	56	25
42	44	42
33	72	31
51	98	29
56	56	
	72	

At the .05 significance level, can we conclude there is a difference in the mean amounts charged per purchase on the three cards?

Solution

There are three populations involved—the three credit cards.

H_0: $\mu_1 = \mu_2 = \mu_3$
H_1: the means are not all equal

There are three "treatments" or columns. Hence, there are $k - 1 = 3 - 1 = 2$ degrees of freedom in the numerator. There are a total of 18 samples, therefore $N = 18$. The number of degrees of freedom in the denominator is 15, found by $N - k = 18 - 3$. The critical value is found in Appendix G. Find the table for the .05 significance level and the column headed by 2 degrees of freedom. Then move down that column to the margin row with 15 degrees of freedom and read the value. It is 3.68. The decision rule is: reject the null hypothesis if the computed value of F exceeds 3.68, otherwise do not reject H_0. Shown graphically, the decision rule is:

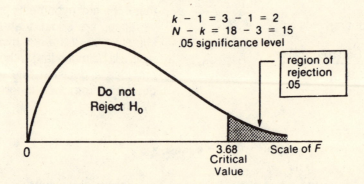

There are two sources of variation in an analysis of variance study. These sources occur between treatments (designated SST) and within treatments (designated SSE). The sum of SST and SSE is the total amount of variation, written SS Total; n_c refers to the number of observations in each column (treatments).

The calculations needed for SST, SSE, and SS Total are:

Amounts Charged

	MasterCard		Visa		Store		Total
	X	X²	X	X²	X	X²	
	$61	3,721	$85	7,225	$61	3,721	
	28	784	56	3,136	25	625	
	42	1,764	44	1,936	42	1,764	
	33	1,089	72	5,184	31	961	
	51	2,601	98	9,604	29	841	
	56	3,136	56	3,136			
			72	5,184			
Column Totals (T_c)	271		483		188		942
Sum of Squares X²		13,095		35,405		7,912	56,412
Sample Size; n_c	6		7		5		$N = 18$

140

The sum of squares total, SS total, is computed using formula 10–4.

$$SS\ Total = \Sigma X^2 - \frac{(\Sigma X)^2}{N} = 56,412 - \frac{(942)^2}{18} = 7,114$$

Recall that ΣX^2 refers to the sum of all observations squared. However, $(\Sigma X)^2$ is found by summing all the observations and then squaring that sum. The total number of observations is N, or 18.

The sum of squares due to treatment (SST) is computed using formula 10–1 where T_c^2 is the square of the column (treatment) totals, and n_c is the number of sample in each treatment.

$$SST = \Sigma \frac{T_c^2}{n_c} - \frac{(\Sigma X)^2}{N}$$

$$= \left[\frac{(271)^2}{6} + \frac{(483)^2}{7} + \frac{(188)^2}{5} \right] - \frac{(942)^2}{18}$$

$$= 3,337.9667$$

The sum of squares error (SSE) is computed as follows using formula 10–2.

$$SSE = \Sigma X^2 - \Sigma \frac{T_c^2}{n_c}$$

$$= 56,412 - \left[\frac{(271)^2}{6} + \frac{(483)^2}{7} + \frac{(188)^2}{5} \right]$$

$$= 3,776.0333$$

As a check, SST + SSE should equal SS Total:

$$SS\ Total = SST + SSE$$
$$= 3,337.9667 + 3,776.0333$$
$$= 7,114$$

which is the same as that computed above.

The next step is to insert these values into the ANOVA table.

Source Variation	Sum of Squares	Degrees of Freedom	Mean Squares
Treatment	SST = 3,337.9667	$k - 1 = 3 - 1 = 2$	$\frac{3,337.9667}{2} = 1,668.9834$
Within	SSE = 3,776.0333	$N - k = 18 - 3 = 15$	$\frac{3,776.0333}{15} = 251.7356$
Total	SS Total = 7,114		

Computing F using formula 10–5:

$$F = \frac{SST/(k - 1)}{SSE/(N - k)} = \frac{3,337.9667/(3 - 1)}{3,776.0333/(18 - 3)} = 6.63$$

Since the computed value of F (6.63) exceeds the critical value of 3.68, the null hypothesis is rejected at the .05 level and the alternate hypothesis is accepted. It is concluded that mean amounts charged by Bon Ton customers is not the same for the three credit cards.

There are many computer software packages that will perform the ANOVA calculations and output the results. MINITAB, SAS, SPSSX, and STATPACK are examples. The following output is from the MINITAB system. Notice that computed F is the same as determined previously.

```
ANALYSIS OF VARIANCE
SOURCE      DF        SS        MS          F
FACTOR       2      3338      1669       6.63
ERROR       15      3776       252
TOTAL       17      7114
                                  INDIVIDUAL 95 PCT CI'S FOR MEAN
                                  BASED ON POOLED STDEV
LEVEL        N      MEAN    STDEV   --------+---------+---------+-------
master       6     45.17    13.08        (------*-----)
visa         7     69.00    18.61                      (------*-----)
store        5     37.60    14.52   (-------*------)
                                    --------+---------+---------+-------
POOLED STDEV =     15.87               40        60        80
```

Exercise 1

Check your answers against those in the ANSWER section.

The accelerating cost of electricity and gas has caused the management at Arvco Electronics to lower the heat in the work areas. The instructor conducting night classes for employees is concerned that this may have an adverse effect on the employees' test scores. Management agreed to investigate. The employees taking the basic electronics were randomly assigned to three groups. One group was in a classroom having a temperature of 60°, another group was placed in a room having a temperature of 70°, and the third group was in a room having a temperature of 80°. At the completion of the chapters on tests of hypotheses a common examination was given consisting of ten questions. The number correct for each of the 20 employees were:

Temperature		
60°	70°	80°
3	7	4
5	6	6
4	8	5
3	9	7
4	6	6
	8	5
	8	4
		3

At the .05 significance level can management conclude that there is a difference in achievement with respect to the three temperatures?

Problem 2

In Problem 1 it was concluded that there was a difference between the mean amounts charged for the three different credit cards, MasterCard, Visa, and the BonTon Store card. Between which credit cards is there a significant difference?

Solution

From the MINITAB output above note that the mean amount charged using the VISA card was $69.00 and $37.60 for the Bon Ton card. Since these means have the largest difference, let's determine if this pair of means differ significantly.

To determine if the means differ, a confidence interval for the difference between the two population means is developed. This confidence interval employs the t distribution and the mean square error (MSE) term. Recall that one of the assumptions for ANOVA is that the standard deviations (or variances) in the sampled populations must be the same. The MSE term is an estimate of this common variance. It is obtained from the MINITAB output. The formula is:

$$(\bar{X}_1 - \bar{X}_2) \pm t \sqrt{MSE\left(\frac{1}{n_1} + \frac{1}{n_2}\right)} \qquad 10\text{--}5$$

where

$\bar{X}_1$ is the mean of the first treatment

$\bar{X}_2$ is the mean of the second treatment

t is obtained from the t table. The degrees of freedom is equal to $N - k$.

MSE is the mean square error term, which is found in the ANOVA table. It is equal to $SSE/(N - k)$ and is an estimate of the common population variance.

n_1 is the number of observations in the first treatment.

n_2 is the number of observations in the second treatment.

If the confidence interval includes 0, there is no difference in the treatment means. However, if both end points of the confidence interval are on the same side of 0 it indicates that pair of means differ.

$$(\bar{X}_1 - \bar{X}_2) \pm t \sqrt{MSE\left(\frac{1}{n_1} + \frac{1}{n_2}\right)}$$

$$(69.00 - 37.60) \pm 2.131 \sqrt{252\left(\frac{1}{7} + \frac{1}{5}\right)}$$

$$31.40 \pm 19.81$$

$$\$11.59 \text{ to } \$51.21$$

Where

$$\bar{X}_1 = 69.00 \qquad \bar{X}_2 = 37.60$$

$$n_1 = 7 \qquad n_2 = 5$$

t is 2.131 from Appendix F with 15 degrees of freedom. MSE is 252, which is in the ANOVA table.

143

Since both end points have the same sign, positive in this case, we conclude that there is a difference in the mean amount charged on VISA and the store charge.

Similar, approximate results can be obtained directly from the MINITAB output. In the lower right corner of the output a confidence interval was developed for each mean. The * indicates the mean of the treatment and the symbols (and) indicate the endpoints of the confidence interval. In comparing treatment means, if there is any common area between the two, they do *not* differ. If there is not any common area between the treatment means, they differ. For the credit card example, MasterCard and VISA have common area and do not differ. MasterCard and the store card do not differ, but the store and VISA do differ.

Problem 3

Teledko Associates is a marketing research firm that specializes in comparative shopping. Teledko is hired by General Motors to compare the selling price of the Pontiac Sunbird with the Chevy Cavalier. Posing as a potential customer, a representative of Teledko visited 8 Pontiac dealerships in Metro City and 6 Chevrolet dealerships and obtained quotes on comparable cars. The standard deviation for the selling prices of 8 Pontiac Sunbirds is $350 and on the six Cavaliers, $290. At the 0.02 significance level is there a difference in the variation in the quotes of the two types of dealerships?

Solution

Let the Sunbird be population 1 and the Cavalier population 2. A two-tailed test is appropriate because we are looking for a difference in the variances. We are not trying to show that one population has a larger variance than the other. The null and alternate hypotheses are:

$$H_0 : \sigma_1^2 = \sigma_2^2$$
$$H_1 : \sigma_1^2 \neq \sigma_2^2$$

The F distribution is the appropriate test statistic for comparing two sample variances. For a two-tailed test, the larger sample variance is placed in the numerator. The critical value of F is found by dividing the significance level in half and then referring to Appendix G and the appropriate degrees of freedom. There are $n - 1 = 8 - 1 = 7$ degrees of freedom in the numerator and $n - 1 = 6 - 1 = 5$ degrees of freedom in the denominator. From Appendix G, using the .01 significance level, the critical value of F is 10.5. If the ratio of the two variances exceeds 10.5, the null hypothesis is rejected and the alternate hypothesis is accepted. The computed value of the test statistics is determined by

$$F = \frac{s_1^2}{s_2^2} = \frac{(350)^2}{(290)^2} = 1.46$$

The null hypothesis is not rejected. There is no difference in the variation in the quotes of the two types of dealerships because the computed value of F (1.46) is less than the critical F value of 10.5.

Exercise 2

Check your answers against those in the ANSWER section.

Thomas Economic Forecasting Inc., and Harmon Econometrics have the same mean error in forecasting the stock market over the last ten years. However, the standard deviation for Thomas is 30 points and 60 points for Harmon. At the .05 significance level can we conclude that there is more variation in the forecast given by Harmon Econometrics?

144

CHAPTER ASSIGNMENT 10

Testing for Differences in Variances

Name _____ Section _____ Score _____

PART I Matching Select the correct answer and write the appropriate letter in the space provided.

_____ 1. Treatment

_____ 2. *F* distribution

_____ 3. ANOVA

_____ 4. *k*

_____ 5. MSE

a. number of treatments

b. technique for comparing means

c. estimate of the common variance

d. positively skewed distribution

e. source of variation

PART II Multiple Choice Select the correct answer and write the appropriate letter in the space provided.

_____ 6. A treatment is

    a. a normal population.
    b. a source of variation.
    c. the explained variation.
    d. the amount of random error.
    e. None of these.

_____ 7. If *k* is the number of treatments in a one way ANOVA and *N* the total number of units sampled, the degrees of freedom for *F* are

    a. $k - 1$ in the numerator and $N - k$ in the denominator.
    b. k in the numerator and n in the denominator.
    c. $N - 1$ in the numerator and k in the denominator.
    d. $N - k$ in the numerator and $k - 1$ in the denominator.

_____ 8. The *F* distribution is

    a. negatively skewed.
    b. nearly normal.
    c. positively skewed.
    d. a discrete distribution.
    e. None of these

_____ 9. The Analysis of Variance (ANOVA) technique is a test to

    a. determine if population means differ.
    b. determine if degrees of freedom differ.
    c. find the *F* distribution.
    d. measure skewness.

_____ 10. The mean square error term (MSE) is the

    a. treatment variation.
    b. estimated standard deviation of the first sample.
    c. estimated common population variance.
    d. estimated common population standard deviation.

11. The rejection of the null hypothesis in a one-way ANOVA indicates that

    a. all the populations have different means.
    b. at least one pair of means differ.
    c. all the populations have the same means.
    d. the blocks are the same.

12. What is the probability for an F value of more than 4.77 with 4 and 16 degrees of freedom?

    a. .05
    b. .025
    c. .10
    d. .01

13. A test for the difference in two sample variances is performed using the

    a. t distribution.
    b. z distribution.
    c. binomial distribution.
    d. F distribution.

14. The computed F ratio for a one-way ANOVA is 1.44. There are 2 degrees of freedom in the numerator and 15 in the denominator. At the .05 significance level we conclude that

    a. the treatment variances differ.
    b. at least one pair of treatment means differ.
    c. at least one pair of block means differ.
    d. the treatment means do not differ.

15. Which of the following is *not* a requirement for ANOVA?

    a. Normal population
    b. Equal mean population
    c. Equal population variances
    d. Independent samples

PART III Problems Record your answer in the space provided. Show essential calculations.

21. An avid golfer maintains information on his scores for 18 holes of golf. When he rides in a golf cart, the standard deviation of his scores is 5.75 for a sample of 25 rounds. When he carries his bag, the standard deviation of his scores is 7.35 for a sample of 21 rounds. At the .05 significance level, is there more variation in his scores when he carries his own bag?

    a. State the null hypothesis and the alternate hypothesis.

    H_0: _____

    H_1: _____

    b. State the decision rule.

    _____

    c. Compute the value of the test statistic.

    Answer

146

d. State your decision regarding H_0. Interpret your result.

_____

_____

22. Soft contact lens accumulate protein from the eye and must be cleaned with a chemical solution. Stan Rudey, the owner of Rudey's Optics, conducted an experiment to determine if there was a difference in the time (in months) three brands of contacts could be worn until they needed cleaning. Fifteen patients were randomly assigned to three brands of lenses and the elapsed number of months until cleaning was necessary recorded. At the .05 significance level, is there a difference in the mean time to cleaning?

Brand	Months of Wear				
A	3	4	6	3	4
B	2	3	2	5	2
C	5	7	5	4	6

a. State the null hypothesis and the alternate hypothesis.

H_0: _____

H_1: _____

b. State the decision rule.

_____

c. Compute the value of the test statistic.

```
┌─────────────┐
│             │
└─────────────┘
```
Answer

d. State your decision regarding H_0. Interpret your result.

_____

_____

11

CORRELATION AND REGRESSION ANALYSIS

CHAPTER GOALS

After completing this chapter, you will be able to:

1. Draw a scatter diagram.
2. Define the terms dependent variable and independent variable.
3. Compute and interpret Pearson's coefficient of correlation.
4. Conduct a significance test for Pearson's coefficient of correlation.
5. Calculate and explain the coefficient of determination.
6. Use the least squares method to determine the regression equation.
7. Determine the standard error of estimate.
8. Determine a confidence interval and a prediction interval for estimated values of the dependent variable.

Introduction

We studied hypothesis testing concerning means and proportions where only a single feature of the sampled item was considered. For example, based on sample evidence we concluded that the beginning annual mean salary for accounting graduates is $26,000. With this chapter we begin our study of the relationship between two variables. We may want to determine if there is a relationship between the number of years of company service and the income of executives. Or we may want to explore the relationship between crime in the inner city and the unemployment rate.

Two techniques are used to study the relationship between two variables: (1) **correlation analysis**, a technique used to measure the strength of the relationship between two variables; and (2) **regression analysis**, which is concerned with estimating one variable based on another.

The variable used as the estimator is called the **independent variable**. The variable being estimated is called the **dependent variable**. Suppose we are attempting to estimate annual income based on years of service with the company. Years of service is the independent variable, income the dependent variable. In essence, we are suggesting that income is related to, or varies with, years of service.

The Scatter Diagram

A useful tool in correlation analysis is to draw a **scatter diagram**. A scatter diagram portrays the relationship between the two variables. The values of the independent variable are portrayed on the horizontal axis (*X*-axis) and the dependent variable along the vertical axis (*Y*-axis). Note in Figure A that as the length of service increases so does income. In Figure B, as employment rises, the crime rate in the inner city declines.

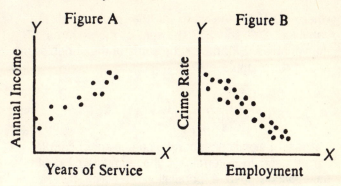

Correlation Coefficient

A measure of the linear (straight-line) strength of the association between two variables is given by the **coefficient of correlation**. It is also called

Pearson's product-moment correlation coefficient or **Pearson's r** after its founder Karl Pearson. The correlation coefficient is usually designated by the lower case *r* and may range from –1.0 to 1.0 inclusive. A value of–1.0 indicates perfect negative correlation and 1.0 perfect positive correlation. A correlation coefficient of 0.0 indicates there is no relationship between the two variables under consideration. This information is summarized in the charts below.

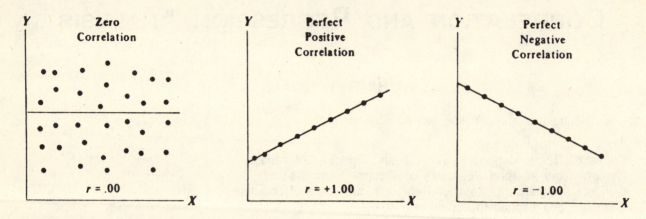

The coefficient of correlation requires that both variables be at least of interval scale.

The degree of strength of the relationship is related to the sign (direction) of the coefficient of correlation. For example, an *r* value of –.60 represents the same degree of correlation as .60. An *r* of –.70 represents a stronger degree of correlation than .40. An *r* of –.90 represents a strong negative correlation and .15 a weak positive correlation.

The coefficient of correlation is computed by the following formula:

$$r = \frac{n(\Sigma XY) - (\Sigma X)(\Sigma Y)}{\sqrt{[n(\Sigma X^2) - (\Sigma X)^2][n(\Sigma Y^2) - (\Sigma Y)^2]}} \qquad [11\text{--}1]$$

where ΣXY is the sum of the product of the variables, ΣX^2 and ΣY^2 the sum of the squares of the variables, ΣX and ΣY the sums of the variables, and *n* the sample size.

A Test of Significance

A test of significance for the coefficient of correlation is used to determine if the computed *r* could have occurred in a population in which the two variables are not related. To put in the form of a question, is the correlation in the population zero?

For a two-tailed test the null hypothesis and the alternate hypothesis are written as follows:

$$H_0: \rho = 0$$
$$H_1: \rho \neq 0$$

The Greek lower case rho, ρ, represents the correlation in the population. The null hypothesis is that there is no association in the population, and alternate that there is correlation.

The alternate hypothesis can also be set up as a one-tailed test. It could read "the correlation coefficient is greater than zero."

The test statistic follows the *t* distribution with $n - 2$ degrees of freedom.

$$t = \frac{r\sqrt{n-2}}{\sqrt{1-r^2}} \qquad [11\text{--}2]$$

The Coefficients of Determination and Nondetermination

Two other measures of association are the coefficient of determination and the coefficient of nondetermination. The **coefficient of determination** is the proportion of the total variation in the dependent variable that is explained or accounted for by the variation in the independent variable. It is usually written as r^2 and may range between 0 and 1.0. It cannot be negative. It is determined by squaring the coefficient of correlation. An r^2 value of .75 indicates that 75 percent of the variation in the dependent variable *(Y)* is explained by the variation in the independent variable *(X)*. The **coefficient of nondetermination**, computed by $1 - r^2$, is the percent of the variation in *Y* that is *not explained* by the variation in *X*. In this example, it would be .25, found by $1 - r^2 = 1 - .75 = .25$.

The Regression Equation

The linear relationship between two variables is given by the equation:

$$Y' = a + bX \qquad 14\text{–}1$$

where

Y' is the predicted value of Y for a selected value of X.

a is the Y intercept. It is the value of Y when $X = 0$.

b is the slope of the line. It measures the change in Y' for each unit change in X. It will always have the same sign as the coefficient of correlation.

X is the value of the independent variable.

The value of a is the **Y intercept** and b is the **regression coefficient**. How do we get these values? They are developed mathematically using the **least squares principle**. The principle minimizes the sum of the squared vertical deviations between Y (the actual value) and Y' (the predicted value).

Computing and Interpreting the a and b Values

Suppose the least squares principle was used to develop an equation expressing the relationship between annual salary and the years of work experience. The equation is:

$$Y' = a + bX = 20{,}000 + 500X \text{ (in dollars)}$$

In the example annual income is the dependent variable Y, and is being predicted on the basis of the employee's years of work experience X, the independent variable. The value of 500 which is b, means that for each additional year of work experience the employee's salary increases by $500. Thus, we would expect an employee with 40 years of work experience to earn $5,000 more than one with 30 years of work experience.

What does the 20,000 dollars represent? It is the value for Y' when $X = 0$. Recall that this is the point where the line intersects the Y-axis. The formulas for computing a and b are:

$$b = \frac{n(\Sigma XY) - (\Sigma X)(\Sigma Y)}{n(\Sigma X^2) - (\Sigma X)^2} \qquad [11\text{–}4]$$

$$a = \frac{\Sigma Y}{n} - b\left(\frac{\Sigma X}{n}\right) \qquad [11\text{–}5]$$

where ΣXY is the sum of the products of the dependent variable and the independent variable; ΣX and ΣY the sum of the independent and dependent variables; ΣX^2 the sum of the squares of the independent variable, and n the size of the sample.

The Standard Error of Estimate

Rarely does the predicted value of Y' agree exactly with the actual Y value. That is, we expect some prediction error. One measure of this error is called the **standard error of estimate**. It is written $s_{y \cdot x}$. A small standard error of estimate indicates that the independent variable is a good predictor of the dependent variable.

The standard error, as it is often called, is similar to the standard deviation described in Chapter 3. Recall that the standard deviation was computed by squaring the difference between the actual value and the mean. This squaring was performed for all n observations. For the standard error of estimate, the difference between the predicted value Y' and the actual value of Y is found and the difference squared and summed over all n observations. The formula is:

$$s_{y \cdot x} = \sqrt{\frac{\Sigma(Y - Y')^2}{n - 2}} \qquad [11\text{–}6]$$

A more convenient computational form is:

$$s_{y \cdot x} = \sqrt{\frac{\Sigma Y^2 - a\Sigma Y - b\Sigma XY}{n - 2}} \qquad [11\text{–}7]$$

where a is the intercept and b the slope, ΣY^2 the sum of the squares of the dependent variable, ΣY the sum of the values of the dependent variable, ΣXY the sum of the products of the dependent and independent variable, and n the sample size.

Establishing a Confidence Interval for Y

The standard error is also used to set confidence intervals for the predicted value of Y'. When the sample size is large and the scatter about the regression line is approximately normally distributed, then the following relationships can be expected:

$Y' \pm 1s_{y \cdot x}$ encompasses about 68% of the points.
$Y' \pm 2s_{y \cdot x}$ encompasses about 95.5% of the points.
$Y' \pm 3s_{y \cdot x}$ encompasses about 99.7% of the points.

Two types of intervals are determined. A **confidence interval** is determined for the *mean* value of Y' for a given value of X. A **prediction interval** is determined for an *individual* value of X. To explain the difference between confidence interval and a prediction interval, suppose we are estimating the salary of management personnel who are 40 years old. The case where we estimate the mean salary and want a range of values for all personnel who are age 40 is a confidence interval. The case where we determine a range of values for the salary of a particular 40 year old employee is called a prediction interval.

The formula for the confidence interval is:

$$Y' \pm t(s_{y \cdot x}) \sqrt{\frac{1}{n} + \frac{(X - \overline{X})^2}{\Sigma X^2 - \frac{(\Sigma X)^2}{n}}} \qquad [11-8]$$

where Y' is the predicted value of Y for a given value of X; X is any selected value of the independent variable; $\overline{X}$ is the mean of the independent variable; n is the sample size; t is the value of the Student t distribution from Appendix F, with $n - 2$ degrees of freedom and the given level of significance.

The formula is modified slightly for the prediction interval. A 1 is placed under the radical and the formula becomes:

$$Y' \pm t(s_{y \cdot x}) \sqrt{1 + \frac{1}{n} + \frac{(X - \overline{X})^2}{\Sigma X^2 - \frac{(\Sigma X)^2}{n}}} \qquad [11-9]$$

Regression Assumptions

Regression is based on four assumptions.

1. For a given value of X, there is a group of Y values and these values are normally distributed about Y'.
2. The standard deviation of each of these normal distributions is the same. The common standard deviation is estimated by $s_{y \cdot x}$.
3. The deviations from the regression line are independent. This means that if there is a large deviation from the regression line for a particular X, it does not necessarily mean that a large deviation must appear for other X values.
4. The relationship between the X and Y values is linear, i.e., a straight line.

The Relationship Among Various Measures of Association

The standard error of estimate measures how closely the actual values of Y are to the predicted values of Y'. When the values are close together the standard error is "small"; when they are spread out the standard error will be large. In the calculation of the standard error, the key term is $\Sigma(Y - Y')^2$. When this term is small, the standard error is also small.

The coefficient of correlation measured the strength of the association between two variables. When the points on a scatter diagram were close to a straight line the correlation coefficient tends to be "large." Thus the standard error and the coefficient of correlation reflect the same information, but use a different scale to report it. The standard error is in the same units as the dependent variable. The correlation coefficient has a range of -1.00 to 1.00.

The coefficient of determination also reports the strength of the association. It is the square of the correlation coefficient and has a range of $.00$ to 1.00.

ANOVA Table

A convenient means of showing the relationships among these measures is an ANOVA Table. This is similar to the table developed in Chapter 10. The total variation $\Sigma(Y - \overline{Y})^2$ is divided into two components: (1) that explained by the regression, and (2) the unexplained or random variation. These two categories are identified in the source column of the following ANOVA table. The column headed *DF* refers to the degrees of freedom associated with each category. The total degrees of freedom is $n - 1$. The degrees of freedom in the regression is 1, because there is one independent variable. The degrees of freedom associated with the error term is $n - 2$. The term *SS*, located in the middle of the table, refers to the variation. These terms are computed as follows.

Total variation = SS total $= \Sigma(Y - \overline{Y})^2$

Error variation = SSE $\quad = \Sigma(Y - Y')^2$

Regression $\quad$ = SSR $\quad = \Sigma(Y' - \overline{Y})^2$

Analysis of Variance Table

SOURCE	DF	SS	MS
Regression	1	SSR	SSR/1
Error	$n - 2$	SSE	SSE/$(n - 2)$
Total	$n - 1$	SS total*	

*SS total = SSR + SSE

The coefficient of determination, r^2, can be computed directly from the ANOVA table.

$$r^2 = \frac{SSR}{SS\ total} = 1 - \frac{SSE}{SS\ total} \quad [11\text{–}9]$$

Note that as SSE decreases r^2 increases. The coefficient of correlation is the square root of this value. Hence, both of these values are related to SSE. The standard error of estimate is obtained using the following equation.

$$s_{y \cdot x} = \sqrt{\frac{SSE}{n-2}}$$

Note again the role played by the SSE term. A small value of SSE will result in a small standard error of estimate.

GLOSSARY

Coefficient of determination—It is the proportion of the variation in the dependent variable explained by the independent variable. It may range between 0 and 1, or 0 and 100 percent in terms of a percent. It is designated r^2.

Coefficient of nondetermination—The proportion of the variation in the dependent variable that is left unexplained by the independent variable, found by $1 - r^2$.

Coefficient of correlation—It is a measure of the degree of linear association between two variables. Designated r, it is found by taking the square root of the coefficient of determination. It may range between -1.0 and $+1.0$.

Correlation analysis—A technique used to measure the strength or the degree of relationship between two variables.

Dependent variable—The variable that is to be predicted or estimated. It is denoted as Y.

Independent variable—The variable that provides the basis for estimation. It is the predictor variable and is denoted as X.

Scatter diagram—A graphic tool which visually portrays the relationship between the independent and dependent variables. The dependent variable is scaled on the Y-axis, the independent variable on the X-axis.

Regression analysis—A technique for predicting or estimating the value of one variable called the dependent variable, based on the value of another variable, the independent variable.

Regression equation—A mathematical equation which defines the linear relationship between the dependent and independent variables. It has the form $Y' = a + bX$ where a is the Y intercept and b the slope of the line.

Least squares—It is a method for determining the regression equation by minimizing the sum of the squares of the vertical distances from the actual Y values to the predicted Y values.

Standard error of estimate—It is a measure of the accuracy of the prediction. It is the square root of the sum of the squared vertical deviations between the observed and predicted observations divided by the number of observations minus two.

CHAPTER PROBLEMS

Problem 1

It is believed that the annual repair cost for the sporty automobile Glockenspiel is related to its age. A sample of 10 automobiles revealed the following:

Repair Cost (in dollars) Y	Age (in years) X
$72	2
99	3
65	1
138	7
170	6
140	8
114	4
83	1
101	2
110	5

Plot these data in a scatter diagram. Does it appear there is a relationship between repair cost and age? Compute the coefficient of correlation. Determine at the .05 significance level whether the correlation in the population is greater than zero.

Solution

The repair cost is the dependent variable and is plotted along the Y-axis. Age is the independent variable and is plotted along the X-axis. To plot the first point move horizontally on the X-axis to 2 and then go vertically to 72 on the Y-axis and place a dot. This procedure is continued until all paired data are plotted. Note that it appears there is a positive relationship between the two variables. That is, as X, the age of the automobile increases, so does the repair cost. But, the relationship is not perfect as evidenced by the scatter of dots.

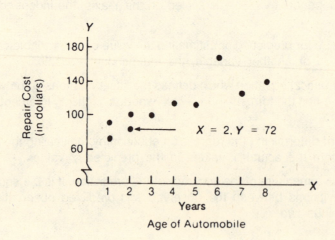

154

The degree of association between age and repair cost is measured by the coefficient of correlation. It is computed by formula 11–1.

$$r = \frac{n(\Sigma XY) - (\Sigma X)(\Sigma Y)}{\sqrt{[n(\Sigma X^2) - (\Sigma X)^2][n(\Sigma Y^2) - (\Sigma Y)^2]}}$$

The calculations and totals in the following table are needed.

	Y	X	XY	X²	Y²
	72	2	144	4	5,184
	99	3	297	9	9,801
	65	1	65	1	4,225
	138	7	966	49	19,044
	170	6	1,020	36	28,900
	140	8	1,120	64	19,600
	114	4	456	16	12,996
	83	1	83	1	6,889
	101	2	202	4	10,201
	110	5	550	25	12,100
Total	1,092	39	4,903	209	128,940

The totals are inserted into the formula and the value of r computed:

$$r = \frac{10(4,903) - (39)(1,092)}{\sqrt{[10(209) - (39)^2][10(128,940) - (1,092)^2]}} = \frac{6,442}{\sqrt{[569][96,936]}} = .867$$

Recall that 0 indicates no correlation and 1.00 perfect correlation. The r of .867 suggests a strong positive correlation between the age of this sports car and annual repair costs. As the age of the car increases so does cost.

The coefficient of determination is the square of the coefficient of correlation. It is .752, found by $(.867)^2$. This value indicates that 75.2 percent of the variation in repair costs can be explained by the age of the car.

A test of hypothesis is used to determine if the correlation in the population could be zero. In this instance, suppose we want to show that there is a positive association between the variables. Recall that the Greek letter ρ refers to the correlation in the population. The null and alternate hypotheses are written as follows:

$$H_0: \rho = 0$$
$$H_1: \rho > 0$$

If the null hypothesis is not rejected, it indicates that the correlation in the population could be zero. If the null hypothesis is rejected, the alternate is accepted. This indicates there is correlation in the population between the two variables and it is positive.

The test statistic follows the student's t distribution with $n - 2$ degrees of freedom. The alternate hypothesis given above specifies a one-tailed test in the positive direction. There are 8 degrees of freedom, found by $n - 2 = 10 - 2$. The critical value for a one-tailed test using the .05 significance level is 1.860 (Appendix F). The decision rule is to reject the null hypothesis if the computed value of t exceeds 1.860. The computed value of t is 4.92, found by using formula 11–2.

$$t = \frac{r\sqrt{n - 2}}{\sqrt{1 - r^2}} = \frac{.867\sqrt{10 - 2}}{\sqrt{1 - (.867)^2}} = 4.92$$

155

Since the computed value (4.92) exceeds the critical value of t, namely 1.860, the null hypothesis is rejected and the alternate accepted. It is concluded that there is a positive association between the age of the automobile and the annual repair cost.

Exercise 1

Check your answers against those in the ANSWER section.

A major oil company is studying the relationship between the daily traffic count and the number of gallons of gasoline pumped at company stations. A sample of eight company owned stations is selected and the following information obtained:

Location	Total Gallons of Gas Pumped (000)	Traffic count (hundreds of cars)
West St.	120	4
Willoughby St.	180	6
Mallard Rd.	140	5
Pheasant Rd.	150	5
I-75	210	8
Kinzua Rd.	100	3
Front St.	90	3
Indiana Ave.	80	2

(a) Develop a scatter diagram with the amount of gasoline pumped as the dependent variable. (b) Compute the coefficient of correlation and the coefficient of determination. (c) Interpret the meaning of the coefficient of determination. (d) Test to determine whether the correlation in the population is zero, versus the alternate hypothesis that the correlation is greater than zero. Use the .05 significance level.

Problem 2

In Problem 1 the relationship between the annual repair cost of the Glockenspiel and its age was examined. The correlation coefficient was computed to be .867, which is considered a strong relationship. Also it was determined that the relationship in the population was not zero.

(a) Use the least squares principle to determine the regression equation. (b) Compute the standard error of estimate. (c) Develop a 95 percent confidence interval for all 4-year-old Glockenspiels and for a prediction interval Ms. Paul's 4-year-old Glockenspiel.

Solution

(a) The first step is to compute the regression equation. The totals for ΣX^2, ΣXY, ΣX, and ΣY for the table in Problem 1 are substituted into formulas 11–4 and 11–5.

$$b = \frac{n(\Sigma XY) - (\Sigma X)(\Sigma Y)}{n(\Sigma X^2) - (\Sigma X)^2} = \frac{10(4,903) - (39)(1,092)}{10(209) - (39)^2} = \frac{6,442}{569} = 11.32$$

$$a = \frac{\Sigma Y}{n} - b\left(\frac{\Sigma X}{n}\right) = \frac{1,092}{10} - 11.32\left(\frac{39}{10}\right) = 65.05$$

Thus, the regression equation is:

$$Y' = a + bX = 65.05 + 11.32X \text{ (in dollars)}$$

Interpreting, repair costs can be expected to increase $11.32 a year on the average. Stated differently, the repair cost of a 4-year-old Glockenspiel can be expected to cost $11.32 more a year than a 3-year-old Glockenspiel.

(b) The standard error of estimate is a measure of the dispersion about the regression line. It is similar to the standard deviation in that it uses squared differences. The differences between the value of Y' and Y are squared and summed over all n observations and then divided by $n - 2$. The positive square root of this value is then obtained. A small value for the standard error of estimate indicates a close association between the dependent and independent variable. The standard error is measured in the same units as the dependent variable. The symbol for the standard error of estimate is $s_{y \cdot x}$.

The standard error is computed using formula 11–57

$$s_{y \cdot x} = \sqrt{\frac{\Sigma Y^2 - a\Sigma Y - b\Sigma XY}{n - 2}}$$

$$= \sqrt{\frac{128,940 - 65.05(1,092) - 11.32(4,903)}{10 - 2}} = 17.33$$

(c) The regression equation is used to estimate the repair cost of a 4-year-old Glockenspiel. The value of 4 is inserted for X in the equation.

$$Y' = 65.05 + 11.32X$$
$$= 65.05 + 11.32(4)$$
$$= 110.33 \text{ (in dollars)}$$

Thus the expected repair cost for a 4-year-old Glockenspiel is $110.33.

Formula 11–8 is used if we want to develop a 95 percent confidence interval for all four-year-old Glockenspiels.

$$Y' \pm ts_{y \cdot x} \sqrt{\frac{1}{n} + \frac{(X - \bar{X})^2}{\Sigma X^2 - \frac{(\Sigma X)^2}{n}}}$$

157

The necessary information for the formula is:

Y'	is 110.33 as previously computed.
t	is 2.306. There are $n - 2$ degrees of freedom, or $n - 2 = 10 - 2 = 8$. From Appendix F, using a two-tailed test and the .05 significance level, move down the .05 column to 8 df and read the value of t.
n	is 10. It is the sample size.
$s_{y \cdot x}$	is 17.33, as computed in an earlier section of this problem.
X	is 4, the age of the Glockenspiel.
$\bar{X}$	is the mean age of the sampled cars. It is 3.9, found by $\bar{X} = 39/10$.
ΣX	is 39, found from the earlier computation in part a.
ΣX^2	is 209, also used in earlier calculations in part a.

Solving for the 95 percent confidence interval:

$$Y' \pm t(s_{y \cdot x}) \sqrt{\frac{1}{n} + \frac{(X - \bar{X})^2}{\Sigma X^2 - \frac{(\Sigma X)^2}{n}}} = \$110.33 \pm 2.306(\$17.33) \sqrt{\frac{1}{10} + \frac{(4 - 3.9)^2}{209 - \frac{(39)^2}{10}}}$$

$$= \$110.33 \pm \$12.65$$
$$= \$\ 97.68 \text{ to } \$122.98$$

The 95 percent confidence interval for the mean amount spent on repairs to a 4-year-old Glockenspiel is between \$97.68 and \$122.98. Interpreting, about 95 percent of the similarly constructed intervals would include the population value.

Recall that Ms. Paul owns a 4-year-old Glockenspiel. The 95 percent prediction interval for her repair costs is computed as follows using formula 11–9.

$$Y' \pm t(s_{y \cdot x}) \sqrt{1 + \frac{1}{n} + \frac{(X - \bar{X})^2}{\Sigma X^2 - \frac{(\Sigma X)^2}{n}}} = \$110.33 \pm 2.306(\$17.33) \sqrt{1 + \frac{1}{10} + \frac{(4 - 3.9)^2}{209 - \frac{(39)^2}{10}}}$$

$$= \$110.33 \pm \$41.92$$
$$= \$\ 68.41 \text{ to } \$152.25$$

Interpreting we would conclude with a 95 percent level of confidence that Ms. Paul will spend between \$68.41 and \$152.25 on repairs this year to her four-year-old Glockenspiel. About 95 percent of the similarly constructed intervals would include the population value.

158

Problem 3

Use the information from Problem 1 to develop an ANOVA Table. Compute the coefficient of determination, the coefficient of correlation, and the standard error of estimate from this table.

Solution

The MINITAB System was used to develop the following output.

Analysis of Variance

SOURCE	DF	SS	MS
Regression	1	7,293.4	7,293.4
Error	8	2,400.2	300.0
Total	9	9,693.6	

The coefficient of determination is computed from formula 11–9.

$$r^2 = \frac{SSR}{SS\ Total} = 1 - \frac{SSE}{SS\ Total} = 1 - \frac{2,400.2}{9,693.6} = 0.752$$

159

The correlation coefficient is .867, found by taking the square root of .752. These two coefficients (.867 and .752) are the same as computed in Problem 3.

The standard error of estimate is computed by the following formula.

$$s_{y \cdot x} = \sqrt{\frac{SSE}{n-2}} = \sqrt{\frac{2,400.2}{10-2}} = 17.32$$

Note again the role played by the SSE term. A small value of SSE will result in a small standard error of estimate.

Exercise 3

Check your answers against those in the ANSWER section.

Refer to Exercise 1, regarding the relationship between the amount of gasoline pumped and the traffic count. The following output was obtained from MINITAB.

Analysis of Variance

SOURCE	DF	SS	MS
Regression	1	14,078	14,078
Error	6	310	52
Total	7	14,388	

Compute the coefficient of determination, the coefficient of correlation, and the standard error of estimate.

CHAPTER ASSIGNMENT 11

Correlation and Regression Analysis

Name _____ Section _____ Score _____

PART I **Matching** Select the correct answer and write the appropriate letter in the space provided.

_____ 1. Correlation coefficient

_____ 2. Coefficient of determination

_____ 3. Standard error of estimate

_____ 4. Intercept

_____ 5. Slope

_____ 6. Least squares

_____ 7. Independent variable

_____ 8. Dependent variable

_____ 9. Scatter diagram

_____ 10 Confidence interval

a. variable being estimated

b. minimizes the term $\Sigma(Y - Y')^2$ to find a and b

c. amount Y' increases when X increases by 1

d. value when $X = 0$

e. percent of explained variation

f. may range from -1.00 to 1.00

g. variable being used to estimate

h. measure of the variation around regression line

i. graphic tool to show the relationship between X and Y

j. shows a range of values of Y'

PART II **Multiple Choice** Select the correct answer and write the appropriate letter in the space provided.

_____ 11. A regression equation is used to

    a. measure the association between two variables.
    b. estimate the value of the dependent variable based on the independent variable.
    c. estimate the value of the independent variable based on the dependent variable.
    d. compute the coefficient of determination.

_____ 12. A regression equation was computed where $b = 0$ and $a = 7.0$. This would mean that the

    a. regression equation is parallel to the X-axis.
    b. regression equation always passes through the origin.
    c. regression equation is parallel to the Y-axis.
    d. None of the above.

_____ 13. The least squares principle means that

    a. the term $\Sigma(Y - Y')^2$ is minimized.
    b. the term $\Sigma(Y - \underline{Y}')^2$ is maximized.
    c. the term $\Sigma(Y - \overline{Y})^2$ is minimized.
    d. the term $\Sigma(\overline{Y} - Y')^2$ is maximized.

_____ 14. The standard error of estimate is

    a. always in the same units as the independent variable.
    b. reported in squared units of the dependent variable.
    c. a measure of the variation around the regression line.
    d. sometimes negative.

_____ 15. The slope of the regression line and the coefficient of correlation

    a. always have the same sign.
    b. are always inversely related.
    c. are measured in the same units.
    d. always have the same sign as the intercept.

_____ 16. If the computed value of the standard error of estimate is 0, this means

    a. there is no relationship between the two variables.
    b. all the points are on the regression line.
    c. you made a mistake in arithmetic.
    d. that the relationship between the two variables is negative.

_____ 17. The coefficient of determination is

    a. determined by SSR/SS total.
    b. usually labeled as r^2.
    c. a measure of the percent of the variation explained by the regression equation.
    d. All of the above.

_____ 18. Which of the following statements are true regarding the coefficient of correlation?

    a. It cannot be negative.
    b. It may range from −1.00 to 1.00.
    c. A value of 50 indicates perfect correlation.
    d. A value of 0.00 indicates perfect correlation.
    e. None of the above.

_____ 19. A coefficient of correlation was computed to be −.70. This means that

    a. as the X value increases the Y value also increases.
    b. the coefficient of determination is also 0.
    c. as the X value increases the Y value decreases.
    d. The X and Y values are not related.

_____ 20. Which value of r indicates a stronger correlation than −.45?

    a. .44
    b. −.34
    c. .67
    d. 0
    e. None of these is correct.

PART III Problems Record your answer in the space provided. Show essential calculations.

21. Bank One of Texas is studying the relationship between the mean account balance for individual checking accounts and the number of transactions per month. (A transaction is an activity to the account, such as writing a check, withdrawing funds, etc.) A sample of twelve accounts revealed:

Customer	Mean Balance $00	Number of Transactions	Show work here
1	9	4	
2	8	4	
3	14	12	
4	11	6	
5	6	2	
6	11	4	
7	12	10	
8	7	4	
9	11	10	
10	9	12	
11	5	6	
12	4	4	

a. Draw a scatter diagram.

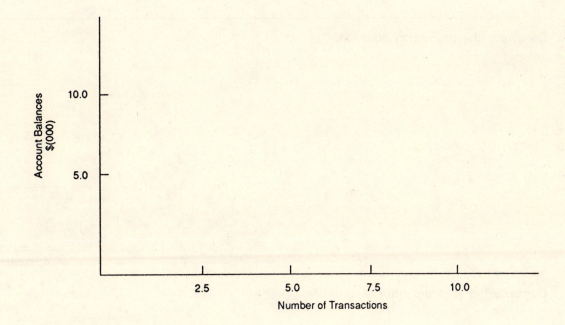

b. Compute the coefficient of correlation.

c. At the .05 significance level can we conclude that there is positive correlation in the population? State the null and the alternate hypotheses.

H_0: _____

H_1: _____

State the decision rule.

_____

Compute the value of the test statistic.

Answer

State your decision regarding H_0. Interpret your result.

_____

_____

d. Determine the regression equation.

a =
b =

Answer

e. Compute the standard error of estimate.

Answer

164

f.   Estimate the account balance for all customers who had five transactions.

  <table><tr><td>   </td></tr></table>
  Answer

d.   Develop a 95 percent confidence interval for the mean account balance of all customers with five transactions at Bank One of Texas.

h.   Develop a 95 percent confidence interval for the account balance of Jim Minitel, a customer of Bank One of Texas who had five transactions last month.

12

MULTIPLE REGRESSION AND CORRELATION

CHAPTER GOALS

After completing this chapter, you will be able to:

1. Describe the relationship between one dependent variable and two or more independent variables.
2. Interpret the MINITAB multiple regression computer output.
3. Understand and interpret the terms correlation matrix, coefficient of multiple determination, net regression coefficient, and multiple standard error of estimate.
4. Conduct a test of hypothesis for each independent variable.
5. Conduct a global test of hypothesis to determine if any of the regression coefficients could be zero.

Introduction

The methods presented in Chapter 11 considered only the relationship between one dependent variable and one independent variable. The possible effect of other independent variables was ignored. For example, we described how the repair cost of a car was related to the age of the car. Are there other factors that affect the repair cost? Does the size of the engine or the number of miles driven affect the repair cost? When several independent variables are used to estimate the value of the dependent variable it is called **multiple regression.**

The Multiple Regression Equation

Recall that for one independent variable the regression equation has the form:

$$Y' = a + bX$$

For more than one independent variable, the equation is extended to include the additional variables. For three independent variables it is:

$$Y' = a + b_1X_1 + b_2X_2 + b_3X_3$$

The values of b_1, b_2, and b_3 are called the **net regression coefficients.** They indicate the change in the estimated value for a unit change in one of the independent variables when the other independent variables are held constant.

For example, suppose the National Sales Manager of General Motors wants to analyze regional sales using the number of autos registered in the region (X_1), the age of the automobiles registered in the region (X_2), and the personal income in the region (X_3). Some of the sample information obtained is:

Region	Sales ($ millions) Y	Number of autos in region (000) X_1	Average age of autos (years) X_2	Personal income in region (billions) X_3
I	$ 9.2	842	5.6	$ 29.5
II	46.8	2,051	5.1	182.6
III	26.2	1,010	5.8	190.7
etc.				

Suppose the multiple regression equation was computed to be:

$$Y' = 41.0 + .0071X_1 + (-3.19)X_2 + .01611X_3$$

In April of this year the automobile registration bureau announced that in a particular region 1,542,000 autos were registered, and their average age was 6.0 years. Another agency announced that personal income in the region was $150 billion. The sales manager could then estimate, as early as April, annual sales for this year by inserting the value of these independent variables in the equation and solving for Y':

$$Y' = 41.0 + .0071(1,542) - 3.19(6.0) + .01611(150)$$
$$= \$35.2 \text{ million}$$

What is the meaning of the regression coefficients? The .0071 associated with number of autos in the region (in thousands) indicates that for each additional 1,000 autos sold, sales will increase .0071 (million), if the other independent variables are held constant. That is, the regression coefficients show change in the dependent variable when the other independent variables are not allowed to change.

Measures of Association in Multiple Regression

It is likely that there is some error in the estimation. This can be measured by the **multiple standard error of estimate.** Like the standard error of estimate described in the previous chapter, it is based on the squared deviations between Y and Y'. The **coefficient of multiple determination**, written R^2, reports the proportion of the variation in Y which is explained by the variation in the set of independent variables. In the example, if the coefficient of multiple determination were .81, it would indicate that the three independent variables, considered jointly, explain 81 percent of the variation in millions of sales dollars. The **coefficient of nondetermination**, found by $1 - R^2$, is the amount of variation that is unexplained by the set of independent variables. In the example, if 81 percent of the variation is explained, then 19 percent is not. The 19 percent is found by $1 - .81$. The unexplained variation is due to random effects and variables not considered in the set of independent variables.

Tests of Hypothesis for Multiple Regression

Two tests of hypotheses are considered in this chapter. The first tests the overall ability of the set of independent variables to explain differences in the dependent variable. This test is often referred to as the **global test.** The null hypothesis is that the net regression coefficients in the population are all zero. If accepted, it would imply that the set of coefficients is of no value in explaining differences in the dependent variable. The alternate hypothesis is that *at least one of the coefficients is not zero*. This test is written in symbolic form for three independent variables as:

$$H_0: \beta_1 = \beta_2 = \beta_3 = 0$$
$$H_1: \text{Not all the } \beta s \text{ are } 0$$

Rejecting H_0 and accepting H_1 implies that one or more of the independent variables is useful in explaining differences in the dependent variable. However, a word of caution, it does not suggest how many or identify which independent variables are not zero.

The test statistic used is the F distribution which was first described in Chapter 10, the ANOVA chapter. To employ the F distribution, two sets of degrees of freedom are required. The degrees of freedom for the numerator is equal to k, the number of independent variables. The degrees of freedom in the denominator is equal to $n - (k + 1)$ where n refers, as usual, to the total number of observations.

The second test of hypothesis identifies which of the set of independent variables are significant predictors of the dependent variable. That is, it tests the independent variables individually rather than as a unit. This test is useful because unimportant variables can be eliminated. The test statistic is the t distribution with $n - (k + 1)$ degrees of freedom. For example, suppose we want to test whether the second independent variable was zero, versus the alternate that it was less than zero. The null and alternate hypotheses would be written as follows:

$$H_0: \beta_2 = 0$$
$$H_1: \beta_2 < 0$$

Rejection of the null hypothesis and acceptance of the alternate hypothesis would imply that variable number two is significant and that its relationship is indirect.

Qualitative Variables

Variables used in regression analysis must be **quantitative.** That is, they must be numerical in nature. However, frequently we want to use variables that are not numeric. These variables are called **qualitative.** For example, we are interested in estimating the selling price of a used automobile based on its age. Selling price is the dependent variable and age is one independent variable. Another variable is whether or not the car was manufactured in the United States. Note that a particular car can assume only two conditions: either it was built in the U.S. or it was not. Qualitative variables are also called **dummy** or **indicator variables.** To employ a qualitative variable a 0 or 1 coding scheme is used. For example, in the study regarding estimated selling prices of used automobiles those made in the U.S. are coded 1 and all others as 0.

Stepwise Regression

In an earlier section we mentioned that a global test can be used to determine whether any of a set of independent variables had regression coefficients different from zero. We also stated that the regression coefficients can be tested individually. If the null hypothesis is rejected, the variable is retained in the analysis. If the null hypothesis is not rejected, the variable can be dropped from the analysis.

The stepwise method provides a direct method of solution of multiple regression and correlation problems. The independent variables are brought into the regression equation in the order in which they will increase R-square the most. Further, only variables that have significant regression coefficients enter the regression equation.

A **correlation matrix** is developed first which gives all possible simple correlations between each independent variable and the dependent variable. Then the independent variable with the largest simple correlation with the dependent variable is entered. The independent variable that will yield the largest increase in R-square is entered into the multiple regression equation next.

The stepwise process continues until all the significant independent variables are entered into the regression equation. The stepwise method tests each independent variable to determine if the regression coefficient is different from zero before entering it into the regression equation. Hence, only independent variables with significant regression coefficients become a part of the final regression equation.

Assumption for Multiple Regression and Correlation

There are six assumptions that must be met in multiple correlation.

1. The independent variable and the dependent variables must have a linear relationship.
2. The dependent variable must be continuous and interval scale.
3. The variation in the difference between the actual value of the dependent variable and the estimated value must be the same for all fitted values of Y. That is, $(Y - Y')$ must be the same for all values of Y'. For example, the $(Y - Y')$ term cannot have a tendency to be larger when Y' is large. The $(Y - Y')$ term is called the **residual**. When the differences are the same it is said to exhibit **homoscedasticity**.
4. The residuals should be approximately normally distributed with a mean of zero. The standard error of estimate is a measure of the dispersion of this distribution.
5. Successive observations of the dependent variable must be unrelated; that is, not correlated. Violation of this assumption is called **autocorrelation.** It frequently occurs when the data are collected over time.
6. The set of independent variables should not be highly correlated. When independent variables are correlated this condition is called **multicollinearity.**

Seldom in a real world example are all of the conditions fully met. However, the technique of regression still works effectively. If there is concern regarding the violation of one or more of the assumptions, it is suggested that a more advanced statistics book, be consulted.

The ANOVA Table

A convenient means of showing the regression output is to use an ANOVA table. The variation in the dependent variable is separated into two components: (1) that explained by the regression and (2) the unexplained variation. The categories are identified in the source column of the following ANOVA table. The column headed "DF" refers to the degrees of freedom associated with each category. The total degrees of freedom is $n - 1$. The degrees of freedom for regression is k, the number of independent variables. The degrees of freedom associated with the error term is $n - (k + 1)$. The MS column refers to the mean square and is obtained by dividing the SS by DF.

$$\text{Total variation} = \text{SS total} = \Sigma(Y - \bar{Y})^2$$
$$\text{Error variation} = \text{SSE} = \Sigma(Y - Y')^2$$
$$\text{Regression} = \text{SSR} = \Sigma(Y' - \bar{Y})^2$$

Analysis of Variance

SOURCE	DF	SS	MS
Regression	k	SSR	$MSR = SSR/k$
Error	$n-(k+1)$	SSE	$MSE = SSE/(n-(k+1))$
Total	$n-1$	SS total	

GLOSSARY

Multiple regression and correlation analysis—A technique used to analyze the relationship between two or more independent variables and a dependent variable.

Multiple regression equation—It defines the relationship between the dependent variable and the independent variables in the form of an equation. For two independent variables it is: $Y' = a + b_1X_1 + b_2X_2$.

Standard error of estimate—It measures the error in the predicted dependent variable.

Multiple coefficient of determination—The proportion of the variation in the dependent variable that is explained by the independent variables.

Multiple coefficient of nondetermination—It is the proportion of the variation in the dependent variable that is not explained by the independent variables.

Multiple coefficient of correlation—It is the square root of the coefficient of determination and is the relative strength of association between the dependent variable and the independent variables. It is also positive.

Quantitative variable—A numeric variable that is at least interval scale.

Dummy Variable—A variable that assumes only certain categorical values (such as 0 and 1).

Stepwise regression—Independent variables enter the regression equation in the order in which they will increase R-square the most. Only independent variables that have significant regression coefficients are entered.

Correlation matrix—A matrix showing all possible simple coefficients of correlation among all the independent variables and the dependent variable.

Residual—The difference between the actual and the estimated value of the dependent variable.

Homoscedasticity—The residuals are the same for all estimated values of the dependent variable.

Autocorrelation—Successive observations of the dependent variable are correlated.

Multicollinearity—The correlation among the independent variables.

CHAPTER PROBLEMS

Problem 1

The Skaff Appliance Company currently has over 1,000 retail outlets throughout the United States and Canada. They sell name brand electronic products, such as TVs, stereos, and microwave ovens. Skaff Appliance is considering opening several additional stores in other large metropolitan areas. Paul Skaff, president, would like to study the relationship between the sales at existing locations, and several factors regarding the existing store or its region. The factors are the population and the unemployment in the region, and the advertising expense of the store. Another variable considered is "mall." Mall refers to whether the existing store is located in an enclosed shopping mall or not. A "1" indicates a mall location; a "0" indicates the store is not located in a mall. A random sample of 30 stores is selected.

Sales ($000)	Population (000,000)	Percent Unemployed	Advertising Expense ($000)	Mall Location
5.17	7.50	5.1	59.0	0
5.78	8.71	6.3	62.5	0
4.84	10.00	4.7	61.0	0
6.00	7.45	5.4	61.0	1
6.00	8.67	5.4	61.0	1
6.12	11.00	7.2	12.5	0
6.40	13.18	5.8	35.8	0
7.10	13.81	5.8	59.9	0
8.50	14.43	6.2	57.2	1
7.50	10.00	5.5	35.8	0
9.30	13.21	6.8	27.9	0
8.80	17.10	6.2	24.1	1
9.96	15.12	6.3	27.7	1
9.83	18.70	0.5	24.0	0
10.12	20.20	5.5	57.2	1
10.70	15.00	5.8	44.3	0
10.45	17.60	7.1	49.2	0
11.32	19.80	7.5	23.0	0
11.87	14.40	8.2	62.7	1
11.91	20.35	7.8	55.8	0
12.60	18.90	6.2	50.0	0
12.60	21.60	7.1	47.6	1
14.24	25.25	0.4	43.5	0
14.41	27.50	4.2	55.9	0
13.73	21.00	0.7	51.2	1
13.73	19.70	6.4	76.6	1
13.80	24.15	0.5	63.0	1
14.92	17.65	8.5	68.1	0
15.28	22.30	7.1	74.4	1
14.41	24.00	0.8	70.1	0

Determine the regression equation using the MINITAB system. Conduct a test of hypothesis to determine if any of the regression coefficients are not equal to zero.

171

Solution

The first step is to determine the correlation matrix. It shows all possible simple coefficients of correlation. The MINITAB output is as follows.

```
              Sales    Popul    %-unemp    Adv
Popul         0.894
%-unemp      -0.198   -0.368
Adv           0.279    0.125    -0.030
Mall          0.155    0.085     0.017    0.259
```

Sales is the dependent variable. Of particular interest is which independent variable has the strongest correlation with sales. In this case it is population (.894). The negative sign between sales and %-unemp indicates that as the unemployment rate increases, sales decrease.

A second use of the correlation matrix is to check for multicollinearity. Multicollinearity can distort the standard error of estimate and lead to incorrect conclusion regarding which independent variables are significant. The strongest correlation among the independent variables is between %-unemp and popul (−0.368). A rule of thumb is that a correlation between −0.70 and 0.70 will not cause problems and can be ignored. At this point it does not appear there is a problem with multicollinearity.

We want to test the overall ability of the set of independent variables to explain the behavior of the dependent variable. Do the independent variables population, percent unemployed, advertising expense, and mall explain a significant amount of the variation in sales? This question can be answered by conducting a global test of the regression coefficients. The null and alternate hypotheses are:

$$H_0: \beta_1 = \beta_2 = \beta_3 = \beta_4 = 0$$
$$H_1: \text{At least one of the } \beta s \text{ is not zero.}$$

The null hypothesis states that the regression coefficients are all zero. If they are all zero, they are of no value in explaining differences in the sales of the various stores. If the null hypothesis is rejected and the alternate accepted the conclusion is that at least one of the regression coefficients is not zero. Hence, we would conclude that at least one of the variables is significant in terms of explaining difference in sales.

The F distribution is used as the test statistic. It is based on the degrees of freedom in the numerator and in the denominator. The degrees of freedom associated with the regression, which is in the numerator, is equal to the number of independent variables. In this case there are four independent variables, so there are 4 degrees of freedom in the numerator. The degrees of freedom in the error row is $n - (k + 1) = 30 - (4 + 1) = 25$. There are 25 degrees of freedom in the denominator. The critical value of F is obtained from Appendix G. Find the column with 4 degrees of freedom and the row with 25 degrees of freedom in the table for the .05 significance level. The value is 2.76. The null hypothesis is rejected if the computed F is greater than 2.76.

The output from MINITAB is as follows.

```
Analysis of Variance

SOURCE        DF      SS        MS        F        p
Regression     4    270.461    67.615    34.71    0.000
Error         25     48.705     1.948
Total         29    319.166
```

The computed value of F is 34.71 as shown above. It is also computed as follows.

$$F = \frac{SSR/k}{SSE/(n-(k+1))} = \frac{270.461/4}{48.705/25} = \frac{67.615}{1.948} = 34.71$$

Since the computed value of 34.71 exceeds the critical value of 2.76, the null hypothesis is rejected and the alternate accepted. The conclusion is that at least one of the regression coefficients does not equal zero.

Exercise 1

Check your answers against those in the ANSWER section.

Todd Heffren, President of Heffren Manufacturing Co., is studying the power usage at his Vanengo Plant. He believes that the amount of electrical power used is a function of the outside temperature during the day, and the number of units produced that day. A random sample of ten days is selected. The power usage in thousands of kilowatt hours of electricity and the production on that date is obtained. The National Weather Service is contacted to obtain the high temperature for the selected dates.

Power Used	Temperature (F)	Units Produced
12	83	120
11	79	110
13	85	128
9	75	101
14	87	105
10	81	108
12	84	110
11	77	107
14	85	112
11	84	119

The MINITAB system was used to compute a correlation matrix and ANOVA table for the Heffren Manufacturing Co. data. Do you see any problems with multicollinearity? Test the hypothesis that all the regression equations are zero. Use the .05 significance level.

	Usage	Temp
Temp	0.838	
Output	0.361	0.506

Analysis of Variance

SOURCE	DF	SS	MS
Regression	2	17.069	8.534
Error	7	7.031	1.004
Total	9	24.100	

Problem 2

In Problem 1 we found that at least one of the four independent variables had a regression coefficient different from zero. Use the MINITAB system to aid in determining which of the regression coefficients is not equal to zero. Would you consider deleting any of the independent variables?

Solution

The following output is from MINITAB.

The regression equation is
Sales = − 1.67 + 0.552 Popul + 0.203 %−unemp + 0.0314 Adv + 0.220 Mall

Predictor	Coef	Stdev	t-ratio	p
Constant	−1.669	1.408	−1.18	0.247
Popul	0.55191	0.05063	10.90	0.000
%−unemp	0.2032	0.1171	1.74	0.095
Adv	0.03135	0.01606	1.95	0.062
Mall	0.2198	0.5400	0.41	0.687

s = 1.396   R−sq = 84.7%   R−sq(adj) = 82.3%

The four independent variables explain 84.7% of the variation in sales. For those coefficients where the null hypothesis that they are equal to zero cannot be rejected we will consider eliminating them from the regression equation. We are actually conducting four tests of hypotheses.

For Population	For % Unemployed	For Advertising	For Mall
$H_0: \beta_1 = 0$	$H_0: \beta_2 = 0$	$H_0: \beta_3 = 0$	$H_0: \beta_4 = 0$
$H_1: \beta_1 \neq 0$	$H_1: \beta_2 \neq 0$	$H_1: \beta_3 \neq 0$	$H_1: \beta_4 \neq 0$

We will use the .05 significance level and a two-tailed test. The test statistic is the t distribution with $n - (k + 1) = 30 - (4 + 1) = 25$ degrees of freedom. The decision rule is to reject the null hypothesis if the computed value of t is less than −2.060 or greater than 2.060.

From the MINITAB output, the column labeled "Coef" reports the regression coefficients. The "Stdev" column reports the standard deviation of the slope coefficients. The "t-ratio" column reports the computed value of the test statistic. The t-ratio for population exceeds the critical value, but the computed values for percent unemployed, advertising expense, and mall are not in the rejection region. This indicates that the independent variable population should be retained and the other three dropped.

However, there is a problem that occurs in many real situations. Note that both percent unemployed and advertising expense are close to being significant. In fact, advertising expense would be significant if we increased the level of significances to .10. (The critical value would be −1.708 and 1.708, and −1.95 is outside the critical region.) Another indicator of trouble is a reversal of a sign of the regression coefficient. Earlier in Problem 1, in the correlation matrix, the correlation between percent unemployed and sales was negative. Note in the above regression equation the sign of the coefficient is positive. (The regression coefficient is 0.203). A reversal of sign such as this is often an indication of multicollinearity. The earlier conclusion that there was not a problem should be reviewed. Perhaps one or both of the independent variables—either advertising expense or percent unemployment—should be included in the regression equation.

An effective method for determining the optimum set of independent variables is to employ the stepwise procedure. In the stepwise procedure variables enter the regression equation in the order in which they will increase the R-square term the most. In addition, tests of significance are conducted at each step to insure that only independent variables that have significant regression coefficients are entered and retained in the regression equation.

The following output is from MINITAB's stepwise procedure.

MTB > step c1 c2–c5

STEPWISE REGRESSION OF Sales ON 4 PREDICTORS, WITH N = 30

STEP	1	2
CONSTANT	1.38697	−0.07874
Popul	0.533	0.521
T-RATIO	10.56	10.83
Adv		0.033
T-RATIO		2.10
s	1.51	1.43
R-sq	79.92	82.75

This procedure indicates that both population and advertising expense should be included in the regression equation.

How does the stepwise procedure work? As noted before, it starts with the correlation matrix. It examines the simple correlations between each of the independent variables and the dependent variable. The variable population has the strongest correlation with sales (.894) so it enters the equation first. In the first step, 79.92% of the variation in sales is explained by the independent variable population. This variable is tested to insure that its regression coefficient is significant.

The next step is to look at the remaining variables.

The independent variable, from those not currently in the regression equation, that will result in the largest increase to R-square is selected. The regression equation is recomputed including this new variable and the newly entered variable is tested to determine if its regression coefficient is significant. This process continues until all possible independent variables with significant regression coefficients are entered into the regression equation. If all the proposed set of independent variables have significant regression coefficients, they are all entered into the regression equation.

In our example the next variable to enter the equation is advertising expense. When advertising expense is added to the regression equation the R-square term is increased from 79.92% to 82.75%. In the column headed "2" in the stepwise output the complete regression equation is given as well as the "T-RATIO." The T-RATIO is the value computed for the test of individual regression coefficients. Can we show these regression coefficients to be significant? To answer this question we employ the test of individual regression coefficients.

	For Population	For Advertising
	$H_0: \beta_1 = 0$	$H_0: \beta_3 = 0$
	$H_1: \beta_1 \neq 0$	$H_1: \beta_3 \neq 0$

There are 2 independent variables in the equation: so the degrees of freedom is 27, found by 30 − (2 + 1). The critical values of t are −2.052 and 2.052. The computed t-ratio is 10.83 for population and 2.10 for advertising expense. Both of these values cause the rejection of the hypothesis that the regression coefficient is zero. We conclude that both of these independent variables have significant regression coefficients. Note that the stepwise method did not introduce the variables mall or percent unemployment, because neither has a significant regression coefficient.

The regression equation with the four independent variables had an R-square term of 84.7% but the stepwise method produced an equation with only two independent variables and that regression equation explained

82.8% of the variation in sales. A simpler equation, with two significant variables, that explains nearly the same amount of variation. Thus by using the stepwise method we were able to obtain nearly the same R-square value with only two variables. Advertising expense and population should be included in the equation and the percent unemployment and mall should be dropped. Using advertising expense and population also removes the sign reversal problem and hence there is no multicollinearity.

Exercise 2

Check your answers against those in the ANSWER section.

Refer to **Exercise 1.** The following output is for the Heffren Manufacturing problem. Conduct a test of hypothesis to determine which of the independent variables have regression coefficients not equal to zero. Use the .05 significance level.

The regression equation is
Usage = $-$ 16.8 + 0.37 Temp $-$ 0.0171 Output

Predictor	Coef	Stdev	t-ratio
Constant	-16.801	7.162	-2.35
Temp	0.37089	0.09962	3.72
Output	-0.01707	0.04791	-0.36

CHAPTER ASSIGNMENT 12

Multiple Regression and Correlation

Name _____ Section _____ Score _____

PART I **Matching** Select the correct answer and write the appropriate letter in the space provided.

_____ 1. Residual

_____ 2. Homoscedasticity

_____ 3. Autocorrelation

_____ 4. Multicollinearity

_____ 5. Correlation matrix

_____ 6. Stepwise

_____ 7. Indicator variable

_____ 8. Quantitative variable

_____ 9. Regression coefficient

_____ 10. Global test

a. successive residuals are correlated

b. correlation among the independent variables

c. all simple correlations among the variables

d. variables entered in the order in which R^2 is increased the fastest

e. may take on values of only 0 or 1

f. tests all regression coefficients to see if any are not 0

g. a numerical value

h. constant variance term

i. $Y - Y'$

j. change in Y' for a unit change in one independent variable with others held constant

PART II **Multiple Choice** Select the correct answer and write the appropriate letter in the space provided.

_____ 11. A multiple regression equation implies that

    a. there is only one independent variable.
    b. there is more than one dependent variable.
    c. there are two or more independent variables.
    d. R^2 is at least .50.
    e. None of these is correct.

_____ 12. A regression coefficient for X_2 shows the amount of change in the dependent variable for a change of 1.0 in X_2 when

    a. the other independent variables are held constant.
    b. the other dependent variables are held constant.
    c. R^2 is increased by 1.
    d. None of the above.

_____ 13. If the multiple standard error of estimate is equal to 0,

    a. the coefficient of determination is also 0.
    b. both the coefficient of determination and the coefficient of correlation equal 0.
    c. R^2 is equal to 1.00.
    d. the regression coefficient is 1.00.

_____ 14. In a global test of hypothesis H_0 states that

     a. all the independent variables are 0.
     b. all the dependent variables are 0.
     c. all the regression coefficients are 0.
     d. R^2 is 1.00.

_____ 15. A qualitative or dummy variable

     a. can assume only the values 0 or 1.
     b. must be at least interval scale.
     c. must be equal to R^2.
     d. must be a numeric value.
     e. None of these is correct.

_____ 16. A residual is the

     a. estimated value of Y'.
     b. actual value of Y.
     c. difference between Y and Y'.
     d. same as the standard deviation.
     e. None of these is correct.

_____ 17. Multicollinearity means that

     a. successive observations are related.
     b. the independent variables are correlated.
     c. the residuals do not have a constant variance.
     d. the dependent variables are correlated.

_____ 18. A correlation matrix reports

     a. only the correlations between the dependent variable and all the independent variables.
     b. all the simple correlation coefficients.
     c. only the positive correlations.
     d. the regression coefficients.

_____ 19. In stepwise regression only independent variables

     a. with significant regression coefficients enter the regression equation.
     b. with correlation coefficients greater than 1.0 are considered.
     c. with residuals greater than 1.0 are considered.
     d. All of the above.

PART III **Problems** Record your answer in the space provided. Show essential calculations.

20. William Clegg is the owner and CEO of Clegg QC Consulting. Mr. Clegg is concerned about the salary structure of his company and has asked the Human Relations Department to conduct a study. Mr. Stan Hire, an analyst in the department, is assigned the project. Stan selects a random sample of 15 employees and gathers information on the salary, the number of years with Clegg Consulting, the employee's performance rating for the previous year, and the number of days absent last year.

Salary ($000)	Years with Firm	Performance Rating	Days Absent
50.3	6	60	8
69.0	9	85	3
50.7	7	60	8
46.9	4	78	12
44.2	5	70	6
50.3	6	73	6
49.2	6	83	6
54.6	5	74	5
52.1	5	85	5
58.3	6	85	4
54.8	4	88	5
63.0	8	78	5
50.1	5	61	6
52.1	4	74	5
36.5	3	65	7

a. The following correlation matrix was developed from the MINITAB System. Do you see any problems? Which independent variable has the strongest correlation with salary?

	Salary	Years	Perform
Years	0.768		
Perform	0.514	0.130	
Absent	−0.587	−0.370	−0.435

_____

_____

_____

_____

_____

b. Conduct a test of hypothesis to determine if any of the regression coefficients are not equal to 0. This analysis of variance table was computed as part of the output. Use the .05 significance level.

Analysis of Variance

SOURCE	DF	SS	MS	F	p
Regression	3	641.10	213.70	13.91	0.000
Error	11	168.94	15.36		
Total	14	810.04			

H_0: _____

H_1: _____

The decision rule is to reject H_0 if _____ .

What is your decision? Interpret.

_____

_____

Determine the R-square value. _____

Interpret it. _____

_____

_____

c. Additional information was obtained from MINITAB. Conduct a test of hypothesis to determine if any of the regression coefficients do not equal 0. Use the .05 significance level.

The regression equation is
Salary = 19.2 + 3.10 Years + 0.269 Perform − 0.704 Absent

Predictor	Coef	Stdev	t-ratio	p
Constant	19.19	12.15	1.58	0.143
Years	3.0962	0.7061	4.38	0.001
Perform	0.2694	0.1196	2.25	0.046
Absent	−0.7043	0.5859	−1.20	0.255

H_0: _____ H_0: _____ H_0: _____

H_1: _____ H_1: _____ H_1: _____

The decision rules are to reject H_0 if _____ .

What is your decision? Interpret.

_____

_____

180

13

ANALYSIS OF NOMINAL-LEVEL DATA: THE CHI-SQUARE DISTRIBUTION

CHAPTER GOALS

After completing this chapter, you will be able to:

1. Explain the characteristics of the chi-square distribution.
2. Test a hypothesis regarding the difference between an observed and an expected set of frequencies.
3. Test whether two criteria of classification in a contingency table are related.
4. Conduct a test for normality.

Introduction

Recall in earlier chapters on hypothesis testing that the level of measurement was assumed to be at least of interval scale and the population from which the sample was drawn was normally distributed. What if these conditions cannot be met? In such instances **nonparametric** or **distribution-free tests** are used. These tests do not require any assumptions about the shape of the population, thus tests of hypothesis can be performed on nominal and ordinal scale data. Recall that the nominal level of measurement requires only that the sample information be categorized, with no order implied. As an example, students are classified by major: business, history, political science, etc.

This chapter considers tests where only the nominal level of measurement is required, although these tests may be used at a higher level of measurement. In the next chapter we discuss tests where at least the ordinal scale of measurement is assumed.

The Chi-Square Distribution

In the previous chapters the standard normal, t and F distributions were used as the test statistics. Recall that a test statistic is quantity, determined from the sample information, used as a basis for deciding whether to reject the null hypothesis. In this chapter another distribution, called chi-square and designated χ^2, is used as the test statistic. It is similar to the t and F distributions in that there is a family of χ^2 distributions, each with a different shape, depending on the number of degrees of freedom. When the number of degrees of freedom is small the distribution is positively skewed, as the number of degrees of freedom increases it becomes symmetrical and approaches the normal distribution. Chi-square is based on squared deviations between an observed frequency and an expected frequency, and therefore is always positive.

Goodness-of-Fit Tests

In the **goodness-of-fit** test the χ^2 distribution is used to determine how well an observed set of observations "fits" an "expected" set of observations. For example, suppose an instructor had told his class that his grading system would be "uniform." That is, that he would give the same number of A's, B's, C's, D's, and F's. Suppose that these were the results at the end of the quarter:

Grade	Number
A	12
B	24
C	23
D	30
F	11
	100

The question to be answered is: Do these final grades depart from those that could be expected if the instructor had graded uniformly? The null and alternate hypotheses are:

H_0: The distribution is uniform.
H_1: The distribution is not uniform.

The sampling distribution follows the χ^2 distribution and the value of the test statistic is computed by:

$$\chi^2 = \sum \frac{(f_o - f_e)^2}{f_e} \qquad 13\text{--}1$$

where f_o is the observed frequency and f_e is the expected frequency.

It is not necessary that the expected frequencies be equal to apply the goodness-of-fit test. For example, at Scandia Technical Institute, over the years 50 percent of the students were classified as freshmen, 40 percent sophomores, and 10 percent unclassified. A sample of 200 students this past semester revealed that 90 were freshmen, 80 were sophomores, and 30 were unclassified. The null and alternate hypotheses are:

H_0: The distribution of students has not changed.
H_1: The distribution of students has changed.

Contingency Tables

The χ^2 distribution is also applicable if we want to determine if there is a relationship between two criteria of classification. As an example, we are interested in whether there is a relationship between job advancement within a company and the sex of the employee. A sample of 100 employees is selected. The survey results revealed: (Each of the boxes is called a "cell.")

Sex	No Advancement	Slow Advancement	Rapid Advancement	Total
Male	7	13	30	50
Female	13	17	20	50
Total	20	30	50	100

Note that an employee is classified two ways: by sex and by advancement. When an individual or item is classified according to two criteria, the resulting table is called a **contingency table.** The null and alternate hypotheses are expressed as follows:

H_0: There is no relationship between sex and advancement.
H_1: There is a relationship between sex and advancement.

Formula 13–1 is used to compute the value of the test statistic. The expected frequency, f_o, is computed by noting that 50/100 or 50 percent of the sample is male. If the null hypothesis is true and advancement is unrelated to the sex of the employee, then it is expected that 50 percent of those who have not advanced will be male. The expected frequency f_e for males who have not advanced is 10, found by .50(20). The other expected frequencies are computed similarly. If the difference between the observed and the expected value is too large to have occurred by chance, the null hypothesis is rejected.

There is a limitation to the use of the χ^2 distribution. The value of f_e should be at least 5 for each cell (box). This requirement is to prevent any cell from carrying an inordinate amount of weight, and causing the null hypothesis to be rejected.

A Test of Normality

The normal probability distribution plays a key role in statistical analysis. In Chapter 6 we devoted an entire chapter to its study. In several other chapters, such as chapters 8, 9, and 10, we assumed the sampled populations were normally distributed. How can we verify the normality assumption? The chi-square distribution offers a method.

The procedure uses the goodness-of-fit test and formula 13–1. With the goodness-of-fit procedure the data are already in categories. When we want to test for normality the usual first step is to organize the data into a frequency distribution. Next, we transform the class limits to a z value by subtracting the class limits from the population mean and dividing by the standard deviation. Thus, we transform the categories of the frequency distribution into deviations from the mean and use the areas in the standard normal distribution to determine the f_e values. For example, we have the following frequency distribution of biweekly salaries. Assume that $\mu = \$1,200$ and $\sigma = \$200$. The frequency distribution of salaries is converted to a z value by $z = (X - \mu)/\sigma$.

Category	Salaries	z values
1	below $800	below −2.00
2	$ 800 to 1,000	−2.00 to −1.00
3	1,000 to 1,200	−1.00 to 0.00
4	1,200 to 1,400	0.00 to 1.00
5	1,400 to 1,600	1.00 to 2.00
6	above 1,600	above 2.00

The expected frequencies are computed by determining the area between the z values and multiplying by the sample size. The null hypothesis is that the sampled population is normal, the alternate is that the sampled population is not normal.

The degrees of freedom is the number of categories minus 1. Further details of the steps are given in **Problem 4**.

GLOSSARY

Nonparametric tests of hypotheses—Also called distribution-free tests. These tests do not require the population to be normally distributed. Appropriate for nominal and ordinal data.

Goodness-of-fit test—A nonparametric test involving a set of observed frequencies and a corresponding set of expected frequencies. The purpose of the test is to determine if there is a difference between the two sets of data one of which is observed, the other expected.

Contingency table—A two-way classification of a particular observation.

CHAPTER PROBLEMS

Problem 1

A distributor of personal computers has five locations in the city of Ashland. The sales in units for the first quarter of the year were as follows. At the .01 significance level do the records suggest that sales are uniformly distributed among the five locations?

Location	Sales (Units)
North Side	70
Pleasant Township	75
Southwyck	70
I-90	50
Venice Ave.	35
	300

Solution

The first step is to state the null hypothesis and the alternate hypothesis. The null hypothesis is that sales are uniformly distributed among the five stores. The alternate hypothesis is that there has been a change and the sales pattern is not uniformly distributed among the five stores. These hypotheses are written as follows:

H_0: Sales are uniformly distributed among the five locations.
H_1: Sales are not uniformly distributed among the five locations

The appropriate test statistic is the χ^2 distribution. The critical value is obtained from Appendix I. The number of degrees of freedom is equal to the number of categories minus 1. There are five categories (locations), therefore there are four degrees found by $k - 1 = 5 - 1 = 4$. The problem states beforehand that the .01 significance level is to be used. To locate the critical value, find the column headed .01 and the row where df, the degree of freedom, is 4. The value at the intersection of this row and column is 13.277. Therefore, the decision rule is: Reject H_0 if the computed value of the test statistic exceeds 13.277. Graphically, the decision rule is:

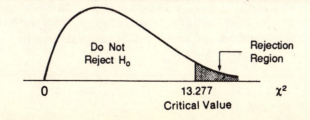

183

The observed frequencies, f_o, are in col. 1 of the following table. The expected frequencies are in col. 2. How are the expected frequencies determined? If the null hypothesis is true (that sales are uniformly distributed among the five locations), then 1/5 of 300, or 60 computers should have been sold at each location.

Location	Col. 1 f_o	Col. 2 f_e	Col. 3 $f_o - f_e$	Col. 4 $(f_o - f_e)^2$	Col. 5 $\dfrac{(f_o - f_e)^2}{f_e}$
North Side	70	60	10	100	1.67
Pleasant Township	75	60	15	225	3.75
Southwyck	70	60	10	100	1.67
I-90	50	60	−10	100	1.67
Venice Ave.	35	60	−25	625	10.42
	300	300	0		19.18

Recall that, the value of the test statistic is computed by formula 13–1.

$$\chi^2 = \sum \frac{(f_o - f_e)^2}{f_e} \qquad\qquad 13\text{--}1$$

The value of the test statistic is found by first taking the difference between the observed frequency and the expected frequency (Col. 3). Next these differences are squared (Col. 4). Then the result is divided by the expected frequency (Col. 5). This result is then summed over the five locations. The total is 19.18. The value of 19.18 is compared to the critical value of 13.277. Since 19.18 is greater than the critical value, H_0 is rejected and H_1 accepted. We conclude that sales are not uniformly distributed among the five locations.

Exercise 1

Check your answers against those in the ANSWER section.

A tire manufacturer is studying the position of tires in blowouts. It seems logical that the tire blowouts will be uniformly distributed among the four positions. For a sample of 100 tire failures, is there any significant difference in that tire's position on the car? Use the .05 significance level.

Location of tire on the car

Left Front	Left Rear	Right Front	Right Rear
28	20	29	23

Problem 2

From past experience the manager of the parking facilities at a major airport knows that 58 percent of the customers stay less than one hour, 23 percent between one and two hours, 10 percent between two and three hours, and nine percent three hours or more.

The manager wants to update this study. A sample of 500 stamped parking tickets is selected. The results showed 300 stayed less than one hour, 100 from one to two hours, 60 from two to three hours, and 40 parked three hours or more. At the .01 significance level does the data suggest there has been a change in the length of time customers use the parking facilities?

Solution

The first step is to state the null hypothesis and alternate hypothesis.

H_0: There has been no change in the distribution of parking times.
H_1: There has been a change in the distribution of parking times.

The next step is to determine the decision rule. Note in the table below that there are four categories. The number of degrees of freedom is the number of categories minus 1. In this problem it is $4 - 1 = 3$ degrees of freedom. Referring to Appendix I, the .01 level and 3 degrees of freedom, the critical value of chi-square is 11.345, so H_0 is rejected if χ^2 is greater than 11.345.

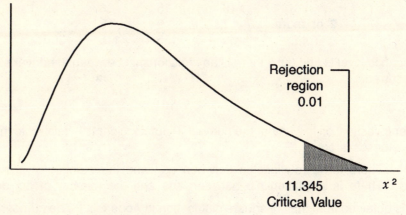

The value of the test statistic is computed as follows:

The observed frequencies from the sample are shown in Column 2 of the following table. Recall that based on past experience 58 percent of the customers parked their car less than one hour. If the null hypothesis is true, then $58\% \times 500$ (in the sample) = 290, the expected frequency. Likewise, 23 percent stayed from one to two hours. Thus, $23\% \times 500$ gives the expected frequency of 115. The complete set of expected frequencies are given in Column 3. Chi-square is computed to be 4.86.

Time in Parking Lot	Col. 1 Percent of Total	Col. 2 Number in Sample f_o	Col. 3 f_e	Col. 4 $f_o - f_e$	Col. 5 $(f_o - f_e)^2$	Col. 6 $\dfrac{(f_o - f_e)^2}{f_e}$
Less than 1 hour	58%	300	290	10	100	100/290 = 0.34
1 up to 2 hours	23%	100	115	−15	225	225/115 = 1.96
2 up to 3 hours	10%	60	50	10	100	100/50 = 2.00
3 hours or more	9%	40	45	− 5	25	25/45 = 0.56
Total	100%	500	500	0		χ^2 = 4.86

Since the computed value of chi-square (4.86) is less than the critical value (11.345), the null hypothesis is not rejected. There has been no change in the lengths of parking time at the airport.

Exercise 2

Check your answers against those in the ANSWER section.

In recent years, 42 percent of the American-made automobiles sold in the United States were manufactured by General Motors, 33 percent by Ford, 22 percent by Chrysler, and 3 percent by all others.

A sample of the sales of American-made automobiles conducted last week revealed that 174 were manufactured by Chrysler, 275 by Ford, 330 by GM, and 21 by all others.

Test the hypothesis at the .05 level that there has been no change in the sales pattern.

185

Problem 3

A study is made by an auto insurance company to determine if there is a relationship between the driver's age and the number of automobile accident claims submitted during a one year period. From a sample of 300 claims, the following sample information was recorded.

No. of Accidents	Less than 25	25-50	Over 50	Total
0	37	101	74	212
1	16	15	28	59
2 or more	7	9	13	29
Total	60	125	115	300

Age (Years)

Use the .05 significance level to find out if there is any relationship between the driver's age and the number of accidents that occurred.

Solution

The question under investigation is whether the number of auto accidents is related to the driver's age. The null and alternate hypotheses are:

H_0: There is no relationship between age and the number of accidents.
H_1: There is a relationship between age and the number of accidents.

The critical value is obtained from the chi-square distribution in Appendix I. The number of degrees of freedom is equal to the number of rows minus one times the number of columns minus one. Hence, the degrees of freedom is $(3 - 1)(3 - 1) = 4$. The significance level, as stated in the problem, is .05. The critical value from Appendix I is 9.488. The null hypothesis is not rejected if the computed value of χ^2 is equal to or less than 9.488.

Formula 13–1, as cited earlier, is used to determine χ^2.

$$\chi^2 = \sum \frac{(f_o - f_e)^2}{f_e}$$

where f_o is the frequency observed and f_e the expected frequency. The first step is to determine the expected frequency for each corresponding observed frequency. If the null hypothesis is true (the number of accidents is not related to age) we can expect 212 out of the 300 sampled, or 70.67 percent of the drivers to have had no accidents. Thus, we can expect 70.67 percent of the 60 drivers under 25 years, or 42.40 drivers, to have had no accidents.

Likewise, if the null hypothesis is true, 70.67 percent of the 125 drivers in the 25 to 50 age bracket, or 88.33 drivers, should have had no accidents.

The table below shows the complete set of observed and expected frequencies.

No. of Accidents	Less than 25 f_o	Less than 25 f_e	25-50 f_o	25-50 f_e	Over 50 f_o	Over 50 f_e	Total
0	37	42.40	101	88.33	74	81.27	212
1	16	11.80	15	24.58	28	22.62	59
2 or more	7	5.80	9	12.08	13	11.12	29
	60	60.00	125	125.00	115	115.00	300

Age

The expected frequency can be calculated by:

$$f_e = \frac{(\text{row total})(\text{column total})}{\text{grand total}}$$

186

The value for the first row and column is used as an example. There are 212 people who did not have any accidents, 60 persons are less than 25 years old, and there is a total of 300 people. These values are inserted into the formula:

$$f_e = \frac{(\text{row total})\ (\text{column total})}{\text{grand total}} = \frac{(212)(60)}{300} = 42.40$$

which is the same value computed previously.

The computed value of χ^2 is 11.03.

$$\chi^2 = \sum \frac{(f_o - f_e)^2}{f_e} = \frac{(37.00 - 42.40)^2}{42.40} + \frac{(101.00 - 88.33)^2}{88.33} + \ldots + \frac{(13 - 11.12)^2}{11.12} = 11.03$$

Since the computed value of χ^2 is greater than the critical value of 9.488, the null hypothesis is rejected and the alternate accepted. We conclude that there is a relationship between age and the number of accidents.

Exercise 3

Check your answers against those in the ANSWER section.

A random sample of 480 male and female adults was asked the amount of time each person spent watching TV last week. Their responses are shown below. At the .05 significance level, does it appear that the amount of time spent watching TV is related to the sex of the viewer?

Hours	Sex of viewer		Total
	Male	Female	
Under 8	70	90	160
8 to 15	100	60	160
15 or more	55	105	160
	225	255	480

Problem 4

The following is the distribution of the number of outpatients surgeries per day for the last 100 days at St. Luke's Hospital, Maumee, Ohio. Assume the population mean is 24 patients per day and the standard deviation is 4 patients per day.

Number of Patients	Number of Days
Less than 18	12
18 up to 22	19
22 up to 26	39
26 up to 30	21
30 or more	9
Total	100

Is it reasonable to assume that the population of the number of patients per day is normally distributed? Use the .05 significance level.

Solution

The null hypothesis and the alternate hypothesis are:

H_0: The population is normal.
H_1: The population is not normal.

There are 5 categories, so there are $5 - 1 = 4$ degrees of freedom. From Appendix I, H_0 is rejected if the computed value of chi-square is greater than 9.488.

Next, we compute the expected values. To do this we determine the areas under a normal curve with $\mu = 24$ and $\sigma = 4$. Recall from Chapter 6, to determine the areas we convert from a normal distribution to the standard normal distribution by $z = (X - \mu)/\sigma$. To find the area below 18 patients:

1. The z value corresponding to 18 is -1.50, found by $(18 - 24)/4$.

2. The area between $z = 0.00$ and 1.50 is .4332, from Appendix D.

3. The area between -1.50 and 0.00 is also .4332, because of symmetry.

4. The area below -1.50 is .0668, found by $.5000 - .4332$.

5. If the distribution is normal with $\mu = 24$ and $\sigma = 4$, then we expect $100(.0668) = 6.68$ days during which there were 18 or less patients.

To determine the expected frequency for 18 up to 22 patients, first find z value for 22 patients. It is -0.50, found by $(22 - 24)/4 = -0.50$. The area between a z value of -0.50 and -1.50 is $.4332 - .1915 = .2417$. We therefore expect $100(.2417) = 24.17$ days to have between 18 and 22 patients.

The remaining expected frequencies are determined similarly.

Number of Patients	z values	f_o	f_e
Less than 18	less than -1.50	12	6.68
18 up to 22	-1.50 up to -0.50	19	24.17
22 up to 26	-0.50 up to 0.50	39	38.30
26 up to 30	0.50 up to 1.50	21	24.17
30 or more	1.50 or more	9	6.68
	Total	100	100.00

188

To determine the value of chi-square we use formula 13–1. The computations are as follows:

Number of Patients	f_o	f_e	$\dfrac{(f_o - f_e)^2}{f_e}$
Less than 18	12	6.68	4.2369
18 up to 22	19	24.17	1.1059
22 up to 26	39	38.30	0.0128
26 up to 30	21	24.17	0.4158
30 or more	9	6.68	0.8057
Total	100	100.00	6.5771

The computed value of chi-square is 6.5771, which is less than the critical value of 9.488. Hence, the null hypothesis is not rejected. We conclude that the sample could have been obtained from a normal population. It is reasonable to conclude that the distribution of days is normal with a mean of 24 and a standard deviation of 4.

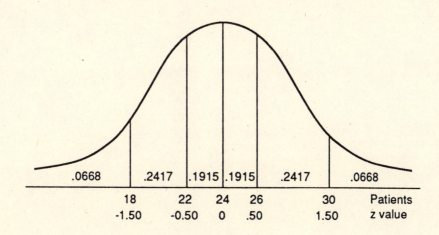

CHAPTER ASSIGNMENT 13

Analysis of Nominal Level Data: The Chi-Square Distribution

Name _____ Section _____ Score _____

PART I Matching Select the correct answer and write the appropriate letter in the space provided.

_____ 1. Contingency table

_____ 2. Goodness-of-fit

_____ 3. Nonparametric tests

_____ 4. Nominal scale

_____ 5. Chi-square distribution

a. continuous distribution

b. each sampled observation is classified according to two criteria

c. no assumptions about the shape of the population is required

d. compares observed and expected frequencies

e. data is only categorized

PART II Multiple Choice Select the correct answer and write the appropriate letter in the space provided.

_____ 6. In a nonparametric test

    a. the population is assumed to be normal.
    b. the sample size must be at least 30.
    c. σ is always known.
    d. no assumption is made about the shape of the population.

_____ 7. A two-way classification of the data is called a

    a. normal distribution.
    b. contingency table.
    c. chi-square distribution.
    d. test for normality.

_____ 8. The chi-square distribution is

    a. symmetric.
    b. positively skewed.
    c. negatively skewed.
    d. a discrete distribution.

_____ 9. In a chi-square test there are 4 degrees of freedom. At the .05 significance level the critical value of chi-square is

    a. 9.488
    b. 7.815
    c. 7.779
    d. 13.388

_____ 10. The level of measurement required for the goodness-of-fit test is

    a. nominal.
    b. ordinal.
    c. interval.
    d. ratio.

_____ 11. A sample of 300 construction workers is classified by years of experience (3 categories) and age (4 categories). How many degrees of freedom are there in a test to determine if experience and age are related?

a. 12
b. 299
c. 4
d. 6
e. None of these is correct.

_____ 12. Which of the following assumptions are required for all nonparametric tests?

a. A normal population
b. Equal population variances
c. Samples of at least 30
d. None of the above.

_____ 13. The shape of the chi-square distribution is based on the

a. number of degrees of freedom.
b. shape of the population.
c. sample size.
d. variation in the population.

_____ 14. The sum of the observed frequencies and the expected frequencies are

a. always equal.
b. never equal.
c. equal to the degrees of freedom.
d. equal the value of chi-square.

_____ 15. In a test to determine if two criteria of classification are related, the expected cell frequencies should be

a. less than 5.
b. less than 5% of n.
c. at least 5.
d. at least 30.

PART III Problems Record your answer in the space provided. Show essential calculations.

16. A market research firm that works with political candidates is investigating whether the order in which the candidate's name appears on the ballot has any influence on the likelihood of being elected. A total of 108 elections were reviewed, and the results are shown below.

	Position on Ballot				
	1	*2*	*3*	*4*	*Total*
Number of Wins	35	30	26	17	108

At the .05 significance level is there a difference in the number of wins in each position?

State the null hypothesis and the alternate hypothesis.

H_0: ______________________________

H_1: ______________________________

State the decision rule.

____

Compute the value of the test statistic.

Answer

State your decision regarding H_0. Interpret your result.

____

____

17. A study is made of men over the age of 50. Each man is classified as to whether or not he has had a heart attack and the amount that he smokes at the present time. The following results were obtained for a sample of 300 men.

Amount Smoked	Heart Attack Yes	No	Total
None	50	150	200
Moderate	45	30	75
Heavy	15	10	25

At the .01 significance level can we conclude that smoking is related to heart attacks?

State the null hypothesis and the alternate hypothesis.

H_0: _____

H_1: _____

State the decision rule.

_____

Compute the value of the test statistic.

┌─────────────────┐
│   │
└─────────────────┘
Answer

State your decision regarding H_0. Interpret your result.

_____

_____

18. Northern Pacific Wood Products, Inc. is a large manufacturer of Office Supplies, such as desks, tables, and office cabinets. A sample of 400 of their manufacturing employees revealed the following distribution of hourly wages. At the .05 significance level can we conclude that the population of hourly wages is normally distributed and that $\mu = \$12$ and $\sigma = \$3.00$?

Hourly wage ($)	Frequency
Below $8.00	25
$ 8.00 to $10.00	70
$10.00 to $12.00	110
$12.00 to $14.00	101
$14.00 to $16.00	57
above $16.00	37

State the null hypothesis and the alternate hypothesis.

H_0: _____

H_1: _____

State the decision rule.

_____

Compute the value of the test statistic.

_____

Answer

State your decision regarding H_0. Interpret your result.

_____

_____

195

14

NONPARAMETRIC METHODS: ANALYSIS OF RANKED DATA

CHAPTER GOALS

After completing this chapter, you will be able to:

1. Conduct a test of hypothesis about the median.
2. Apply the Wilcoxon rank-sum test.
3. Apply the Kruskal-Wallis one-way ANOVA test.
4. Apply the Wilcoxon matched-pairs signed rank test.

Introduction

This chapter continues our study of nonparametric tests of hypotheses. Recall that for nonparametric tests there is no assumption required regarding the shape of the population. The data can be either of the nominal or the ordinal scale. In Chapter 13, applications of the chi-square distribution, which requires only the nominal scale of measurement were presented. In this chapter four additional nonparametric tests are considered. The first is for the median of a population. The Wilcoxon rank-sum test compares two independent samples to determine if they came from equal populations, and the Kruskal-Wallis test compares more than two independent samples to determine if they came from equal populations. The Wilcoxon signed-rank test considers the magnitude of the difference between dependent observations.

Median Test

The median of population of unknown shape is proposed. A single random sample is selected from the population and the number of values in the sample that are above (or below) the hypothesized median is determined. The standard normal distribution is used as the test statistic. The following formula (14-1) is used as the test statistic.

$$z = \frac{(X \pm .50) - \mu}{\sigma} \qquad [14\text{-}1]$$

X is the number of observations larger (or smaller) than the hypothesized median, μ is the population mean, found by $n\pi$, and σ is the population standard deviation, found by $\sqrt{n\pi(1-\pi)}$.

The Wilcoxon Rank-Sum Test

This test is the nonparametric alternative to the Student t test for independent samples described in Chapter 9. The purpose of Student's t test was to determine if the two independent populations had the same mean. Recall we assumed that two independent random samples were selected from normally distributed populations with equal standard deviations. What if the equal standard deviations or the normality assumption cannot be met? The student t is not appropriate an a nonparametric alternative the **Wilcoxon rank-sum** test is used.

The Wilcoxon rank-sum test is based on the sum of the ranks of the independent samples. If the populations are the same, then the combined rankings of the two samples will be nearly evenly divided between the two samples, and the total of the ranks will be about the same. If the populations are not the same, one of the samples will have a predominance of the larger ranks and its total (rank-sum) will be larger. When both samples are at least 8, the standard normal distribution is used as the test statistic. The formula (14-2) is used.

$$z = \frac{W - \dfrac{n_1(n_1 + n_2 + 1)}{2}}{\sqrt{\dfrac{n_1 n_2(n_1 + n_2 + 1)}{12}}} \quad [14\text{-}2]$$

W is the sum of the ranks in the first population, n_1 is the number of samples from the first population, and n_2 is the number of samples from the second population.

The Kruskal-Wallis Test

The Wilcoxon rank-sum test compares two independent populations. The **Kruskal-Wallis** test allows for the simultaneous comparison of *more* than two independent populations. It is an alternative to the ANOVA, described in Chapter 10, for comparing more than two population means. Recall from Chapter 10 that to apply ANOVA it was necessary that, in addition to independent samples, (1) the data be of interval scale (2) the population be normally distributed, and (3) the population variances be equal. The Kruskal-Wallis test should be used if one or more of these cannot be met. It requires at least five observations in each sample and uses χ^2 with the degrees of freedom equal to the number of populations minus 1, as the test statistic.

To employ the Kruskal-Wallis test, we substitute the rankings of the sampled items for the actual values. The test statistic, designated by H is computed using formula 14–3, as follows.

$$H = \frac{12}{N(N + 1)}\left(\frac{\Sigma R_1^2}{n_1} + \frac{\Sigma R_2^2}{n_2} + \ldots + \frac{\Sigma R_k^2}{n_k}\right) - 3(N + 1)$$

where

ΣR_1 is the sum of the ranks for the sample designated 1, ΣR_2 is the sum of the ranks for the sample designated 2, and so on.

n_1 is the number in the sample designated 1, n_2 is the number in the sample designated 2, and so on.

N is the combined number of observations for all samples.

k is the number of populations.

The Wilcoxon Signed-Rank Test

The t-test for paired observations, discussed in Chapter 9, assumed that the differences in the paired observations were normally distributed. If this assumption cannot be met the **Wilcoxon signed-rank test** is used. To use this test the first step is to determine the *absolute value* of the paired differences. Next these absolute values are ranked from smallest to largest. The sign of the original differences in the paired observation is reintroduced. The sum of the negative and the positive ranks is determined and, finally the smaller rank sum is compared to the critical value, found in Appendix K.

GLOSSARY

Wilcoxon rank-sum test—A test devised to determine whether there is a difference between two independent populations. No assumption is made regarding the shape of the population is necessary.

Kruskal-Wallis test—A test to determine whether there is a difference among more than two populations. No assumption regarding the shape of the populations is necessary.

Wilcoxon signed-rank test—A test for determining whether there is a difference between two sets of data, one of which is based on a "before" situation and the other an "after" situation. The two sets of data must be related in some way.

Median test—A testing used to determine if it's reasonable to conclude that the sample data came from a population with the proposed median.

CHAPTER PROBLEMS

Problem 1

The national sales manager for a major publisher of college level textbooks believes that a sales person should make more than 8 calls per day on faculty in an attempt to sell their texts. A sample of 20 sales representatives showed they made the following number of calls yesterday.

13	11	11	9	5	7	10	10	6	8	15
9	12	6	14	6	7	13	6	15		

At the .05 significance level can the sales manager conclude that the median number of calls is more than 8 in the population.

Solution

We do not have any information on the shape of the population, but we will assume that it is not normal. So instead of testing whether the mean is 8 we will test whether the median is 8. The null and the alternate hypotheses are:

$$H_0: \text{ Median} = 8$$
$$H_1: \text{ Median} > 8$$

The first step is to insure that the binomial conditions are met. Recall that these conditions are:

1. There are only two possible outcomes. Either a sales person made more than 8 calls yesterday or he or she did not. If exactly 8 calls were made that observation is dropped from the study and the sample size reduced.

2. The trials are independent. For example, the number of sales calls made by the third person does not affect how many calls the fourth person makes.

3. The sample size is fixed. In this case there are 20 observations. However, any values that are equal to the hypothesized median are dropped from the study. So, the one observation equal to 8 is deleted and the sample is reduced to 19.

4. The probability of a success is constant. It is .50. The chance that the number of calls is more than 8 is .50 and the chance that it is less than 8 is also .50, if the median is 8.

The normal distribution is used to approximate the binomial distribution when np and $n(1-p)$ are both greater than 5, where n is the sample size and p is .50. Here $np = 19(.50) = 9.5$ and $n(1-p) = 19(.50) = 9.5$, so the criterion is met. Using formulas 5-4 and 5-5 from Chapter 5, the mean and the variance of binomial distribution are determined.

$$\mu = np = 19(.50) = 9.5$$
$$\sigma^2 = np(1-p) = 19(.50)(.50) = 4.75$$

The standard deviation is 2.179, found by $\sqrt{4.75}$.

Formula 14-1 is used to find the value of the test statistic. To explain, X is the number of observations that are larger than the hypothesized median. The .50 is the correction for continuity, discussed in Chapter 5. It is used when a discrete distribution, such as the binomial, is approximated by a continuous distribution, such as the normal. If the value of X is larger than $n/2$ then .50 is subtracted from X. If the value of X is less than $n/2$ then .50 is added. Formula 14-1 is:

$$z = \frac{(X \pm .50) - \mu}{\sigma}$$

In this case 12 of the 19 sales people made more than 8 calls, so $X = 12$. The critical value is 1.645, using the .05 significance level. So the null hypothesis is rejected if the computed value of z is greater than 1.645.

The value of the test statistic is 0.918, found by

$$z = \frac{11.5 - 9.5}{2.179} = 0.918$$

The decision is not to reject the null hypothesis. We cannot conclude that the typical sales person is making more than 8 calls.

Exercise 1

Check your answers against those in the ANSWER section.

The specifications for an Everlife AAA battery call for a median life of 500 hours. The quality assurance manager selected a random sample of 30 batteries from today's production and found that 6 did not last the 500 hours. At the .05 significance level can the quality assurance manager conclude that the median life of the Everlife AAA battery is less than 500 hours?

Problem 2

A manufacturer of candy, gum and other snacks recently completed a sales campaign designed to increase the amounts spent by women in vending machines, where many of their products are sold. To evaluate the effectiveness of the campaign samples of eight men and nine women are selected. Each person is asked to keep a record of the amount they spend in vending machines for a week. The results are as follows:

Amount Spent by Men	Amount Spent by Women
$ 4.32	$ 2.81
6.05	3.45
7.21	4.16
8.57	4.32
9.80	5.54
10.10	6.93
12.76	7.54
13.65	8.32
15.87	10.76
	11.21

Assume that the distribution of the amounts spent for men and women is not normally distributed. At the .05 significance level can we conclude that men spend more?

Solution

The first step is to determine which test to use. Because the populations are not normally distributed the *t* test for independent samples is not appropriate. The Wilcoxon rank-sum test allows for two independent samples and does not require any assumptions regarding the shape of the population, so it is appropriate.

The next step is to state the null and the alternate hypotheses. A one-tailed test is used because we want to show that the distribution of the amounts spent by the men is larger, or to the right of, that of the women. To put it another way, the median amount spent by the men is larger than the median amount spent by the women.

H_0: The distributions are the same
H_1: The distribution of the men is located to the right of that of the women.

When the two independent samples both have at least eight observations the test statistic is the standard normal distribution. the formula for z is:

$$z = \frac{W - \dfrac{n_1(n_1 + n_2 + 1)}{2}}{\sqrt{\dfrac{n_1 n_2(n_1 + n_2 + 1)}{12}}}$$

n_1 is the number of observations in the first sample, n_2 the number of observations in the second sample, and W the sum of the ranks in one of the samples.

At the .05 significance level the null hypothesis is rejected if z is greater than 1.645.

The test is based on the sum of the ranks. The two samples are ranked as if they belonged to a single sample. If the null hypothesis is true—that the two populations are the same—then the sum of the ranks for the two groups would be about the same. If the null hypothesis is not true, then there will be a disparity in the rank sums.

The data on the amounts spent by both the men and the women are ranked in the following table and the rank sums determined.

Amount Spent by Men		Amount Spent by Women	
Dollars	Rank	Dollars	Rank
4.32	4.5	2.81	1.0
6.05	7.0	3.45	2.0
7.21	9.0	4.16	3.0
8.57	12.0	4.32	4.5
9.80	13.0	5.54	6.0
10.10	14.0	6.93	8.0
12.76	17.0	7.54	10.0
13.65	18.0	8.32	11.0
15.87	19.0	10.76	15.0
		11.21	16.0
	113.5		76.5

The value of z is computed where $W = 113.5$, $n_1 = 9$ and $n_2 = 10$. Note that there was a man and a woman who each spent \$4.32. That is there is a tie for this position. To resolve the tie, the ranks involved are averaged. That is, the ranks of 4 and 5 are average and the value of 4.5 is assigned to those involved.

$$z = \frac{W - \dfrac{n_1(n_1 + n_2 + 1)}{2}}{\sqrt{\dfrac{n_1 n_2(n_1 + n_2 + 1)}{12}}}$$

$$z = \frac{113.5 - \dfrac{9(9 + 10 + 1)}{2}}{\sqrt{\dfrac{9(10)(9 + 10 + 1)}{12}}} = 1.919$$

Since the computed value of z (1.919) is greater than the critical value of 1.645, the null hypothesis is rejected. The distribution of the amounts spent by the men is to the right of that of the women. The median of the distribution of the amounts spent by the men is larger than the median of the amounts spent by the women.

Exercise 2

Check your answers against those in the ANSWER section.

The Continental Muffler Company manufactures two different mufflers, the Tough Muffler and the Long Last Muffler. As an experiment, they installed Tough Mufflers on eight of their employees' automobiles and the Long Last on nine cars. The number of miles driven before a muffler needed replacing is recorded below (in thousands of miles).

Tough Muffler	Long Last Muffler
24	35
31	46
37	49
44	52
36	41
30	40
28	32
21	29
	27

Assume the distributions of miles driven are not normal. Does the evidence suggest a difference in the number of miles driven using the two mufflers before replacement? Use the .05 significance level.

Problem 3

A study is made regarding the reaction time (in seconds) to danger among four groups of professional drivers: cab drivers, bus drivers, truck drivers, and race car drivers. The results are as follows:

Reaction Time (seconds)

Cab Drivers	Bus Drivers	Truck Drivers	Race Car Drivers
3.4	4.5	3.7	2.8
3.3	4.0	3.0	2.7
1.9	2.9	2.1	3.8
3.1	3.1	2.9	2.2
2.5	3.7	1.8	1.7
	4.4	3.6	

Assume that the reaction times are not normally distributed. At the .05 significance level, is there a difference in reaction times?

Solution

The ANOVA technique described in Chapter 10 for comparing several population means assumed that the populations are normally distributed. In this case the normality assumption cannot be made. Hence a nonparametric alternative, the Kruskal-Wallis test, is used. The null and alternate hypotheses are:

H_0: The distributions of reaction times are the same.
H_1: The distributions of reaction times are not the same.

202

The χ^2 distribution is the test statistic. For this test there are $k - 1$ degrees of freedom, where $k = 4$ is the number of treatments (groups of professional drivers), so the degrees of freedom is $k - 1 = 4 - 1 = 3$. The critical value from Appendix I is 7.815 given a significance level of .05.

The value of the test statistic is computed using formula 14–4.

$$H = \frac{12}{N(N+1)} \left(\frac{\Sigma R_1^2}{n_1} + \frac{\Sigma R_2^2}{n_2} + \ldots + \frac{\Sigma R_k^2}{n_k} \right) - 3(N+1)$$

where N refers to the toal number sampled (22 in this instance), ΣR_1^2 to the square of the sum of the ranks in the first sample, n_1 to the number of observations in the first sample, ΣR_2^2 to the square of the sum of the ranks of the second sample, and so on.

The value of the test statistic is computed by first ranking the reaction times of the four groups as though they were a single group. Note that there are several instances involving tied ranks. The third bus driver and the fourth truck driver each had a reaction time of 2.9 seconds. These two drivers involve the 9th and 10th rank. To resolve the tie the ranks involved are averaged and the average rank assigned to each. Hence both drivers are assigned the rank of 9.5, found by $(9 + 10)/2$. The other ties are resolved in a similar fashion.

Reaction Times and Ranks for Professional Drivers

Cab Drivers		Bus Drivers		Truck Drivers		Race Car Drivers	
Time	Rank	Time	Rank	Time	Rank	Time	Rank
3.4	15	4.5	22	3.7	17.5	2.8	8
3.3	14	4.0	20	3.0	11	2.7	7
1.9	3	2.9	9.5	2.1	4	3.8	19
3.1	12.5	3.1	12.5	2.9	9.5	2.2	5
2.5	6	3.7	17.5	1.8	2	1.7	1
		4.4	21	3.6	16		
Totals	50.5		102.5		60		40

Next, these results are substituted into the formula for H and its value is computed:

$$H = \frac{12}{N(N+1)} \left(\frac{\Sigma R_1^2}{n_1} + \frac{\Sigma R_2^2}{n_2} + \frac{\Sigma R_3^2}{n_3} + \frac{\Sigma R_4^2}{n_4} \right) - 3(N+1)$$

$$= \frac{12}{22(22+1)} \left(\frac{(50.5)^2}{5} + \frac{(102.5)^2}{6} + \frac{(60)^2}{6} + \frac{(40)^2}{5} \right) - 3(22+1)$$

$$= 6.44$$

Since the computed value (6.44) is less than the critical value of 7.815, the null hypothesis cannot be rejected. The evidence does not suggest a difference in the distribution of reaction times to emergency situations among various types of professional drivers.

Exercise 3

Check your answers against those in the ANSWER section.

A travel agency selected samples of hotels from each of three major chains and recorded the occupancy rate for each hotel on a specific date. The occupancy rate is the percentage of the total number of rooms that were occupied the previous night. The results are as follows:

Best Eastern	Comfort Inn	Quality Court
58%	69%	72%
57	67	80
67	62	84
63	69	94
61	77	86
64		

Do these data suggest any difference in the occupancy rates? Use the .05 significance level. Assume that the percentage of occupancy rates are not normally distributed.

Problem 4

A sample of ten Army recruits was given a test to determine how well they liked the Army. Later that same day they were taken on a march—very long and very strenuous. On their return they were given a similar test to again measure how well they liked the Army. The scores are shown below. At the .05 significance level, can we conclude that the recruits liked the Army less after the march? Assume the scores are not normally distributed.

	Test Score	
Recruit	Before	After
Barrett	132	122
Bier	150	165
Spitler	139	127
Contact	108	101
Walker	106	99
Stasiak	105	92
Soto	133	110
Lopez	157	139
Kies	114	99
Landrum	122	113

Solution

First note that the samples are dependent. That is, we have a score for Barrett before the march and after the march. We are concerned with the distribution of the differences and are not willing to assume that the differences are normally distributed. Thus the paired t test, described in Chapter 9, which requires the normality assumption cannot be used.

The Wilcoxon signed-rank test considers the magnitude of the difference. The null and alternate hypothesis are stated as follows.

H_0: There was no change in how well the recruits liked the Army.
H_1: The recruits liked the Army better before the march.

The steps to complete the Wilcoxon signed-rank test are as follows.

1. The difference between each paired observation is found. If any difference is 0, it is eliminated and the size of the sample is reduced by the number of 0 differences.

2. These differences are ranked from highest to lowest, without regard to their signs. If ties occur, the ranks involved are averaged and each tied observation is awarded the mean rank.

3. The ranks with a positive difference are assigned to one column and those with a negative difference to another.

4. The sums of the positive (R^+) and negative (R^-) ranks are determined.

5. The smaller of the two sums (R^+ and R^-) is compared with the critical values found in Appendix K. This critical value is called T.

Appendix K is used to formulate the decision rule. First locate the column headed by .05 using a one-tailed test. Next move down that column to the row where $N = 10$. The critical value is 10. The decision is to reject H_0 if the smaller of R^+ and R^- is 10 or less.

The values for R^+ and R^- are computed as follows:

Recruit	Before	After	Difference	Rank	R^+	R^-
Barrett	132	122	10	4	4	
Bier	150	165	−15	7.5		7.5
Spitler	139	127	12	5	5	
Contact	108	101	7	1.5	1.5	
Walker	106	99	7	1.5	1.5	
Stasiak	105	92	13	6	6	
Soto	133	110	23	10	10	
Lopez	157	139	18	9	9	
Kies	114	99	15	7.5	7.5	
Landrum	122	113	9	3	3	
					47.5	7.5

Since $R^- = 7.5$, H_0 is rejected and H_1 accepted. It is concluded that recruits like the Army better before the march.

Exercise 4

Check your answers against those in the ANSWER section.

Twelve persons whose IQs were measured in college between 1960 and 1965 were located recently and retested with an equivalent IQ test. The information is given below.

Student	Recent Score	Original Score
John Barr	119	112
Bill Sedwick	103	108
Marcia Elmquist	115	115
Ginger Thealine	109	100
Larry Clark	131	120
Jim Redding	110	108
Carol Papalia	109	113
Victor Suppa	113	126
Dallas Paul	94	95
Carol Kozoloski	119	110
Joe Sass	118	117
P. S. Sundar	112	102

At the .05 significance level can we conclude that the IQ scores have increased in over 20 years? Use the Wilcoxon signed-rank test.

CHAPTER ASSIGNMENT 14

Nonparametric Methods: Analysis of Ranked Data

Name _____ Section _____ Score _____

PART I **Matching** Select the correct answer and write the appropriate letter in the space provided.

_____ 1. Median test

_____ 2. Ordinal scale

_____ 3. Nonparametric tests

_____ 4. Wilcoxon signed-rank test

_____ 5. Wilcoxon rank-sum test

a. ranked data

b. uses only one sample

c. requires independent samples

d. Requires dependent samples

e. normal population not required

PART II **Multiple Choice** Select the correct answer and write the appropriate letter in the space provided.

_____ 6. For a nonparametric test

    a. the populations must be normal.
    b. the data must be at least interval scale.
    c. the populations must be independent.
    d. assumptions regarding the population are not necessary.

_____ 7. Which of the following is *not* a nonparametric test?

    a. median test
    b. ANOVA
    c. Kruskal-Wallis
    d. chi-square goodness-of-fit test

_____ 8. Which of the following tests require dependent samples?

    a. median test
    b. Kruskal-Wallis
    c. Wilcoxon signed-rank test
    d. Wilcoxon rank-sum test

_____ 9. Which of the following conditions must be met for the median test?

    a. normal population
    b. equal population variances
    c. at least 30 observations
    d. np and $n(1-p)$ are greater than 5

_____ 10. Which of the following tests require independent samples?

    a. median test
    b. Kruskal-Wallis
    c. Wilcoxon signed-rank test
    d. paired *t*-test

_____ 11. The *z* distribution is used as the test statistic for the Wilcoxon rank-sum test when

    a. there are at least eight observations in each sample.
    b. the population is normal.
    c. if one of the samples is at least 30.
    d. the samples have equal variances.

_____ 12. Which of the following tests uses the chi-square distribution as the test statistic?

   a. median test
   b. Kruskal-Wallis
   c. Wilcoxon signed-rank test
   d. paired t-test

_____ 13. The Kruskal-Wallis test is a replacement for

   a. the sign test.
   b. ANOVA.
   c. paired t-test.
   d. the binomial distribution.

_____ 14. A difference between the Wilcoxon rank-sum test and the Kruskal-Wallis test is

   a. the Wilcoxon rank-sum test uses dependent samples and the Kruskal-Wallis test independent sample.
   b. the Wilcoxon rank-sum test uses independent samples and the Kruskal-Wallis test dependent sample.
   c. the Kruskal-Wallis test requires the interval scale of measurement.
   d. the Wilcoxon rank-sum test uses two independent samples and the Kruskal-Wallis test two or more independent samples.

_____ 15. We want to test the H_0 that the median equal $12.40 and the H_1 that the median does not equal $12.40. The critical value of z at the .10 significance level is

   a. ±1.96
   b. ±1.645
   c. ±2.33
   d. ±2.58

PART III Problems Record your answer in the space provided. Show essential calculations.

16. The building specifications in Tontogony require that the sewer pipe used in residential areas have a median breaking strength of at least 2,500 pounds per lineal foot. The drainline Pipe and Supply Company would like to become a supplier for Tontogony. The city testing agency collected 15 pieces of pipe and found that 12 had a breaking strength of more than 2,500 pounds per linear foot. At the .05 significance level does this company meet the specification?

State the null hypothesis and the alternate hypothesis.

H_0:______________________________________

H_1:______________________________________

State the decision rule.

____

Compute the value of the test statistic.

Answer

State your decision regarding H_0. Interpret your result.

____

____

17. The Internal Revenue Service selects a sample of 8 individual tax returns where a home office deduction is claimed. Copies of the 8 returns are sent the Rooney Tax Service and Swanson's Tax Associates, and both firms are asked to compute the tax owed. The information is shown below. Using the Wilcoxon signed-rank test and the .10 significance level, is there a difference in the tax estimates of the two firms?

Taxpayer	Rooney Tax Service	Swanson Tax Associates
Back	$1,600	$1,910
Bodomus	1,970	1,920
Collins	2,120	2,080
Draves	2,140	2,340
Ellerbruck	2,340	2,390
Grimm	2,510	2,850
Holley	2,560	2,980
LaPorte	2,710	3,340

State the null hypothesis and the alternate hypothesis.

H_0: _____

H_1: _____

State the decision rule.

_____

Compute the value of the test statistic.

┌─────────────┐
│   │
└─────────────┘
Answer

State your decision regarding H_0. Interpret your result.

_____
_____

18. The owner of Steve's Grille, a short order restaurant located near Northlands University believes that male students spend more than female students. A sample of ten male and seven female students revealed the following amounts spent in his grille. At the .05 significance level can Steve conclude that male students spend more? Assume the populations are not normally distributed.

Male	Female
$ 9.90	$ 9.10
10.10	9.50
11.30	9.60
11.70	10.30
12.10	10.40
12.80	10.50
14.60	10.70
14.80	11.21
15.40	
17.10	

State the null hypothesis and the alternate hypothesis.

H_o:_____

H_1:_____

State the decision rule.

_____

Compute the value of the test statistic.

```
┌─────────────────┐
│                 │
└─────────────────┘
      Answer
```

State your decision regarding H_o. Interpret your result.

_____

_____

19. The chief packaging engineer for a cereal manufacturer is considering changing the basic color of the package from red to either blue or green. He selects a sample of 20 supermarkets, and randomly assigns the red packages to 7 locations, the blue to 7 locations, and the green to 6 locations. After a week the following number of packages of each cereal were sold. Assume the distribution of the number sold is not normal. At the .05 significance level is there a difference in the distributions of packages sold?

Red	Blue	Green
437	448	402
450	455	452
460	469	553
464	513	560
464	519	567
477	539	580
530	607	

State the null hypothesis and the alternate hypothesis.

H_o:_____

H_1:_____

State the decision rule.

_____

Compute the value of the test statistic.

Answer

State your decision regarding H_o. Interpret your result.

_____

_____

212

15

STATISTICAL QUALITY CONTROL

CHAPTER GOALS

After completing this chapter, you will be able to:

1. Discuss the role of statistical quality control in evaluating the quality of production in a manufacturing or service operation.
2. Define the quality control terms chance causes, assignable causes, in control, and out of control.
3. Distinguish between variable and attribute control charts.
4. Construct two charts for variables—a mean chart and a range chart.
5. Construct two charts for attributes—a percent defective chart and a chart for the number of defects per unit.
6. Construct an operating characteristic curve for various sampling plans.

Introduction

Prior to the Industrial Revolution, a craftsman was in complete charge of the quality of the finished product. Before selling a buggy, the craftsman made sure the wheels were round, all the bolts were tight, etc. The Industrial Revolution changed the way clothing, furniture, farm implements, shoes, and other consumer items were manufactured. Employees were organized in assembly lines and each employee performed one or two tasks. To control the quality of the output, all of the finished products were inspected, that is, there was 100 percent inspection after the manufacturing operation was completed.

During the 1930s and 1940s the concept of **statistical quality control** was developed. Instead of 100 percent inspection, a sample of the parts produced is selected and inspected during production and a decision made regarding the quality of the production. The goal was to minimize the amount of defective material produced.

Causes of Variation

On a production line there is no such thing as two identical parts. The difference between two parts may be very small but they are different. The tensile strength of a roll of steel wire varies throughout the length of wire, and not every MacDonald's Quarter Pounder has exactly 0.25 lbs. of meat. There are two general categories of variation in a process: chance causes and assignable causes. **Chance causes** are usually large in number and random in nature and usually cannot be eliminated. The amount of material or "shot" of plastic used in the injection molding of a plastic bottle varies due to many conditions. Conditions such as temperature, dust and dirt, etc. are not always constant causing the amount of plastic to vary slightly. An **assignable cause** of variation is nonrandom variation which can be eliminated or greatly reduced. Suppose the sample boxes of breakfast cereal are significantly overweight. An investigation revealed that the lever controlling the weight of the cereal had become loose. Thus, the assignable cause is a loose lever, and it can be easily reset and tightened.

In recent years competition from foreign manufacturers, especially in the automotive industry, has caused American firms to revamp and strengthen their quality control programs.

Control Charts

A useful tool for insuring that a product is manufactured properly is a **statistical control chart**. Control charts are based on the theory of sampling. Random samples of the product are obtained during the production process and the results portrayed in chart form. These control charts are useful for separating random causes of variation from those that are assignable to some particular condition.

On a chart there is an *in control* area and an *out of control* area. If the plot on the chart representing production is in the "in control" area, it is assumed that the production is satisfactory. If the plot on the chart is in the "out of control" area, it is assumed that the production is unsatisfactory. There is an **upper control limit** (UCL), and a **lower control limit** (LCL). A typical chart before any plots are made appears as:

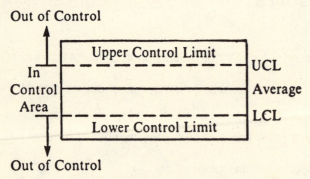

If we are concerned with the mean outside diameter and if the manufacturing process is "in control," the sample mean will fall between the UCL and LCL 99.73 percent of time by chance, which is the same as ± three standard deviations from the arithmetic mean.

Types of Control Charts

There are two basic types of control charts. Control charts for **variables** are used when the characteristic under investigation can be measured, such as the outside diameter of a pipe or the weight of the contents of a bottle of cola. Outside diameter, weights, etc., vary. Two charts designed to control these variables are the **mean chart** and the **range chart.** The mean chart shows management, production engineers, machine operators, and others whether the arithmetic mean weight, length, outside diameter, inside diameter, etc., is in control (satisfactory), or out of control (unsatisfactory).

A **range chart** has a similar purpose, that is, to depict graphically whether the ranges are in control or out of control. As examples, the two charts for variables might appear as:

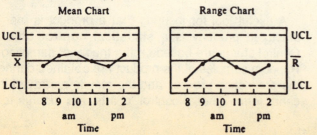

An analysis of the two charts reveals that both the arithmetic mean length of a piece of steel and the range of the lengths of the pieces are satisfactory (in control).

Some products can only be classified as being "acceptable" or "unacceptable." Charts developed for these products are called **attribute charts**. For example, a light bulb is either defective or not defective. When this type of classification is used, control charts for these attributes include the **percent defective chart** and **c̄ chart**. The **percent defective chart** drawn to control the percent defective for a ball bearing might appear as:

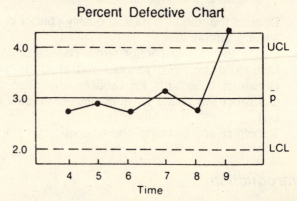

Percent Defective Chart

The process was in control from 4 p.m. until 8 p.m. The 9 p.m. check revealed that the percent defective exceeded the upper control limit of 4 percent. The quality control engineer would no doubt take steps to bring the process back into control (below 4 percent).

It is difficult for many processes to manufacture all the units without a defect appearing. For example, the exterior of an automobile being manufactured might have a paint glob on the hood, the trunk lid might not be centered correctly, and there might be a steel sliver protruding on the left front door. In that case, there would be three defects per unit. A chart designed to portray the number of defects per unit is called a c̄-bar chart. For this problem it might appear as:

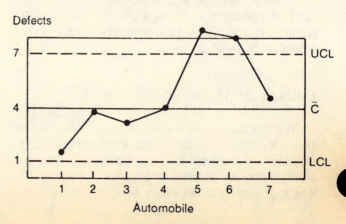

Based on the above chart, between 1 and 7 defects per car is expected. The mean is 4. However, the number of defects in car 5 and car 6 exceeded the upper control limit and the process would be declared "out of control." It was brought under control for car 7. That is, the process was back "in control."

Acceptance Sampling

In any business situation there is concern over the quality of an incoming shipment of a product. For example, a cola manufacturer purchases plastic 2 liter bottles from a blow molding supplier. The plastic bottles are received in lots of 2,400. The manufacturer does not expect each bottle to be perfect, but he has an agreement with the supplier regarding the percent of the bottles that are defective. The usual procedure is to check the quality of the incoming product using a statistical sampling plan. A random sample of n units is selected from the lot of N units. The inspection will determine the number of defective parts in the sample. This number is compared to the predetermined number called the **critical number** or the **acceptance number.** If the number of defects exceeds the critical number, the lot is rejected. As an example, the cola manufacturer might take a random sample of 30 bottles and inspect each. If 3 or less are defective the entire lot of bottles is accepted. Otherwise, the shipment is returned to the supplier.

Acceptance sampling is a decision-making process. According to the specific sampling plan, the lot is either acceptable or not acceptable. So there are two decisions that can be made. In addition, there are two **states of nature**. If the lot is acceptable and the sampling process reveals it to be good, or the lot is unacceptable and the sampling process shows the lot to be unacceptable then a correct decision has been made. However, there are two additional possibilities. The lot may actually contain more defects than it should, but the sampling process reveals it to be acceptable. This is called a **beta error** or **consumer's error**. If the lot is actually within agreed upon limits, but the sampling process reveals that it should be rejected, this is called the **producer's error.**

An **operating characteristic** curve is developed to show the probabilities of accepting incoming lots with various quality levels. The binomial distribution is used to determine the probabilities corresponding to the various quality levels.

GLOSSARY

Statistical quality control—Developed in the 1930s and 1940s, it was a new concept for controlling the quality of mass-produced items. Instead of inspecting each item, a sample of the production is taken and a decision regarding all the production during a given time period is made.

Quality control charts—They portray graphically the results of samples taken during the production period. They have two areas—an area of "in control" and an area of "out of control." If the sample result falls in the "in control" area it means that production is satisfactory. Otherwise, it is "out of control" (unsatisfactory).

Upper control limit and lower control limit—The two points which separate the in control area from the out of control area.

Attributes—A product or service is classified as acceptable or unacceptable. No reading or measurement is obtained.

Variable—A reading or measurement on the product or service is obtained.

Acceptance sampling—A random sample of n units is selected from a lot of N units. If c or less units are found defective among the n sampled units the lot is accepted, otherwise it is rejected.

Acceptance number—The maximum number of defective units allowed in a sample and still accept the lot. The number is usually designated as c.

Operating characteristic curve—A graph developed to show the probability of accepting lots of various quality levels. The horizontal axis shows the proportion of defective units in the population and the vertical axis the probability that a lot of that quality level is accepted.

Producer's risk—The likelihood that an acceptable lot is rejected.

Consumer's risk—The likelihood that a lot that should be accepted is actually rejected.

CHAPTER PROBLEMS

Problem 1

A machine set to fill a bottle with 60.0 grams of liquid was started at 7 a.m. today. Slight variations (called chance variations) were expected. The quality control inspector made her initial check of the weights at 8 a.m. She selected five bottles from the first hour of production and weighed each one. The results of the first seven inspections follows:

	Sample				
Time	1	2	3	4	5
8 a.m.	60.0	59.9	60.0	60.0	60.1
9 a.m.	60.0	60.2	60.1	60.2	60.0
10 a.m.	60.1	60.1	60.0	59.8	60.0
11 a.m.	60.0	59.8	60.0	60.0	60.2
12 noon	60.2	60.0	59.8	60.1	59.8
1 p.m.	60.3	60.1	59.9	60.1	59.8
2 p.m.	60.1	59.8	59.7	59.9	59.8

Develop a control chart for (a) the sample means and (b) the sample ranges.

Solution

a. The upper and lower control limits for the mean are determined using formula 15–1.

$$\text{UCL and UCL} = \overline{\overline{X}} \pm A_2 \overline{R} \qquad [15\text{--}1]$$

$\overline{\overline{X}}$ is the mean of the sample means, $\overline{R}$ is the mean of the ranges, and A_2 is a factor which is related to the standard deviation. A_2 is based on the number of observations taken each hour, that is the sample size.

Statistical theory has shown that there is a constant relationship between the range and the standard deviation, for a given sample size. A_2 expresses this constant relationship. To obtain find the specific value for A_2 refer to Appendix L where the number of items in the sample is 5. The value is 0.577 in this example.

Refer to the table below. The sample values for 8 a.m. are 60.0, 59.9, 60.0, 60.0 and 60.1 grams respectively. The sum of those five values is 300.0, so the mean is 60.0 grams (found by 300.0/5). The means for all remaining hours are computed. The sum of the seven means is 419.98 and the mean of these seven means ($\overline{\overline{X}}$) is 59.997, found by 419.98/7.

For the 8 a.m. check the highest weight is 60.1 grams, the lowest 59.9. The difference between the highest and lowest (the range) is 0.2. The sum of the seven ranges is 2.4 and the mean 0.343, found by 2.4/7. This information is summarized in the following table.

	Sample							
Time	1	2	3	4	5	ΣX	$\overline{X}$	R
8 a.m.	60.0	59.9	60.0	60.0	60.1	300.0	60.00	0.2
9 a.m.	60.0	60.2	60.1	60.2	60.0	300.5	60.10	0.2
10 a.m.	60.1	60.1	60.0	59.8	60.0	300.0	60.00	0.3
11 a.m.	60.0	59.8	60.0	60.0	60.2	300.0	60.00	0.4
12 noon	60.2	60.0	59.8	60.1	59.8	299.9	59.98	0.4
1 p.m.	60.3	60.1	59.9	60.1	59.8	300.2	60.04	0.5
2 p.m.	60.1	59.8	59.7	59.9	59.8	299.3	59.86	0.4
							419.98	2.4

As noted, the control limits for the hourly sample means are determined using formula 15–1.

$$\text{UCL and LCL} = \overline{\overline{X}} \pm A_2\overline{R}$$
$$= 59.997 \pm 0.577(0.343)$$
$$= 59.997 \pm 0.198$$

So the lower control limit is set at 59.799 and the upper control limit is set at 60.195. The MINITAB software system was used to generate the following control chart. There is a small difference in the limits due to rounding, but it is clear that the process is in control until 2 p.m. At that time the sample mean drops to 59.86 grams. This is still greater than the lower limit on the chart of 59.80 grams. However, this rather dramatic downward shift is likely an indicator of trouble and should be investigated.

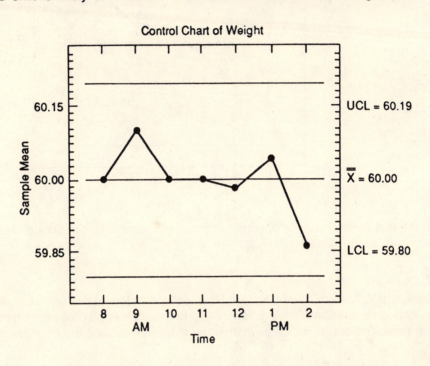

Control Chart of Weight

b. The LCL and UCL of the control chart for ranges is constructed using formula 15–2.

$$\text{Upper control limit UCL} = D_4\overline{R}$$

$$\text{Lower control limit LCL} = D_3\overline{R}$$

The factors D_3 and D_4 (like A_2) are developed from the constant relationship between the range and the standard deviation. The factors D_3 and D_4 are also given in Appendix L. To find the values go down the left column to the number in the sample (5) and then go across to the columns headed D_3 and D_4. The factor $D_4 = 2.115$ and $D_3 = 0$. To determine the UCL and LCL for the range chart:

$$\text{UCL} = D_4\overline{R} = 2.115(0.343) = 0.725$$

$$\text{LCL} = D_3\overline{R} = 0(0.343) = 0$$

217

The following chart for the range was developed using MINITAB.

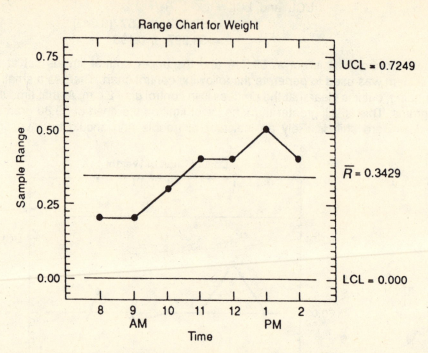

Range Chart for Weight

Based on the first seven hours of operation the process variability is in control. None of the observations are outside the control limits.

Problem 2

The Administration at Rossford General Hospital is investigating the quality of meals served to patients. A ten-day survey is conducted by submitting a questionnaire to a sample of 50 patients with the noon meal each day. The patients are required only to indicate whether the meal was satisfactory or unsatisfactory. The results are as follows:

Date	Sample Size	Number of Unsatisfactory Meals
May 1	50	2
2	50	3
3	50	1
4	50	4
5	50	8
6	50	2
7	50	5
8	50	4
9	50	7
10	50	4

Construct a control chart for the proportion defective. In this case, the chart is reporting the proportion of the patients dissatisfied with the meal.

Solution

This problem requires the use of an attribute chart because a meal is classified only as satisfactory or unsatisfactory. No "measurement" is obtained.

The upper and lower control limits are determined using formula 15–3.

$$\text{UCL and LCL} = \bar{p} \pm 3 \sqrt{\frac{\bar{p}\,(1 - \bar{p})}{n}} \qquad [15\text{-}3]$$

where $\bar{p}$ is the proportion defective over all the samples and n is the number in each sample.

The value of $\bar{p}$, the proportion unsatisfactory, is computed by first determining the proportion of unsatisfactory meals for each sample.

Date	Sample Size	Number of Unsatisfactory Meals	Proportion of Unsatisfactory Meals
May 1	50	2	.04
2	50	3	.06
3	50	1	.02
4	50	4	.08
5	50	8	.16
6	50	2	.04
7	50	5	.10
8	50	4	.08
9	50	7	.14
10	50	4	.08
			.80

Then, to compute the mean percent defective:

$$\bar{p} = \frac{\text{Sum of proportion defective}}{\text{Number of samples}} = \frac{0.80}{10} = 0.08$$

$$\text{UCL and LCL} = \bar{p} \pm 3 \sqrt{\frac{\bar{p}\,(1 - \bar{p})}{n}}$$

$$= .08 \pm 3 \sqrt{\frac{.08\,(1 - .08)}{50}}$$

$$= .08 \pm .115$$

$$= 0 \text{ and } .195$$

Thus, the control limits for the proportion of unsatisfactory meals are set at 0 and .195. The lower control limit could not logically be a negative number. The following MINITAB chart indicates that the proportion of unsatisfactory meals is well within the control limit.

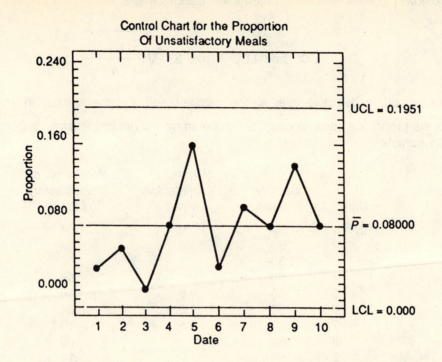

Control Chart for the Proportion
Of Unsatisfactory Meals

UCL = 0.1951

$\bar{P}$ = 0.08000

LCL = 0.000

Proportion

Date

Problem 3

A new automobile assembly line was put into operation. The number of defects on the exterior of the first ten cars off the assembly line were: 3, 5, 4, 6, 2, 3, 5, 4, 2, and 4. Construct a $\bar{c}$ bar chart for the number of defects per unit.

Solution

The formula for the upper and lower control limits for a $\bar{c}$ bar chart are determined using 15–4.

$$\text{UCL and LCL} = \bar{c} \pm 3 \sqrt{\bar{c}}$$

The total number of defects in the first ten cars is 38, found by 3 + 5 + 4 + 6 + 2 + 3 + 5 + 4 + 2 + 4. The mean number of defects per car ($\bar{c}$) is:

$$\bar{c} = \frac{\Sigma \text{ of the number of defects}}{\text{Total number of cars}}$$

$$= \frac{38}{10} = 3.8$$

The upper and lower control limits are:

$$\text{UCL and LCL} = \bar{c} \pm 3 \sqrt{\bar{c}}$$

$$= 3.8 \pm 3\sqrt{3.8}$$

$$= 3.8 \pm 5.848$$

$$\text{UCL} = 9.648$$

$$\text{LCL} = 0 \text{ (since the number of defects cannot be less than 0)}$$

220

Based on the sample data for the $\bar{c}$ bar chart, more than 99 percent of the cars will have between 0 and 9.648 defects.

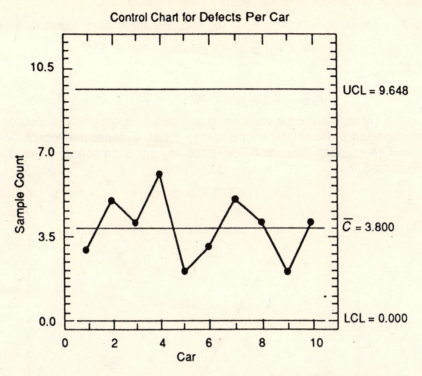

Control Chart for Defects Per Car

Problem 4

The Berry Cola Company processes a soft drink with a blueberry flavor added to the cola. It is packaged in 2-liter plastic bottles. The bottles are purchased from Persall Plastics in lots of 2400. Berry Cola has agreed to select a sample of 25 incoming bottles and inspect them for all quality characteristics. If 2 or less defective bottles are found in the sample, the lot is considered acceptable. Suppose we want to develop an operating characteristic curve showing the likelihood that lots will be accepted that are 5%, 10%, or 20% defective.

Solution

This is an example of attribute sampling, because each bottle sampled is classified as either acceptable or not acceptable. No measurement or "reading" is obtained on the bottle.

The binomial distribution is used to compute the various probabilities. Recall that to employ the binomial distribution four requirements must be met.

1. There are only two possible outcomes. A bottle is either acceptable or not acceptable.
2. There is a fixed number of trials. The number of trials is the sample size, 25 in this case.
3. There is constant probability of success. A success is the probability of finding a defective part. In this case, Berry Cola is concerned about lots that are 5 percent, 10 percent and 20 percent defective.
4. The trials are independent. The probability the fifth bottle is defective is not related to the probability the eighth bottle is defective.

The binomial probabilities are given in Appendix A. First, let's assume the lot is actually 5% defective, so $p = .05$, n, the size of the sample, is 25, and the acceptance number is 2. We usually let c refer to the acceptance number, so here $c = 2$. To find the probability turn to Appendix A, an n of 25, and the column where $p = .05$. Berry Cola will allow 0, 1, or 2 defects in the sample and still consider the lot of 2,400 acceptable. Thus, we add the probability of 0, 1, or 2 defects in the sample of 25. Find the row where r, the number of defects, is 0 and read the probability. It is .277. The probability of 1 defect in a sample of 25 where $p = .05$ is .365. The probability of 2 defects is .231. Adding these three probabilities (0, 1, and 2) gives the probability of accepting a lot that is actually 5 percent defective. The result is .873, found by $.277 + .365 + .231$. Hence, the probability of accepting a lot that is actually 5 percent defective is .873. This is often written in the following shorthand form.

221

$$P(X \le 2 \mid p = .05 \text{ and } n = 25) = .873$$

where X is the number of defects and the slash | means "given that."

The probability of 2 or fewer defects with $p = .10$, and $n = 25$ is also found by using Appendix A.

$$P(X \le 2 \mid p = .10 \text{ and } n = 25) = .537.$$

For the case where $p = .20$:

$$P(X \le 2 \mid p = .20 \text{ and } n = 25) = .098.$$

The following OC curve shows the various values of p and their corresponding probability of accepting a lot of that quality. The management of Berry Cola will be able to quickly evaluate the acceptance probabilities for the various quality levels. Other probabilities can be developed by using the normal approximation to the binomial distribution (not discussed here).

OC Curve

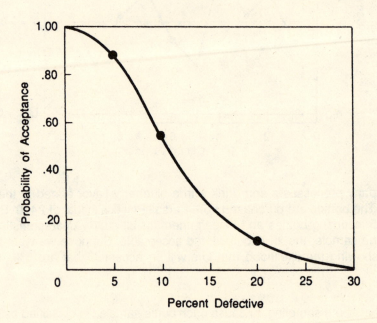

Exercise 1

Check your answers against those in the ANSWER section.

Use the sampling plan developed above and compute the probability that a lot 30% defective is accepted.

CHAPTER ASSIGNMENT 15

Correlation and Regression Analysis

Name _____ Section _____ Score _____

PART I **Matching** Select the correct answer and write the appropriate letter in the space provided.

_____ 1. Attribute

_____ 2. Acceptance sampling

_____ 3. Variable chart

_____ 4. Acceptance number

_____ 5. OC curve

_____ 6. Consumer risk

_____ 7. UCL

_____ 8. Chance variation

_____ 9. Assignable variation

_____ 10. Producer risk

a. item considered acceptable or defective

b. chart based on a measurement

c. acceptable lot rejected

d. rejectable lot accepted

e. upper control limit

f. random variation

g. variation due to a particular cause

h. number of defective units allowed in a sample

i. graph that shows the likelihood of accepting lots at various quality levels

j. system for controlling the quality of items as they are produced

PART II **Multiple Choice** Select the correct answer and write the appropriate letter in the space provided.

_____ 11. The purpose of a quality control chart is to

   a. inspect quality into the product.
   b. monitor the quality of a product as it is being produced.
   c. determine the probability of acceptance.
   d. determine the mean.

_____ 12. An attribute control chart is

   a. based on a measurement.
   b. based on whether the product or service is acceptable or unacceptable.
   c. useful for estimating the probability of acceptance.
   d. based on estimating the standard deviation from the range.

_____ 13. The mean and the range charts are
   a. attribute charts.
   b. operating characteristic charts.
   c. variable charts.
   d. used to compute acceptance probabilities.

_____ 14. Chance variation is

   a. due to some specific cause, such as a worn tool.
   b. measured by a sampling plan.
   c. the height of the OC curve.
   d. random in nature.

_____ 15. In acceptance sampling the

    a. letter c is the acceptance number.
    b. binomial distribution is used.
    c. sample size is n.
    d. All of the above.

_____ 16. A c-bar chart is an example of a(n)

    a. attribute chart.
    b. acceptance plan.
    c. variable chart.
    d. OC curve.

_____ 17. A particular sampling plan consists of selecting a sample of 20 items. The lot is considered acceptable if 0 or 1 defect is found in the sample. The probability of accepting a lot 20 percent defective is

    a. .20
    b. .058
    c. .070
    d. None of the above.

_____ 18. Refer to Question 17. If the lot is 10 percent defective instead of 20 percent the probability of acceptance will

    a. increase.
    b. decrease.
    c. remain the same.
    d. be equal to the standard deviation.

_____ 19. Refer to Question 7. If the acceptance number is increased from 1 to 2 the probability of acceptance will

    a. increase.
    b. decrease.
    c. remain the same.
    d. be equal to the standard deviation.

_____ 20. The producer's risk is

    a. the likelihood an acceptable lot is rejected.
    b. the likelihood an unacceptable lot is accepted.
    c. also called the consumer's risk.
    d. an example of the Poission distribution.

21. The North Central Insurance Company is studying recent claim history. A sample of 5 claims for each of the last 5 months is obtained. Develop a control chart for the mean and the range of the amount (in $000) of settled claims for each month. Does it appear that any of the months are unusual?

Month	Samples 1	2	3	4	5	Total	Mean	Range
January	1.1	0.9	1.3	1.5	1.2			
February	0.5	1.4	1.4	1.3	1.1			
March	0.4	0.3	0.9	0.9	1.0			
April	1.3	1.6	1.6	1.5	0.6			
May	1.2	0.3	1.1	0.7	0.6			

a. Determine the upper and lower control limits for the mean.

b. Determine the upper and lower control limits for the range.

22. A high speed machine produces a small plastic spacer. To check on the machine's performance, a sample of 30 spacers is selected each hour and the number of defects in the sample determined. On the basis of the ten samples taken yesterday determine the control limits for a percent defective chart.

Sample Number	Number in Sample	Number of Defects	Proportion Defective
1	30	1	
2	30	5	
3	30	5	
4	30	1	
5	30	5	
6	30	9	
7	30	5	
8	30	10	
9	30	7	
10	30	3	

23. Dr. Sundar is chairman of the Sociology Department at Southeast State University. He is studying the number of students who drop a sociology course after they initially registered. The following is the number of drops per section for the 15 courses offered last semester in the department:

4, 9, 3, 4, 4, 4, 8, 6, 8, 2, 1, 2, 2, 3, 5

What are the control limits for a c-bar chart of the number of drops?

24. The Mills Hardware Company purchases various types of pliers, in lots of 5,000, for sale in the Home Improvement Department. The Purchasing Department inspects 20 pliers at random before accepting each lot. If 2 or less of the pliers are defective the lot is accepted. If 3 or more of the sample are defective the lot is returned to the manufacturer. Determine the probability of accepting a lot that is 10 percent defective. A lot that is 20 percent defective.

ANSWERS TO EXERCISES
Chapter 2

1.
Stated Class Limits	True Class Limits	Midpoint	Class Frequency
15-24	14.5-24.5	19.5	6
25-34	24.5-34.5	29.5	11
35-44	34.5-44.5	39.5	3
			20

2.

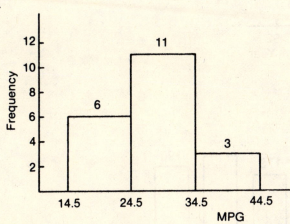

3.

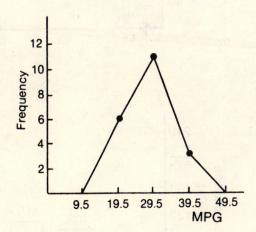

4.
Stem	Leaf
1	899
2	013577899
3	0002267
4	0

5.
True Class Limits	Class Frequency	Cum. Frequency	Percent Cum. Freq.
14.5-24.5	6	6	30
24.5-34.5	11	17	85
34.5-44.5	3	20	100

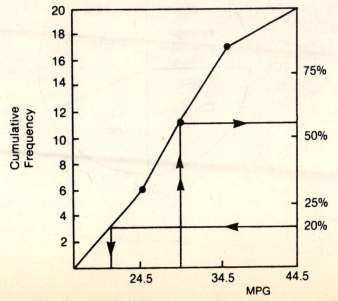

a. about 57% of the cars get less than 30 MPG
b. 20% of the cars obtain about 20 MPG or less

227

6.

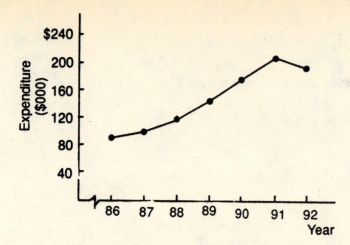

7.

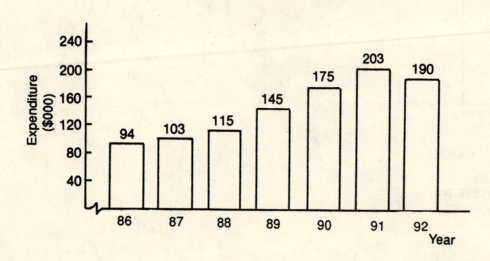

8.

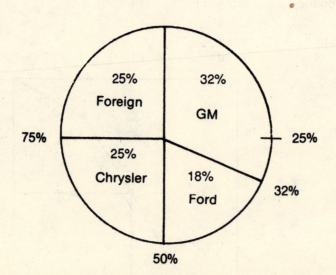

Chapter 3

1. $\overline{X} = 6$, Median $= 5$, Modes are 4 and 8

2.

Stated Limits	True Limits	Midpoint X	Frequency f	fX	Cum. Freq.
$ 6– 8	$ 5.5– 8.5	7	2	14	2
9–11	8.5–11.5	10	8	80	10
12–14	11.5–14.5	13	20	260	30
15–17	14.5–17.5	16	14	224	44
18–20	17.5–20.5	19	6	114	50
				692	

a. $\overline{X} = \dfrac{692}{50} = 13.84$

b. Median $= 11.5 + \left(\dfrac{\frac{50}{2} - 10}{20}\right)(3) = 13.75$

c. Mode $= 13$

3. $GM = \sqrt[45]{159/51} - 1 = \sqrt[45]{3.117647} - 1$

$\qquad = 1.02559 - 1.0$

$\qquad = .026$

4.

X	$X - \overline{X}$	$|X - \overline{X}|$	$(X - \overline{X})^2$
$ 2	$-2	$2	4
5	1	1	1
6	2	2	4
4	0	0	0
3	−1	1	1
20	0	6	10

$\overline{X} = \dfrac{\$20}{5} = \$4.00$

$\qquad$ range $= 6 - 2 = 4$

$\qquad$ MAD $= \dfrac{6}{5} = \$1.20$

$\qquad s^2 = \dfrac{10}{5 - 1} = 2.5$

$\qquad s = \sqrt{2.5} = \$1.58$

5.

Weekly Income	f	Midpoint X	fX	fX²	CF
$100–$149	5	$124.5	$ 622.5	77,501.25	5
150– 199	9	174.5	1,570.5	274,052.25	14
200– 249	20	224.5	4,490.0	1,008,005.00	34
250– 299	18	274.5	4,941.0	1,356,304.50	52
300– 349	5	324.5	1,622.5	526,501.25	57
350– 399	3	374.5	1,123.5	420,750.75	60
	60		$14,370.0	3,663,115.00	

a. $s = \sqrt{\dfrac{3,663,115.00 - \dfrac{(14,370)^2}{60}}{60 - 1}} = \$61.27$

b. $Q_1 = \$199.5 + \left(\dfrac{\dfrac{60}{4} - 14}{20}\right)(\$50) = \$202.00$

$Q_3 = \$249.5 + \left(\dfrac{\dfrac{3}{4}(60) - 34}{18}\right)(\$50) = \$280.06$

$QD = \dfrac{\$280.06 - \$202.00}{2} = \$39.03$

6.   positively skewed, $sk = \dfrac{3(\$990 - \$950)}{\$700} = 1.71$

Chapter 4

1.   a. $\dfrac{90}{300} = .30$

    b. $\dfrac{270}{300} = .90$

2.   .68, found by .60 + .20 − .12

3.   a. $P(3) = (.10)(.10)(.10) = .001$
    b. $P(None) = (.90)(.90)(.90) = .729$
    c. $P(At\ least\ one) = 1 - P(None) = 1 - .729 = .271$

4.   a. $P(Both\ female) = \left(\dfrac{6}{10}\right)\left(\dfrac{5}{9}\right) = .33$

    b. $P(At\ least\ one\ male) = \left(\dfrac{4}{10}\right)\left(\dfrac{3}{9}\right) + \left(\dfrac{4}{10}\right)\left(\dfrac{6}{9}\right) + \left(\dfrac{6}{10}\right)\left(\dfrac{4}{9}\right) = .67$

5.   a. $P(Heart\ attack\ or\ heavy\ smoker) = \dfrac{180}{500} + \dfrac{125}{500} - \dfrac{90}{500} = .43$

    b. $P(Heavy\ smoker\ no\ heart\ attack) = \dfrac{35}{500} = .07$

6.

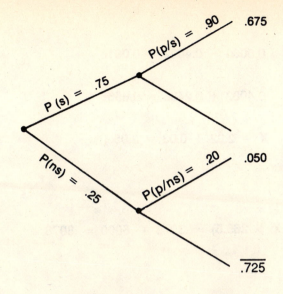

$$P(s/p) = \frac{(.75)(.90)}{(.75)(.90) + (.25)(.20)} = \frac{.675}{.725} = .931$$

Chapter 5

1. $\mu = \Sigma X \cdot P(X) = 0(.60) + 1(.30) + 2(.10) = .50$

$\sigma^2 = \Sigma (X - \mu)^2 P(X) = (0 - .50)^2(.60) + (1 - .50)^2(.30) + (2 - .50)_2(.30)$
$= .45$

2.   *Probability*

   R,R,NR   (.60) (.60) (.40) =   .144
   R,NR,R   (.60) (.40) (.60) =   .144
   NR,R,R   (.40) (.60) (.60) =   .144
                                         .432

$$P(2) = \frac{3!}{2!\,(3 - 2)!}(.60)^2(.40)^1 = .432$$

3. a. $P(0) = .014$
   b. $P(r \geqslant 5) = P(5) + P(6) + \cdots = .158 + .079 + .029 + .008 + .001$
                                        $= .275$
   c. $P(2 \leqslant r \leqslant 4) = .168 + .240 + .231 = .639$

4. $\mu = (1,000)(.002) = 2.00$

   a. $P(0) = 0.1353$
   b. $P(X \geq 2) = 1 - [P(0) + P(1)] = 1 - [0.1353 + 0.2707] = 0.594$

5. $N = 30,\ s = 5,\ n = 4,\ r = 2$

$$P(z) = \frac{\binom{5}{2}\binom{30 - 5}{4 - 2}}{\binom{30}{4}} = 0.109$$

Chapter 6

1. a. $z = \dfrac{2.00 - 2.02}{0.015} = -1.33$ $0.5000 - 0.4082 = 0.0918$

   b. $z = \dfrac{2.03 - 2.02}{0.015} = 0.67$ $0.4082 + 0.2486 = 0.6568$

   c. $2.05 = \dfrac{X - 2.02}{0.015}$ $X = 2.02 + 0.03 = 2.05$

2. $\mu = (300)(0.90) = 270$

   $\sigma = \sqrt{300\,(0.90)\,(0.10)} = 5.20$

   $z = \dfrac{265.5 - 270}{5.20} = -0.87$ $P(X > 265.5) = .3078 + .5000 = .8078$

Chapter 7

1. a. $_5C_3 = \dfrac{5!}{3!\,2!} = 10$

   b.
Sample Number	Homes Sold	Total Homes Sold	Mean Number of Homes Sold
1	ABC	13	4.33
2	ABD	17	5.67
3	ABE	11	3.67
4	BCD	16	5.33
5	BCE	10	3.33
6	CDE	17	5.67
7	CDA	20	6.67
8	DEA	18	6.00
9	DEB	14	4.67
10	ACE	14	4.67

   c.
Mean Preparation Time	Frequency	Probability
3.33	1	0.1
3.67	1	0.1
4.33	1	0.1
4.67	2	0.2
5.33	1	0.1
5.67	2	0.2
6.00	1	0.1
6.67	1	0.1
	10	1.0

d.

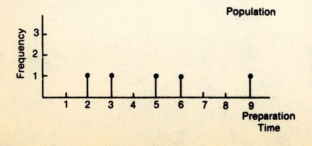

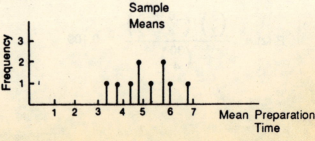

2. $\$150 \pm 2.33 \left(\dfrac{\$20}{\sqrt{36}} \right) = 150 \pm 7.77 = \$142.23$ to $\$157.77$

3. $\$150 \pm 2.33 \left(\dfrac{\$20}{\sqrt{36}} \right) \left(\sqrt{\dfrac{200 - 36}{200 - 1}} \right) = \$150 \pm \$7.05 = \$142.95$ to $\$157.05$

4. $0.60 \pm 1.645 \sqrt{\dfrac{(0.60)(1 - 0.60)}{100}} = .60 \pm .08 = .52$ and $.68$

5. $n = \left[\dfrac{(2.58)(0.25)}{0.20} \right]^2 = 10.4 = 11$

6. $n = (.33)(1 - .33) \left(\dfrac{2.33}{0.04} \right)^2 = 751$

Chapter 8

1. $H_0: \mu = \$30$
   $H_1: \mu > \$30$
   H_0 is rejected if z is greater than 1.645.

   $z = \dfrac{\$33 - \$30}{\dfrac{\$12}{\sqrt{40}}} = 1.58$

   H_0 is not rejected. No increase in the mean amount spent.

   p-value $= P(z > 1.58) = .5000 - .4429 = .0571$

2. Let Youngsville be population 1.
   $H_0: \mu_1 = \mu_2$
   $H_1: \mu_1 > \mu_2$
   H_0 is rejected if z is greater than 1.645.

   $z = \dfrac{6.9 - 4.9}{\sqrt{\dfrac{(3.8)^2}{60} + \dfrac{(3.0)^2}{70}}} = 3.29$

   H_0 is rejected. It takes Youngsville longer to respond to fires.

3. $H_0: p = .40$
$H_1: p < .40$
H_0 is rejected if z is less than -1.28

$$z = \frac{\frac{60}{200} - .40}{\sqrt{\frac{(.40)\ (.60)}{200}}} = -2.89$$

H_0 is rejected. Less than 40 percent of the viewing audience watched the concert.

p-value = $P(z < 2.89) = .5000 - .4981 = .0019$

4. Let population 1 be women

$H_0: p_1 = p_2$
$H_1: p_1 > p_2$

H_0 is rejected if z is greater than 1.645.

$$\bar{p}_c = \frac{45 + 25}{150 + 100} = .28$$

$$z = \frac{.30 - .25}{\sqrt{\frac{(.28)(.72)}{150} + \frac{(.28)(.72)}{100}}} = .86$$

H_0 is not rejected. The proportion of smokers is the same.

p-value = $P(z > 0.86) = .5000 - .3051 = .1949$

Chapter 9

1. $H_0: \mu = 10$
$H_1: \mu > 10$

H_0 is rejected if t is greater than 3.365.

X	X^2
9	81
12	144
14	196
15	225
10	100
12	144
72	890

$$\bar{X} = \frac{72}{6} = 12$$

$$s = \sqrt{\frac{890 - \frac{(72)^2}{6}}{5}} = 2.28$$

$$t = \frac{12 - 10}{2.28/\sqrt{6}} = 2.15$$

H_0 is not rejected. Employee breaks are not longer than ten minutes.

The p-value is between .050 and .025.

2. Let population 1 refer to the mall.

$H_0: \mu_1 = \mu_2$
$H_1: \mu_1 > \mu_2$
H_0 is rejected if t is greater than 2.552.

$$s_p^2 = \frac{(10 - 1)(12)^2 + (10 - 1)(10)^2}{10 + 10 - 2} = 122$$

$$t = \frac{40 - 36}{\sqrt{122\left(\frac{1}{10} + \frac{1}{10}\right)}} = 0.81$$

H_0 is not rejected. No difference in amount spent.

p-value is greater than .10.

3. $H_0: \mu_d = 0$
$H_1: \mu_d \neq 0$

Reject H_0 if t is less than −2.365 or greater than 2.365

Electric	Gas	d	d^2
265	260	5	25
271	270	1	1
260	250	10	100
250	255	−5	25
248	250	−2	4
280	275	5	25
257	260	−3	9
262	260	2	4
		13	193

$$\bar{d} = \frac{13}{8} = 1.625$$

$$s_d = \sqrt{\frac{193 - \frac{(13)^2}{8}}{7}} = 4.96$$

$$t = \frac{1.625}{\frac{4.96}{\sqrt{8}}} = 0.93$$

H_0 is not rejected. There is no difference in the heating cost.

Chapter 10

1. $H_0: \mu_1 = \mu_2 = \mu_3$
   $H_1:$ Not all means are equal.

   H_0 is rejected if F is greater than 3.59.

   $$\text{SS Total} = 681 - \frac{(111)^2}{20} = 64.95$$

   $$\text{SST} = \frac{(19)^2}{5} + \frac{(52)^2}{7} + \frac{(40)^2}{8} - \frac{(111)^2}{20} = 42.4357$$

   $$\text{SSE} = 64.95 - 42.4357 = 22.5143$$

   $$F = \frac{\dfrac{42.4357}{2}}{\dfrac{22.5143}{17}} = 16.02$$

   H_0 is rejected. There is a difference in the mean number correct.

2. $H_0: \sigma_H^2 \le \sigma_T^2 \ ; H_1: \sigma_H^2 > \sigma_T^2$

   H_0 is rejected if $F > 3.18$

   $$F = \frac{(60)^2}{(30)^2} = 4.00$$

   H_0 is rejected. There is more variation in the Harmon forecast.

Chapter 11

1.   a.

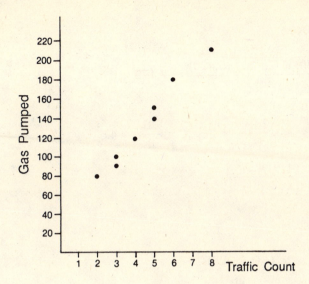

b.

Y	X	XY	X^2	Y^2
120	4	480	16	14,400
180	6	1,080	36	32,400
140	5	700	25	19,600
150	5	750	25	22,500
210	8	1,680	64	44,100
100	3	300	9	10,000
90	3	270	9	8,100
80	2	160	4	6,400
1,070	36	5,420	188	157,500

$$r = \frac{8\,(5,420) - (36)\,(1,070)}{\sqrt{[8\,(188) - (36)^2][8\,(157,500) - (1,070)^2]}} = .989$$

c. $r^2 = (.989)^2$ About 97.8 percent of the variation in gasoline pumped is explained by the traffic count.

d. $H_0 : \rho = 0$
     $H_1 : \rho > 0$

H_0 is rejected if t is greater than 1.943.

$$t = \frac{0.989 \sqrt{6}}{\sqrt{1 - (.989)^2}} = 16.38$$

H_0 is rejected. There is positive correlation in the population.

2. a. $b = \dfrac{8\,(5{,}420) - (36)\,(1{,}070)}{8\,(188) - (36)^2} = 23.269$

$a = \dfrac{1{,}070}{8} - 23.269 \left(\dfrac{36}{8}\right) = 29.040$

$s_{y,x} = \sqrt{\dfrac{157{,}500 - 29.040\,(1{,}070) - 23.269\,(5{,}420)}{8 - 2}} = 7.179$

b. $Y' = 29.040 + 23.269\,(4) = 122.116$

$\Sigma X^2 - \dfrac{(\Sigma X)^2}{n} = 188 - \dfrac{(36)^2}{8} = 26,\quad \bar{X} = \dfrac{36}{8} = 4.5$

$122.116 \pm 2.447\,(7.179)\sqrt{\dfrac{1}{8} + \dfrac{(4 - 4.5)^2}{26}}$

122.116 ± 6.445

c. $122.116 \pm 2.447\,(7.179)\sqrt{1 + \dfrac{1}{8} + \dfrac{(4.0 - 4.5)^2}{26}}$

122.116 ± 18.712

3. $R^2 = \dfrac{14{,}078}{14{,}388} = .9785$

$r = \sqrt{.9785} = .9892$

$s_{y \cdot x} = \sqrt{310/6} = 7.1880$

Chapter 12

1. No problem with multicollinearity

   $H_0: \beta_1 = \beta_2 = 0$
   $H_1:$ Not all β's are zero

   H_0 is rejected if $F > 4.74$

   $F = 8.534/1.004 = 8.5$

H_0 is rejected. At least one regression coefficient is not equal to zero.

2. $H_0: \beta_1 = 0$ $H_0: \beta_2 = 0$
   $H_1: \beta_1 \neq 0$ $H_1: \beta_2 \neq 0$

   Reject H_0 if $t < -2.365$ or $t > 2.365$

   H_0 for β_1 is rejected but H_0 is not rejected for β_2. It appears temperature is related to usage but output is not.

Chapter 13

1. $H_0:$ Distribution is uniform.
   $H_1:$ Distribution is not uniform.

   Reject H_0 if the computed value of χ^2 is greater than 7.815.

Location	f_o	f_e	$\dfrac{(f_o - f_e)^2}{f_e}$
Left front	28	25	0.36
Left rear	20	25	1.00
Right front	29	25	0.64
Right rear	23	25	0.16
	100		2.16

H_0 is not rejected. There is no difference in the failure rates.

2. $H_0:$ There has been no change in the distribution
   $H_1:$ There has been a change in the distribution

   H_0 is rejected if $\chi^2 > 7.815$.

Company	f_o	f_e	$\dfrac{(f_o - f_e)^2}{f_e}$
GM	330	336	.107
Ford	275	264	.458
Chysler	174	176	.023
Other	21	24	.375
Total	800	800	0.963

H_0 is not rejected. There has been no change in the distribution.

3. H_0: There is no relationship between sex and amount of time spent watching T.V.
H_1: There is a relationship between sex and amount of time spent watching TV.
H_0 is rejected if $\chi^2 > 5.991$

f_o	f_e	$\dfrac{(f_o - f_e)^2}{f_e}$
70	75	0.333
90	85	0.294
100	75	8.333
60	85	7.353
55	75	5.333
105	85	4.706
		26.352

H_0 is rejected because χ^2 is greater than 5.991. There is a relationship between sex and the amount of time spent watching TV.

Chapter 14

1. H_0: Median = 500
H_a: Median < 500
Reject H_0 if $z < -1.645$

$$\mu = 30(.5) = 15$$

$$\sigma = \sqrt{30(.5)(.5)} = 2.7386$$

$$z = \frac{6.5 - 15}{2.7386} = -3.10$$

H_0 is rejected. The median is less than 500 hours.

2. H_0: The two populations are the same
H_1: The two populations are not the same
Reject H_0 if $\beta < -1.96$ or $\beta > 1.96$

Tough		Long Last	
Miles	Rank	Miles	Rank
24	2	35	9
31	7	46	15
37	11	49	16
44	14	52	17
36	10	41	13
30	6	40	12
28	4	32	8
21	1	29	5
	55	27	3
			98

$$z = \frac{55 - \dfrac{8(8 + 9 + 1)}{2}}{\sqrt{\dfrac{(8 + 9 + 1)}{12}}} = -1.636$$

H_0 is not rejected. The distributions of miles driven are the same.

3. H_0: The distributions of occupancy rates are the same.
    H_1: The distributions of occupancy rates are not the same.

    H_0 is rejected if χ^2 is greater than 5.991.

    $$H = \frac{12}{16\,(17)} \left(\frac{(24.5)^2}{6} + \frac{(42.5)^2}{5} + \frac{(69.0)^2}{5} \right) - 3\,(17) = 11.36$$

    H_0 is rejected. The occupancy rates are not the same.

4. H_0: There is no difference in the IQ scores.
    H_1: The IQ scores have increased.

    H_0 is rejected if the smaller of R^+ and R^- is 13 or less.

Student	Recent	Original	Diff.	Rank	R^+	R^-
Barr	119	112	7	6	6.0	
Sedwick	103	108	−5	5		5.0
Elmquist	115	115	0			
Thealine	109	100	9	7.5	7.5	
Clark	131	120	11	10	10.0	
Redding	110	108	2	3	3.0	
Papalia	109	113	−4	4		4.0
Suppa	113	126	−13	11		11.0
Paul	94	95	−1	1.5		1.5
Kozoloski	119	110	9	7.5	7.5	
Sass	118	117	1	1.5	1.5	
Sundar	112	102	10	9	9.0	
					44.5	21.5

Since 21.5 is not less than or equal to 13, H_o is not rejected. There has been no change in IQ scores.

Chapter 15

1. $P\,(X \le 2 /\ p = .30 \text{ and } n = 25) = .008$
    from Appendix A where
    $c = 2$, $n = 25$ and $p = .30$.

BINOMIAL PROBABILITY DISTRIBUTION

$n = 1$
PROBABILITY

r	0.05	0.10	0.20	0.30	0.40	0.50	0.60	0.70	0.80	0.90	0.95
0	0.950	0.900	0.800	0.700	0.600	0.500	0.400	0.300	0.200	0.100	0.050
1	0.050	0.100	0.200	0.300	0.400	0.500	0.600	0.700	0.800	0.900	0.950

$n = 2$
PROBABILITY

r	0.05	0.10	0.20	0.30	0.40	0.50	0.60	0.70	0.80	0.90	0.95
0	0.903	0.810	0.640	0.490	0.360	0.250	0.160	0.090	0.040	0.010	0.003
1	0.095	0.180	0.320	0.420	0.480	0.500	0.480	0.420	0.320	0.180	0.095
2	0.003	0.010	0.040	0.090	0.160	0.250	0.360	0.490	0.640	0.810	0.903

$n = 3$
PROBABILITY

r	0.05	0.10	0.20	0.30	0.40	0.50	0.60	0.70	0.80	0.90	0.95
0	0.857	0.729	0.512	0.343	0.216	0.125	0.064	0.027	0.008	0.001	0.000
1	0.135	0.243	0.384	0.441	0.432	0.375	0.288	0.189	0.096	0.027	0.007
2	0.007	0.027	0.096	0.189	0.288	0.375	0.432	0.441	0.384	0.243	0.135
3	0.000	0.001	0.008	0.027	0.064	0.125	0.216	0.343	0.512	0.729	0.857

$n = 4$
PROBABILITY

r	0.05	0.10	0.20	0.30	0.40	0.50	0.60	0.70	0.80	0.90	0.95
0	0.815	0.656	0.410	0.240	0.130	0.063	0.026	0.008	0.002	0.000	0.000
1	0.171	0.292	0.410	0.412	0.346	0.250	0.154	0.076	0.026	0.004	0.000
2	0.014	0.049	0.154	0.265	0.346	0.375	0.346	0.265	0.154	0.049	0.014
3	0.000	0.004	0.026	0.076	0.154	0.250	0.346	0.412	0.410	0.292	0.171
4	0.000	0.000	0.002	0.008	0.026	0.063	0.130	0.240	0.410	0.656	0.815

$n = 5$
PROBABILITY

r	0.05	0.10	0.20	0.30	0.40	0.50	0.60	0.70	0.80	0.90	0.95
0	0.774	0.590	0.328	0.168	0.078	0.031	0.010	0.002	0.000	0.000	0.000
1	0.204	0.328	0.410	0.360	0.259	0.156	0.077	0.028	0.006	0.000	0.000
2	0.021	0.073	0.205	0.309	0.346	0.313	0.230	0.132	0.051	0.008	0.001
3	0.001	0.008	0.051	0.132	0.230	0.313	0.346	0.309	0.205	0.073	0.021
4	0.000	0.000	0.006	0.028	0.077	0.156	0.259	0.360	0.410	0.328	0.204
5	0.000	0.000	0.000	0.002	0.010	0.031	0.078	0.168	0.328	0.590	0.774

$n = 6$
PROBABILITY

r	0.05	0.10	0.20	0.30	0.40	0.50	0.60	0.70	0.80	0.90	0.95
0	0.735	0.531	0.262	0.118	0.047	0.016	0.004	0.001	0.000	0.000	0.000
1	0.232	0.354	0.393	0.303	0.187	0.094	0.037	0.010	0.002	0.000	0.000
2	0.031	0.098	0.246	0.324	0.311	0.234	0.138	0.060	0.015	0.001	0.000
3	0.002	0.015	0.082	0.185	0.276	0.313	0.276	0.185	0.082	0.015	0.002
4	0.000	0.001	0.015	0.060	0.138	0.234	0.311	0.324	0.246	0.098	0.031
5	0.000	0.000	0.002	0.010	0.037	0.094	0.187	0.303	0.393	0.354	0.232
6	0.000	0.000	0.000	0.001	0.004	0.016	0.047	0.118	0.262	0.531	0.735

BINOMIAL PROBABILITY DISTRIBUTION (*continued*)

n = 7
PROBABILITY

r	0.05	0.10	0.20	0.30	0.40	0.50	0.60	0.70	0.80	0.90	0.95
0	0.698	0.478	0.210	0.082	0.028	0.008	0.002	0.000	0.000	0.000	0.000
1	0.257	0.372	0.367	0.247	0.131	0.055	0.017	0.004	0.000	0.000	0.000
2	0.041	0.124	0.275	0.318	0.261	0.164	0.077	0.025	0.004	0.000	0.000
3	0.004	0.023	0.115	0.227	0.290	0.273	0.194	0.097	0.029	0.003	0.000
4	0.000	0.003	0.029	0.097	0.194	0.273	0.290	0.227	0.115	0.023	0.004
5	0.000	0.000	0.004	0.025	0.077	0.164	0.261	0.318	0.275	0.124	0.041
6	0.000	0.000	0.000	0.004	0.017	0.055	0.131	0.247	0.367	0.372	0.257
7	0.000	0.000	0.000	0.000	0.002	0.008	0.028	0.082	0.210	0.478	0.698

n = 8
PROBABILITY

r	0.05	0.10	0.20	0.30	0.40	0.50	0.60	0.70	0.80	0.90	0.95
0	0.663	0.430	0.168	0.058	0.017	0.004	0.001	0.000	0.000	0.000	0.000
1	0.279	0.383	0.336	0.198	0.090	0.031	0.008	0.001	0.000	0.000	0.000
2	0.051	0.149	0.294	0.296	0.209	0.109	0.041	0.010	0.001	0.000	0.000
3	0.005	0.033	0.147	0.254	0.279	0.219	0.124	0.047	0.009	0.000	0.000
4	0.000	0.005	0.046	0.136	0.232	0.273	0.232	0.136	0.046	0.005	0.000
5	0.000	0.000	0.009	0.047	0.124	0.219	0.279	0.254	0.147	0.033	0.005
6	0.000	0.000	0.001	0.010	0.041	0.109	0.209	0.296	0.294	0.149	0.051
7	0.000	0.000	0.000	0.001	0.008	0.031	0.090	0.198	0.336	0.383	0.279
8	0.000	0.000	0.000	0.000	0.001	0.004	0.017	0.058	0.168	0.430	0.663

n = 9
PROBABILITY

r	0.05	0.10	0.20	0.30	0.40	0.50	0.60	0.70	0.80	0.90	0.95
0	0.630	0.387	0.134	0.040	0.010	0.002	0.000	0.000	0.000	0.000	0.000
1	0.299	0.387	0.302	0.156	0.060	0.018	0.004	0.000	0.000	0.000	0.000
2	0.063	0.172	0.302	0.267	0.161	0.070	0.021	0.004	0.000	0.000	0.000
3	0.008	0.045	0.176	0.267	0.251	0.164	0.074	0.021	0.003	0.000	0.000
4	0.001	0.007	0.066	0.172	0.251	0.246	0.167	0.074	0.017	0.001	0.000
5	0.000	0.001	0.017	0.074	0.167	0.246	0.251	0.172	0.066	0.007	0.001
6	0.000	0.000	0.003	0.021	0.074	0.164	0.251	0.267	0.176	0.045	0.008
7	0.000	0.000	0.000	0.004	0.021	0.070	0.161	0.267	0.302	0.172	0.063
8	0.000	0.000	0.000	0.000	0.004	0.018	0.060	0.156	0.302	0.387	0.299
9	0.000	0.000	0.000	0.000	0.000	0.002	0.010	0.040	0.134	0.387	0.630

BINOMIAL PROBABILITY DISTRIBUTION (*continued*)

$n = 10$
PROBABILITY

r	0.05	0.10	0.20	0.30	0.40	0.50	0.60	0.70	0.80	0.90	0.95
0	0.599	0.349	0.107	0.028	0.006	0.001	0.000	0.000	0.000	0.000	0.000
1	0.315	0.387	0.268	0.121	0.040	0.010	0.002	0.000	0.000	0.000	0.000
2	0.075	0.194	0.302	0.233	0.121	0.044	0.011	0.001	0.000	0.000	0.000
3	0.010	0.057	0.201	0.267	0.215	0.117	0.042	0.009	0.001	0.000	0.000
4	0.001	0.011	0.088	0.200	0.251	0.205	0.111	0.037	0.006	0.000	0.000
5	0.000	0.001	0.026	0.103	0.201	0.246	0.201	0.103	0.026	0.001	0.000
6	0.000	0.000	0.006	0.037	0.111	0.205	0.251	0.200	0.088	0.011	0.001
7	0.000	0.000	0.001	0.009	0.042	0.117	0.215	0.267	0.201	0.057	0.010
8	0.000	0.000	0.000	0.001	0.011	0.044	0.121	0.233	0.302	0.194	0.075
9	0.000	0.000	0.000	0.000	0.002	0.010	0.040	0.121	0.268	0.387	0.315
10	0.000	0.000	0.000	0.000	0.000	0.001	0.006	0.028	0.107	0.349	0.599

$n = 11$
PROBABILITY

r	0.05	0.10	0.20	0.30	0.40	0.50	0.60	0.70	0.80	0.90	0.95
0	0.569	0.314	0.086	0.020	0.004	0.000	0.000	0.000	0.000	0.000	0.000
1	0.329	0.384	0.236	0.093	0.027	0.005	0.001	0.000	0.000	0.000	0.000
2	0.087	0.213	0.295	0.200	0.089	0.027	0.005	0.001	0.000	0.000	0.000
3	0.014	0.071	0.221	0.257	0.177	0.081	0.023	0.004	0.000	0.000	0.000
4	0.001	0.016	0.111	0.220	0.236	0.161	0.070	0.017	0.002	0.000	0.000
5	0.000	0.002	0.039	0.132	0.221	0.226	0.147	0.057	0.010	0.000	0.000
6	0.000	0.000	0.010	0.057	0.147	0.226	0.221	0.132	0.039	0.002	0.000
7	0.000	0.000	0.002	0.017	0.070	0.161	0.236	0.220	0.111	0.016	0.001
8	0.000	0.000	0.000	0.004	0.023	0.081	0.177	0.257	0.221	0.071	0.014
9	0.000	0.000	0.000	0.001	0.005	0.027	0.089	0.200	0.295	0.213	0.087
10	0.000	0.000	0.000	0.000	0.001	0.005	0.027	0.093	0.236	0.384	0.329
11	0.000	0.000	0.000	0.000	0.000	0.000	0.004	0.020	0.086	0.314	0.569

$n = 12$
PROBABILITY

r	0.05	0.10	0.20	0.30	0.40	0.50	0.60	0.70	0.80	0.90	0.95
0	0.540	0.282	0.069	0.014	0.002	0.000	0.000	0.000	0.000	0.000	0.000
1	0.341	0.377	0.206	0.071	0.017	0.003	0.000	0.000	0.000	0.000	0.000
2	0.099	0.230	0.283	0.168	0.064	0.016	0.002	0.000	0.000	0.000	0.000
3	0.017	0.085	0.236	0.240	0.142	0.054	0.012	0.001	0.000	0.000	0.000
4	0.002	0.021	0.133	0.231	0.213	0.121	0.042	0.008	0.001	0.000	0.000
5	0.000	0.004	0.053	0.158	0.227	0.193	0.101	0.029	0.003	0.000	0.000
6	0.000	0.000	0.016	0.079	0.177	0.226	0.177	0.079	0.016	0.000	0.000
7	0.000	0.000	0.003	0.029	0.101	0.193	0.227	0.158	0.053	0.004	0.000
8	0.000	0.000	0.001	0.008	0.042	0.121	0.213	0.231	0.133	0.021	0.002
9	0.000	0.000	0.000	0.001	0.012	0.054	0.142	0.240	0.236	0.085	0.017
10	0.000	0.000	0.000	0.000	0.002	0.016	0.064	0.168	0.283	0.230	0.099
11	0.000	0.000	0.000	0.000	0.000	0.003	0.017	0.071	0.206	0.377	0.341
12	0.000	0.000	0.000	0.000	0.000	0.000	0.002	0.014	0.069	0.282	0.540

Binomial Probability Distribution (continued)

n = 13
PROBABILITY

r	0.05	0.10	0.20	0.30	0.40	0.50	0.60	0.70	0.80	0.90	0.95
0	0.513	0.254	0.055	0.010	0.001	0.000	0.000	0.000	0.000	0.000	0.000
1	0.351	0.367	0.179	0.054	0.011	0.002	0.000	0.000	0.000	0.000	0.000
2	0.111	0.245	0.268	0.139	0.045	0.010	0.001	0.000	0.000	0.000	0.000
3	0.021	0.100	0.246	0.218	0.111	0.035	0.006	0.001	0.000	0.000	0.000
4	0.003	0.028	0.154	0.234	0.184	0.087	0.024	0.003	0.000	0.000	0.000
5	0.000	0.006	0.069	0.180	0.221	0.157	0.066	0.014	0.001	0.000	0.000
6	0.000	0.001	0.023	0.103	0.197	0.209	0.131	0.044	0.006	0.000	0.000
7	0.000	0.000	0.006	0.044	0.131	0.209	0.197	0.103	0.023	0.001	0.000
8	0.000	0.000	0.001	0.014	0.066	0.157	0.221	0.180	0.069	0.006	0.000
9	0.000	0.000	0.000	0.003	0.024	0.087	0.184	0.234	0.154	0.028	0.003
10	0.000	0.000	0.000	0.001	0.006	0.035	0.111	0.218	0.246	0.100	0.021
11	0.000	0.000	0.000	0.000	0.001	0.010	0.045	0.139	0.268	0.245	0.111
12	0.000	0.000	0.000	0.000	0.000	0.002	0.011	0.054	0.179	0.367	0.351
13	0.000	0.000	0.000	0.000	0.000	0.000	0.001	0.010	0.055	0.254	0.513

n = 14
PROBABILITY

r	0.05	0.10	0.20	0.30	0.40	0.50	0.60	0.70	0.80	0.90	0.95
0	0.488	0.229	0.044	0.007	0.001	0.000	0.000	0.000	0.000	0.000	0.000
1	0.359	0.356	0.154	0.041	0.007	0.001	0.000	0.000	0.000	0.000	0.000
2	0.123	0.257	0.250	0.113	0.032	0.006	0.001	0.000	0.000	0.000	0.000
3	0.026	0.114	0.250	0.194	0.085	0.022	0.003	0.000	0.000	0.000	0.000
4	0.004	0.035	0.172	0.229	0.155	0.061	0.014	0.001	0.000	0.000	0.000
5	0.000	0.008	0.086	0.196	0.207	0.122	0.041	0.007	0.000	0.000	0.000
6	0.000	0.001	0.032	0.126	0.207	0.183	0.092	0.023	0.002	0.000	0.000
7	0.000	0.000	0.009	0.062	0.157	0.209	0.157	0.062	0.009	0.000	0.000
8	0.000	0.000	0.002	0.023	0.092	0.183	0.207	0.126	0.032	0.001	0.000
9	0.000	0.000	0.000	0.007	0.041	0.122	0.207	0.196	0.086	0.008	0.000
10	0.000	0.000	0.000	0.001	0.014	0.061	0.155	0.229	0.172	0.035	0.004
11	0.000	0.000	0.000	0.000	0.003	0.022	0.085	0.194	0.250	0.114	0.026
12	0.000	0.000	0.000	0.000	0.001	0.006	0.032	0.113	0.250	0.257	0.123
13	0.000	0.000	0.000	0.000	0.000	0.001	0.007	0.041	0.154	0.356	0.359
14	0.000	0.000	0.000	0.000	0.000	0.000	0.001	0.007	0.044	0.229	0.488

BINOMIAL PROBABILITY DISTRIBUTION (continued)

$n = 15$
PROBABILITY

r	0.05	0.10	0.20	0.30	0.40	0.50	0.60	0.70	0.80	0.90	0.95
0	0.463	0.206	0.035	0.005	0.000	0.000	0.000	0.000	0.000	0.000	0.000
1	0.366	0.343	0.132	0.031	0.005	0.000	0.000	0.000	0.000	0.000	0.000
2	0.135	0.267	0.231	0.092	0.022	0.003	0.000	0.000	0.000	0.000	0.000
3	0.031	0.129	0.250	0.170	0.063	0.014	0.002	0.000	0.000	0.000	0.000
4	0.005	0.043	0.188	0.219	0.127	0.042	0.007	0.001	0.000	0.000	0.000
5	0.001	0.010	0.103	0.206	0.186	0.092	0.024	0.003	0.000	0.000	0.000
6	0.000	0.002	0.043	0.147	0.207	0.153	0.061	0.012	0.001	0.000	0.000
7	0.000	0.000	0.014	0.081	0.177	0.196	0.118	0.035	0.003	0.000	0.000
8	0.000	0.000	0.003	0.035	0.118	0.196	0.177	0.081	0.014	0.000	0.000
9	0.000	0.000	0.001	0.012	0.061	0.153	0.207	0.147	0.043	0.002	0.000
10	0.000	0.000	0.000	0.003	0.024	0.092	0.186	0.206	0.103	0.010	0.001
11	0.000	0.000	0.000	0.001	0.007	0.042	0.127	0.219	0.188	0.043	0.005
12	0.000	0.000	0.000	0.000	0.002	0.014	0.063	0.170	0.250	0.129	0.031
13	0.000	0.000	0.000	0.000	0.000	0.003	0.022	0.092	0.231	0.267	0.135
14	0.000	0.000	0.000	0.000	0.000	0.000	0.005	0.031	0.132	0.343	0.366
15	0.000	0.000	0.000	0.000	0.000	0.000	0.000	0.005	0.035	0.206	0.463

$n = 16$
PROBABILITY

r	0.05	0.10	0.20	0.30	0.40	0.50	0.60	0.70	0.80	0.90	0.95
0	0.440	0.185	0.028	0.003	0.000	0.000	0.000	0.000	0.000	0.000	0.000
1	0.371	0.329	0.113	0.023	0.003	0.000	0.000	0.000	0.000	0.000	0.000
2	0.146	0.275	0.211	0.073	0.015	0.002	0.000	0.000	0.000	0.000	0.000
3	0.036	0.142	0.246	0.146	0.047	0.009	0.001	0.000	0.000	0.000	0.000
4	0.006	0.051	0.200	0.204	0.101	0.028	0.004	0.000	0.000	0.000	0.000
5	0.001	0.014	0.120	0.210	0.162	0.067	0.014	0.001	0.000	0.000	0.000
6	0.000	0.003	0.055	0.165	0.198	0.122	0.039	0.006	0.000	0.000	0.000
7	0.000	0.000	0.020	0.101	0.189	0.175	0.084	0.019	0.001	0.000	0.000
8	0.000	0.000	0.006	0.049	0.142	0.196	0.142	0.049	0.006	0.000	0.000
9	0.000	0.000	0.001	0.019	0.084	0.175	0.189	0.101	0.020	0.000	0.000
10	0.000	0.000	0.000	0.006	0.039	0.122	0.198	0.165	0.055	0.003	0.000
11	0.000	0.000	0.000	0.001	0.014	0.067	0.162	0.210	0.120	0.014	0.001
12	0.000	0.000	0.000	0.000	0.004	0.028	0.101	0.204	0.200	0.051	0.006
13	0.000	0.000	0.000	0.000	0.001	0.009	0.047	0.146	0.246	0.142	0.036
14	0.000	0.000	0.000	0.000	0.000	0.002	0.015	0.073	0.211	0.275	0.146
15	0.000	0.000	0.000	0.000	0.000	0.000	0.003	0.023	0.113	0.329	0.371
16	0.000	0.000	0.000	0.000	0.000	0.000	0.000	0.003	0.028	0.185	0.440

BINOMIAL PROBABILITY DISTRIBUTION (*continued*)

$n = 17$
PROBABILITY

r	0.05	0.10	0.20	0.30	0.40	0.50	0.60	0.70	0.80	0.90	0.95
0	0.418	0.167	0.023	0.002	0.000	0.000	0.000	0.000	0.000	0.000	0.000
1	0.374	0.315	0.096	0.017	0.002	0.000	0.000	0.000	0.000	0.000	0.000
2	0.158	0.280	0.191	0.058	0.010	0.001	0.000	0.000	0.000	0.000	0.000
3	0.041	0.156	0.239	0.125	0.034	0.005	0.000	0.000	0.000	0.000	0.000
4	0.008	0.060	0.209	0.187	0.080	0.018	0.002	0.000	0.000	0.000	0.000
5	0.001	0.017	0.136	0.208	0.138	0.047	0.008	0.001	0.000	0.000	0.000
6	0.000	0.004	0.068	0.178	0.184	0.094	0.024	0.003	0.000	0.000	0.000
7	0.000	0.001	0.027	0.120	0.193	0.148	0.057	0.009	0.000	0.000	0.000
8	0.000	0.000	0.008	0.064	0.161	0.185	0.107	0.028	0.002	0.000	0.000
9	0.000	0.000	0.002	0.028	0.107	0.185	0.161	0.064	0.008	0.000	0.000
10	0.000	0.000	0.000	0.009	0.057	0.148	0.193	0.120	0.027	0.001	0.000
11	0.000	0.000	0.000	0.003	0.024	0.094	0.184	0.178	0.068	0.004	0.000
12	0.000	0.000	0.000	0.001	0.008	0.047	0.138	0.208	0.136	0.017	0.001
13	0.000	0.000	0.000	0.000	0.002	0.018	0.080	0.187	0.209	0.060	0.008
14	0.000	0.000	0.000	0.000	0.000	0.005	0.034	0.125	0.239	0.156	0.041
15	0.000	0.000	0.000	0.000	0.000	0.001	0.010	0.058	0.191	0.280	0.158
16	0.000	0.000	0.000	0.000	0.000	0.000	0.002	0.017	0.096	0.315	0.374
17	0.000	0.000	0.000	0.000	0.000	0.000	0.000	0.002	0.023	0.167	0.418

$n = 18$
PROBABILITY

r	0.05	0.10	0.20	0.30	0.40	0.50	0.60	0.70	0.80	0.90	0.95
0	0.397	0.150	0.018	0.002	0.000	0.000	0.000	0.000	0.000	0.000	0.000
1	0.376	0.300	0.081	0.013	0.001	0.000	0.000	0.000	0.000	0.000	0.000
2	0.168	0.284	0.172	0.046	0.007	0.001	0.000	0.000	0.000	0.000	0.000
3	0.047	0.168	0.230	0.105	0.025	0.003	0.000	0.000	0.000	0.000	0.000
4	0.009	0.070	0.215	0.168	0.061	0.012	0.001	0.000	0.000	0.000	0.000
5	0.001	0.022	0.151	0.202	0.115	0.033	0.004	0.000	0.000	0.000	0.000
6	0.000	0.005	0.082	0.187	0.166	0.071	0.015	0.001	0.000	0.000	0.000
7	0.000	0.001	0.035	0.138	0.189	0.121	0.037	0.005	0.000	0.000	0.000
8	0.000	0.000	0.012	0.081	0.173	0.167	0.077	0.015	0.001	0.000	0.000
9	0.000	0.000	0.003	0.039	0.128	0.185	0.128	0.039	0.003	0.000	0.000
10	0.000	0.000	0.001	0.015	0.077	0.167	0.173	0.081	0.012	0.000	0.000
11	0.000	0.000	0.000	0.005	0.037	0.121	0.189	0.138	0.035	0.001	0.000
12	0.000	0.000	0.000	0.001	0.015	0.071	0.166	0.187	0.082	0.005	0.000
13	0.000	0.000	0.000	0.000	0.004	0.033	0.115	0.202	0.151	0.022	0.001
14	0.000	0.000	0.000	0.000	0.001	0.012	0.061	0.168	0.215	0.070	0.009
15	0.000	0.000	0.000	0.000	0.000	0.003	0.025	0.105	0.230	0.168	0.047
16	0.000	0.000	0.000	0.000	0.000	0.001	0.007	0.046	0.172	0.284	0.168
17	0.000	0.000	0.000	0.000	0.000	0.000	0.001	0.013	0.081	0.300	0.376
18	0.000	0.000	0.000	0.000	0.000	0.000	0.000	0.002	0.018	0.150	0.397

BINOMIAL PROBABILITY DISTRIBUTION (continued)

n = 19
PROBABILITY

r	0.05	0.10	0.20	0.30	0.40	0.50	0.60	0.70	0.80	0.90	0.95
0	0.377	0.135	0.014	0.001	0.000	0.000	0.000	0.000	0.000	0.000	0.000
1	0.377	0.285	0.068	0.009	0.001	0.000	0.000	0.000	0.000	0.000	0.000
2	0.179	0.285	0.154	0.036	0.005	0.000	0.000	0.000	0.000	0.000	0.000
3	0.053	0.180	0.218	0.087	0.017	0.002	0.000	0.000	0.000	0.000	0.000
4	0.011	0.080	0.218	0.149	0.047	0.007	0.001	0.000	0.000	0.000	0.000
5	0.002	0.027	0.164	0.192	0.093	0.022	0.002	0.000	0.000	0.000	0.000
6	0.000	0.007	0.095	0.192	0.145	0.052	0.008	0.001	0.000	0.000	0.000
7	0.000	0.001	0.044	0.153	0.180	0.096	0.024	0.002	0.000	0.000	0.000
8	0.000	0.000	0.017	0.098	0.180	0.144	0.053	0.008	0.000	0.000	0.000
9	0.000	0.000	0.005	0.051	0.146	0.176	0.098	0.022	0.001	0.000	0.000
10	0.000	0.000	0.001	0.022	0.098	0.176	0.146	0.051	0.005	0.000	0.000
11	0.000	0.000	0.000	0.008	0.053	0.144	0.180	0.098	0.017	0.000	0.000
12	0.000	0.000	0.000	0.002	0.024	0.096	0.180	0.153	0.044	0.001	0.000
13	0.000	0.000	0.000	0.001	0.008	0.052	0.145	0.192	0.095	0.007	0.000
14	0.000	0.000	0.000	0.000	0.002	0.022	0.093	0.192	0.164	0.027	0.002
15	0.000	0.000	0.000	0.000	0.001	0.007	0.047	0.149	0.218	0.080	0.011
16	0.000	0.000	0.000	0.000	0.000	0.002	0.017	0.087	0.218	0.180	0.053
17	0.000	0.000	0.000	0.000	0.000	0.000	0.005	0.036	0.154	0.285	0.179
18	0.000	0.000	0.000	0.000	0.000	0.000	0.001	0.009	0.068	0.285	0.377
19	0.000	0.000	0.000	0.000	0.000	0.000	0.000	0.001	0.014	0.135	0.377

n = 20
PROBABILITY

r	0.05	0.10	0.20	0.30	0.40	0.50	0.60	0.70	0.80	0.90	0.95
0	0.358	0.122	0.012	0.001	0.000	0.000	0.000	0.000	0.000	0.000	0.000
1	0.377	0.270	0.058	0.007	0.000	0.000	0.000	0.000	0.000	0.000	0.000
2	0.189	0.285	0.137	0.028	0.003	0.000	0.000	0.000	0.000	0.000	0.000
3	0.060	0.190	0.205	0.072	0.012	0.001	0.000	0.000	0.000	0.000	0.000
4	0.013	0.090	0.218	0.130	0.035	0.005	0.000	0.000	0.000	0.000	0.000
5	0.002	0.032	0.175	0.179	0.075	0.015	0.001	0.000	0.000	0.000	0.000
6	0.000	0.009	0.109	0.192	0.124	0.037	0.005	0.000	0.000	0.000	0.000
7	0.000	0.002	0.055	0.164	0.166	0.074	0.015	0.001	0.000	0.000	0.000
8	0.000	0.000	0.022	0.114	0.180	0.120	0.035	0.004	0.000	0.000	0.000
9	0.000	0.000	0.007	0.065	0.160	0.160	0.071	0.012	0.000	0.000	0.000
10	0.000	0.000	0.002	0.031	0.117	0.176	0.117	0.031	0.002	0.000	0.000
11	0.000	0.000	0.000	0.012	0.071	0.160	0.160	0.065	0.007	0.000	0.000
12	0.000	0.000	0.000	0.004	0.035	0.120	0.180	0.114	0.022	0.000	0.000
13	0.000	0.000	0.000	0.001	0.015	0.074	0.166	0.164	0.055	0.002	0.000
14	0.000	0.000	0.000	0.000	0.005	0.037	0.124	0.192	0.109	0.009	0.000
15	0.000	0.000	0.000	0.000	0.001	0.015	0.075	0.179	0.175	0.032	0.002
16	0.000	0.000	0.000	0.000	0.000	0.005	0.035	0.130	0.218	0.090	0.013
17	0.000	0.000	0.000	0.000	0.000	0.001	0.012	0.072	0.205	0.190	0.060
18	0.000	0.000	0.000	0.000	0.000	0.000	0.003	0.028	0.137	0.285	0.189
19	0.000	0.000	0.000	0.000	0.000	0.000	0.000	0.007	0.058	0.270	0.377
20	0.000	0.000	0.000	0.000	0.000	0.000	0.000	0.001	0.012	0.122	0.358

BINOMIAL PROBABILITY DISTRIBUTION (concluded)

$n = 25$

PROBABILITY

r	0.05	0.10	0.20	0.30	0.40	0.50	0.60	0.70	0.80	0.90	0.95
0	0.277	0.072	0.004	0.000	0.000	0.000	0.000	0.000	0.000	0.000	0.000
1	0.365	0.199	0.024	0.001	0.000	0.000	0.000	0.000	0.000	0.000	0.000
2	0.231	0.266	0.071	0.007	0.000	0.000	0.000	0.000	0.000	0.000	0.000
3	0.093	0.226	0.136	0.024	0.002	0.000	0.000	0.000	0.000	0.000	0.000
4	0.027	0.138	0.187	0.057	0.007	0.000	0.000	0.000	0.000	0.000	0.000
5	0.006	0.065	0.196	0.103	0.020	0.002	0.000	0.000	0.000	0.000	0.000
6	0.001	0.024	0.163	0.147	0.044	0.005	0.000	0.000	0.000	0.000	0.000
7	0.000	0.007	0.111	0.171	0.080	0.014	0.001	0.000	0.000	0.000	0.000
8	0.000	0.002	0.062	0.165	0.120	0.032	0.003	0.000	0.000	0.000	0.000
9	0.000	0.000	0.029	0.134	0.151	0.061	0.009	0.000	0.000	0.000	0.000
10	0.000	0.000	0.012	0.092	0.161	0.097	0.021	0.001	0.000	0.000	0.000
11	0.000	0.000	0.004	0.054	0.147	0.133	0.043	0.004	0.000	0.000	0.000
12	0.000	0.000	0.001	0.027	0.114	0.155	0.076	0.011	0.000	0.000	0.000
13	0.000	0.000	0.000	0.011	0.076	0.155	0.114	0.027	0.001	0.000	0.000
14	0.000	0.000	0.000	0.004	0.043	0.133	0.147	0.054	0.004	0.000	0.000
15	0.000	0.000	0.000	0.001	0.021	0.097	0.161	0.092	0.012	0.000	0.000
16	0.000	0.000	0.000	0.000	0.009	0.061	0.151	0.134	0.029	0.000	0.000
17	0.000	0.000	0.000	0.000	0.003	0.032	0.120	0.165	0.062	0.002	0.000
18	0.000	0.000	0.000	0.000	0.001	0.014	0.080	0.171	0.111	0.007	0.000
19	0.000	0.000	0.000	0.000	0.000	0.005	0.044	0.147	0.163	0.024	0.001
20	0.000	0.000	0.000	0.000	0.000	0.002	0.020	0.103	0.196	0.065	0.006
21	0.000	0.000	0.000	0.000	0.000	0.000	0.007	0.057	0.187	0.138	0.027
22	0.000	0.000	0.000	0.000	0.000	0.000	0.002	0.024	0.136	0.226	0.093
23	0.000	0.000	0.000	0.000	0.000	0.000	0.000	0.007	0.071	0.266	0.231
24	0.000	0.000	0.000	0.000	0.000	0.000	0.000	0.001	0.024	0.199	0.365
25	0.000	0.000	0.000	0.000	0.000	0.000	0.000	0.000	0.004	0.072	0.277

FACTORS FOR CONTROL CHARTS

Number of Items in Sample, n	Chart for Averages	Chart for Ranges		
	Factors for Control Limits	Factors for Central Line	Factors for Control Limits	
	A₂	d₂	D₃	D₄

Number of Items in Sample, n	A_2	d_2	D_3	D_4
2	1.880	1.128	0	3.267
3	1.023	1.693	0	2.575
4	.729	2.059	0	2.282
5	.577	2.326	0	2.115
6	.483	2.534	0	2.004
7	.419	2.704	.076	1.924
8	.373	2.847	.136	1.864
9	.337	2.970	.184	1.816
10	.308	3.078	.223	1.777
11	.285	3.173	.256	1.744
12	.266	3.258	.284	1.716
13	.249	3.336	.308	1.692
14	.235	3.407	.329	1.671
15	.223	3.472	.348	1.652

Source: Adapted from American Society for Testing and Materials, *Manual on Quality Control of Materials,* 1951, Table B2, p. 115. For a more detailed table and explanation, see Acheson J. Duncan, *Quality Control and Industrial Statistics,* 3d ed. (Homewood, Ill.: Richard D. Irwin, 1974), Table M, p. 927.

POISSON DISTRIBUTION: PROBABILITY OF EXACTLY X OCCURRENCES

x					μ				
	0.1	0.2	0.3	0.4	0.5	0.6	0.7	0.8	0.9
0	0.9048	0.8187	0.7408	0.6703	0.6065	0.5488	0.4966	0.4493	0.4066
1	0.0905	0.1637	0.2222	0.2681	0.3033	0.3293	0.3476	0.3595	0.3659
2	0.0045	0.0164	0.0333	0.0536	0.0758	0.0988	0.1217	0.1438	0.1647
3	0.0002	0.0011	0.0033	0.0072	0.0126	0.0198	0.0284	0.0383	0.0494
4	0.0000	0.0001	0.0003	0.0007	0.0016	0.0030	0.0050	0.0077	0.0111
5	0.0000	0.0000	0.0000	0.0001	0.0002	0.0004	0.0007	0.0012	0.0020
6	0.0000	0.0000	0.0000	0.0000	0.0000	0.0000	0.0001	0.0002	0.0003
7	0.0000	0.0000	0.0000	0.0000	0.0000	0.0000	0.0000	0.0000	0.0000

x					μ				
	1.0	2.0	3.0	4.0	5.0	6.0	7.0	8.0	9.0
0	0.3679	0.1353	0.0498	0.0183	0.0067	0.0025	0.0009	0.0003	0.0001
1	0.3679	0.2707	0.1494	0.0733	0.0337	0.0149	0.0064	0.0027	0.0011
2	0.1839	0.2707	0.2240	0.1465	0.0842	0.0446	0.0223	0.0107	0.0050
3	0.0613	0.1804	0.2240	0.1954	0.1404	0.0892	0.0521	0.0286	0.0150
4	0.0153	0.0902	0.1680	0.1954	0.1755	0.1339	0.0912	0.0573	0.0337
5	0.0031	0.0361	0.1008	0.1563	0.1755	0.1606	0.1277	0.0916	0.0607
6	0.0005	0.0120	0.0504	0.1042	0.1462	0.1606	0.1490	0.1221	0.0911
7	0.0001	0.0034	0.0216	0.0595	0.1044	0.1377	0.1490	0.1396	0.1171
8	0.0000	0.0009	0.0081	0.0298	0.0653	0.1033	0.1304	0.1396	0.1318
9	0.0000	0.0002	0.0027	0.0132	0.0363	0.0688	0.1014	0.1241	0.1318
10	0.0000	0.0000	0.0008	0.0053	0.0181	0.0413	0.0710	0.0993	0.1186
11	0.0000	0.0000	0.0002	0.0019	0.0082	0.0225	0.0452	0.0722	0.0970
12	0.0000	0.0000	0.0001	0.0006	0.0034	0.0113	0.0263	0.0481	0.0728
13	0.0000	0.0000	0.0000	0.0002	0.0013	0.0052	0.0142	0.0296	0.0504
14	0.0000	0.0000	0.0000	0.0001	0.0005	0.0022	0.0071	0.0169	0.0324
15	0.0000	0.0000	0.0000	0.0000	0.0002	0.0009	0.0033	0.0090	0.0194
16	0.0000	0.0000	0.0000	0.0000	0.0000	0.0003	0.0014	0.0045	0.0109
17	0.0000	0.0000	0.0000	0.0000	0.0000	0.0001	0.0006	0.0021	0.0058
18	0.0000	0.0000	0.0000	0.0000	0.0000	0.0000	0.0002	0.0009	0.0029
19	0.0000	0.0000	0.0000	0.0000	0.0000	0.0000	0.0001	0.0004	0.0014
20	0.0000	0.0000	0.0000	0.0000	0.0000	0.0000	0.0000	0.0002	0.0006
21	0.0000	0.0000	0.0000	0.0000	0.0000	0.0000	0.0000	0.0001	0.0003
22	0.0000	0.0000	0.0000	0.0000	0.0000	0.0000	0.0000	0.0000	0.0001

AREAS UNDER THE NORMAL CURVE

Example:
If $z = 1.96$, then
$P(0$ to $z) = 0.4750$

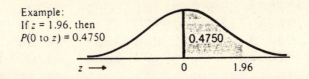

0.4750

$z \longrightarrow$ 0   1.96

Z	0.00	0.01	0.02	0.03	0.04	0.05	0.06	0.07	0.08	0.09
0.0	0.0000	0.0040	0.0080	0.0120	0.0160	0.0199	0.0239	0.0279	0.0319	0.0359
0.1	0.0398	0.0438	0.0478	0.0517	0.0557	0.0596	0.0636	0.0675	0.0714	0.0753
0.2	0.0793	0.0832	0.0871	0.0910	0.0948	0.0987	0.1026	0.1064	0.1103	0.1141
0.3	0.1179	0.1217	0.1255	0.1293	0.1331	0.1368	0.1406	0.1443	0.1480	0.1517
0.4	0.1554	0.1591	0.1628	0.1664	0.1700	0.1736	0.1772	0.1808	0.1844	0.1879
0.5	0.1915	0.1950	0.1985	0.2019	0.2054	0.2088	0.2123	0.2157	0.2190	0.2224
0.6	0.2257	0.2291	0.2324	0.2357	0.2389	0.2422	0.2454	0.2486	0.2517	0.2549
0.7	0.2580	0.2611	0.2642	0.2673	0.2704	0.2734	0.2764	0.2794	0.2823	0.2852
0.8	0.2881	0.2910	0.2939	0.2967	0.2995	0.3023	0.3051	0.3078	0.3106	0.3133
0.9	0.3159	0.3186	0.3212	0.3238	0.3264	0.3289	0.3315	0.3340	0.3365	0.3389
1.0	0.3413	0.3438	0.3461	0.3485	0.3508	0.3531	0.3554	0.3577	0.3599	0.3621
1.1	0.3643	0.3665	0.3686	0.3708	0.3729	0.3749	0.3770	0.3790	0.3810	0.3830
1.2	0.3849	0.3869	0.3888	0.3907	0.3925	0.3944	0.3962	0.3980	0.3997	0.4015
1.3	0.4032	0.4049	0.4066	0.4082	0.4099	0.4115	0.4131	0.4147	0.4162	0.4177
1.4	0.4192	0.4207	0.4222	0.4236	0.4251	0.4265	0.4279	0.4292	0.4306	0.4319
1.5	0.4332	0.4345	0.4357	0.4370	0.4382	0.4394	0.4406	0.4418	0.4429	0.4441
1.6	0.4452	0.4463	0.4474	0.4484	0.4495	0.4505	0.4515	0.4525	0.4535	0.4545
1.7	0.4554	0.4564	0.4573	0.4582	0.4591	0.4599	0.4608	0.4616	0.4625	0.4633
1.8	0.4641	0.4649	0.4656	0.4664	0.4671	0.4678	0.4686	0.4693	0.4699	0.4706
1.9	0.4713	0.4719	0.4726	0.4732	0.4738	0.4744	0.4750	0.4756	0.4761	0.4767
2.0	0.4772	0.4778	0.4783	0.4788	0.4793	0.4798	0.4803	0.4808	0.4812	0.4817
2.1	0.4821	0.4826	0.4830	0.4834	0.4838	0.4842	0.4846	0.4850	0.4854	0.4857
2.2	0.4861	0.4864	0.4868	0.4871	0.4875	0.4878	0.4881	0.4884	0.4887	0.4890
2.3	0.4893	0.4896	0.4898	0.4901	0.4904	0.4906	0.4909	0.4911	0.4913	0.4916
2.4	0.4918	0.4920	0.4922	0.4925	0.4927	0.4929	0.4931	0.4932	0.4934	0.4936
2.5	0.4938	0.4940	0.4941	0.4943	0.4945	0.4946	0.4948	0.4949	0.4951	0.4952
2.6	0.4953	0.4955	0.4956	0.4957	0.4959	0.4960	0.4961	0.4962	0.4963	0.4964
2.7	0.4965	0.4966	0.4967	0.4968	0.4969	0.4970	0.4971	0.4972	0.4973	0.4974
2.8	0.4974	0.4975	0.4976	0.4977	0.4977	0.4978	0.4979	0.4979	0.4980	0.4981
2.9	0.4981	0.4982	0.4982	0.4983	0.4984	0.4984	0.4985	0.4985	0.4986	0.4986
3.0	0.4987	0.4987	0.4987	0.4988	0.4988	0.4989	0.4989	0.4989	0.4990	0.4990

TABLE OF RANDOM NUMBERS

02711	08182	75997	79866	58095	83319	80295	79741	74599	84379
94873	90935	31684	63952	09865	14491	99518	93394	34691	14985
54921	78680	06635	98689	17306	25170	65928	87709	30533	89736
77640	97636	37397	93379	56454	59818	45827	74164	71666	46977
61545	00835	93251	87203	36759	49197	85967	01704	19634	21898
17147	19519	22497	16857	42426	84822	92598	49186	88247	39967
13748	04742	92460	85801	53444	65626	58710	55406	17173	69776
87455	14813	50373	28037	91182	32786	65261	11173	34376	36408
08999	57409	91185	10200	61411	23392	47797	56377	71635	08601
78804	81333	53809	32471	46034	36306	22498	19239	85428	55721
82173	26921	28472	98958	07960	66124	89731	95069	18625	92405
97594	25168	89178	68190	05043	17407	48201	83917	11413	72920
73881	67176	93504	42636	38233	16154	96451	57925	29667	30859
46071	22912	90326	42453	88108	72064	58601	32357	90610	32921
44492	19686	12495	93135	95185	77799	52441	88272	22024	80631
31864	72170	37722	55794	14636	05148	54505	50113	21119	25228
51574	90692	43339	65689	76539	27909	05467	21727	51141	72949
35350	76132	92925	92124	92634	35681	43690	89136	35599	84138
46943	36502	01172	46045	46991	33804	80006	35542	61056	75666
22665	87226	33304	57975	03985	21566	65796	72915	81466	89205
39437	97957	11838	10433	21564	51570	73558	27495	34533	57808
77082	47784	40098	97962	89845	28392	78187	06112	08169	11261
24544	25649	43370	28007	06779	72402	62632	53956	24709	06978
27503	15558	37738	24849	70722	71859	83736	06016	94397	12529
24590	24545	06435	52758	45685	90151	46516	49644	92686	84870
48155	86226	40359	28723	15364	69125	12609	57171	86857	31702
20226	53752	90648	24362	83314	00014	19207	69413	97016	86290
70178	73444	38790	53626	93780	18629	68766	24371	74639	30782
10169	41465	51935	05711	09799	79077	88159	33437	68519	03040
81084	03701	28598	70013	63794	53169	97054	60303	23259	96196
69202	20777	21727	81511	51887	16175	53746	46516	70339	62727
80561	95787	89426	93325	86412	57479	54194	52153	19197	81877
08199	26703	95128	48599	09333	12584	24374	31232	61782	44032
98883	28220	39358	53720	80161	83371	15181	11131	12219	55920
84568	69286	76054	21615	80883	36797	82845	39139	90900	18172
04269	35173	95745	53893	86022	77722	52498	84193	22448	22571
10538	13124	36099	13140	37706	44562	57179	44693	67877	01549
77843	24955	25900	63843	95029	93859	93634	20205	66294	41218
12034	94636	49455	76362	83532	31062	69903	91186	65768	55949
10524	72829	47641	93315	80875	28090	97728	52560	34937	79548
68935	76632	46984	61772	92786	22651	07086	89754	44143	97687
89450	65665	29190	43709	11172	34481	95977	47535	25658	73898
90696	20451	24211	97310	60446	73530	62865	96574	13829	72226
49006	32047	93086	00112	20470	17136	28255	86328	07293	38809
74591	87025	52368	59416	34417	70557	86746	55809	53628	12000
06315	17012	77103	00968	07235	10728	42189	33292	51487	64443
62386	09184	62092	46617	99419	64230	95034	85481	07857	42510
86848	82122	04028	36959	87827	12813	08627	80699	13345	51695
65643	69480	46598	04501	40403	91408	32343	48130	49303	90689
11084	46534	78957	77353	39578	77868	22970	84349	09184	70603

STUDENT *t* DISTRIBUTION

df	Level of significance for one-tailed test					
	0.100	0.050	0.025	0.010	0.005	0.0005
	Level of significance for two-tailed test					
	0.20	0.10	0.05	0.02	0.01	0.001
1	3.078	6.314	12.706	31.821	63.657	636.619
2	1.886	2.920	4.303	6.965	9.925	31.599
3	1.638	2.353	3.182	4.541	5.841	12.924
4	1.533	2.132	2.776	3.747	4.604	8.610
5	1.476	2.015	2.571	3.365	4.032	6.869
6	1.440	1.943	2.447	3.143	3.707	5.959
7	1.415	1.895	2.365	2.998	3.499	5.408
8	1.397	1.860	2.306	2.896	3.355	5.041
9	1.383	1.833	2.262	2.821	3.250	4.781
10	1.372	1.812	2.228	2.764	3.169	4.587
11	1.363	1.796	2.201	2.718	3.106	4.437
12	1.356	1.782	2.179	2.681	3.055	4.318
13	1.350	1.771	2.160	2.650	3.012	4.221
14	1.345	1.761	2.145	2.624	2.977	4.140
15	1.341	1.753	2.131	2.602	2.947	4.073
16	1.337	1.746	2.120	2.583	2.921	4.015
17	1.333	1.740	2.110	2.567	2.898	3.965
18	1.330	1.734	2.101	2.552	2.878	3.922
19	1.328	1.729	2.093	2.539	2.861	3.883
20	1.325	1.725	2.086	2.528	2.845	3.850
21	1.323	1.721	2.080	2.518	2.831	3.819
22	1.321	1.717	2.074	2.508	2.819	3.792
23	1.319	1.714	2.069	2.500	2.807	3.768
24	1.318	1.711	2.064	2.492	2.797	3.745
25	1.316	1.708	2.060	2.485	2.787	3.725
26	1.315	1.706	2.056	2.479	2.779	3.707
27	1.314	1.703	2.052	2.473	2.771	3.690
28	1.313	1.701	2.048	2.467	2.763	3.674
29	1.311	1.699	2.045	2.462	2.756	3.659
30	1.310	1.697	2.042	2.457	2.750	3.646
40	1.303	1.684	2.021	2.423	2.704	3.551
60	1.296	1.671	2.000	2.390	2.660	3.460
120	1.289	1.658	1.980	2.358	2.617	3.373
∞	1.282	1.645	1.960	2.326	2.576	3.291

Appendix G

CRITICAL VALUES OF THE *F* DISTRIBUTION AT A **5** PERCENT LEVEL OF SIGNIFICANCE, $\alpha = .05$

Degrees of freedom for the numerator

	1	2	3	4	5	6	7	8	9	10	12	15	20	24	30	40	60	120	∞
1	161	200	216	225	230	234	237	239	241	242	244	246	248	249	250	251	252	253	254
2	18.5	19.0	19.2	19.2	19.3	19.3	19.4	19.4	19.4	19.4	19.4	19.4	19.4	19.5	19.5	19.5	19.5	19.5	19.5
3	10.1	9.55	9.28	9.12	9.01	8.94	8.89	8.85	8.81	8.79	8.74	8.70	8.66	8.64	8.62	8.59	8.57	8.55	8.53
4	7.71	6.94	6.59	6.39	6.26	6.16	6.09	6.04	6.00	5.96	5.91	5.86	5.80	5.77	5.75	5.72	5.69	5.66	5.63
5	6.61	5.79	5.41	5.19	5.05	4.95	4.88	4.82	4.77	4.74	4.68	4.62	4.56	4.53	4.50	4.46	4.43	4.40	4.37
6	5.99	5.14	4.76	4.53	4.39	4.28	4.21	4.15	4.10	4.06	4.00	3.94	3.87	3.84	3.81	3.77	3.74	3.70	3.67
7	5.59	4.74	4.35	4.12	3.97	3.87	3.79	3.73	3.68	3.64	3.57	3.51	3.44	3.41	3.38	3.34	3.30	3.27	3.23
8	5.32	4.46	4.07	3.84	3.69	3.58	3.50	3.44	3.39	3.35	3.28	3.22	3.15	3.12	3.08	3.04	3.01	2.97	2.93
9	5.12	4.26	3.86	3.63	3.48	3.37	3.29	3.23	3.18	3.14	3.07	3.01	2.94	2.90	2.86	2.83	2.79	2.75	2.71
10	4.96	4.10	3.71	3.48	3.33	3.22	3.14	3.07	3.02	2.98	2.91	2.85	2.77	2.74	2.70	2.66	2.62	2.58	2.54
11	4.84	3.98	3.59	3.36	3.20	3.09	3.01	2.95	2.90	2.85	2.79	2.72	2.65	2.61	2.57	2.53	2.49	2.45	2.40
12	4.75	3.89	3.49	3.26	3.11	3.00	2.91	2.85	2.80	2.75	2.69	2.62	2.54	2.51	2.47	2.43	2.38	2.34	2.30
13	4.67	3.81	3.41	3.18	3.03	2.92	2.83	2.77	2.71	2.67	2.60	2.53	2.46	2.42	2.38	2.34	2.30	2.25	2.21
14	4.60	3.74	3.34	3.11	2.96	2.85	2.76	2.70	2.65	2.60	2.53	2.46	2.39	2.35	2.31	2.27	2.22	2.18	2.13
15	4.54	3.68	3.29	3.06	2.90	2.79	2.71	2.64	2.59	2.54	2.48	2.40	2.33	2.29	2.25	2.20	2.16	2.11	2.07
16	4.49	3.63	3.24	3.01	2.85	2.74	2.66	2.59	2.54	2.49	2.42	2.35	2.28	2.24	2.19	2.15	2.11	2.06	2.01
17	4.45	3.59	3.20	2.96	2.81	2.70	2.61	2.55	2.49	2.45	2.38	2.31	2.23	2.19	2.15	2.10	2.06	2.01	1.96
18	4.41	3.55	3.16	2.93	2.77	2.66	2.58	2.51	2.46	2.41	2.34	2.27	2.19	2.15	2.11	2.06	2.02	1.97	1.92
19	4.38	3.52	3.13	2.90	2.74	2.63	2.54	2.48	2.42	2.38	2.31	2.23	2.16	2.11	2.07	2.03	1.98	1.93	1.88
20	4.35	3.49	3.10	2.87	2.71	2.60	2.51	2.45	2.39	2.35	2.28	2.20	2.12	2.08	2.04	1.99	1.95	1.90	1.84
21	4.32	3.47	3.07	2.84	2.68	2.57	2.49	2.42	2.37	2.32	2.25	2.18	2.10	2.05	2.01	1.96	1.92	1.87	1.81
22	4.30	3.44	3.05	2.82	2.66	2.55	2.46	2.40	2.34	2.30	2.23	2.15	2.07	2.03	1.98	1.94	1.89	1.84	1.78
23	4.28	3.42	3.03	2.80	2.64	2.53	2.44	2.37	2.32	2.27	2.20	2.13	2.05	2.01	1.96	1.91	1.86	1.81	1.76
24	4.26	3.40	3.01	2.78	2.62	2.51	2.42	2.36	2.30	2.25	2.18	2.11	2.03	1.98	1.94	1.89	1.84	1.79	1.73
25	4.24	3.39	2.99	2.76	2.60	2.49	2.40	2.34	2.28	2.24	2.16	2.09	2.01	1.96	1.92	1.87	1.82	1.77	1.71
30	4.17	3.32	2.92	2.69	2.53	2.42	2.33	2.27	2.21	2.16	2.09	2.01	1.93	1.89	1.84	1.79	1.74	1.68	1.62
40	4.08	3.23	2.84	2.61	2.45	2.34	2.25	2.18	2.12	2.08	2.00	1.92	1.84	1.79	1.74	1.69	1.64	1.58	1.51
60	4.00	3.15	2.76	2.53	2.37	2.25	2.17	2.10	2.04	1.99	1.92	1.84	1.75	1.70	1.65	1.59	1.53	1.47	1.39
120	3.92	3.07	2.68	2.45	2.29	2.18	2.09	2.02	1.96	1.91	1.83	1.75	1.66	1.61	1.55	1.50	1.43	1.35	1.25
∞	3.84	3.00	2.60	2.37	2.21	2.10	2.01	1.94	1.88	1.83	1.75	1.67	1.57	1.52	1.46	1.39	1.32	1.22	1.00

Degrees of freedom for the denominator

CRITICAL VALUES OF THE *F* DISTRIBUTION AT A 1 PERCENT LEVEL OF SIGNIFICANCE, $\alpha = .01$

Degrees of freedom for the numerator

	1	2	3	4	5	6	7	8	9	10	12	15	20	24	30	40	60	120	∞
1	4052	5000	5403	5625	5764	5859	5928	5981	6022	6056	6106	6157	6209	6235	6261	6287	6313	6339	6366
2	98.5	99.0	99.2	99.2	99.3	99.3	99.4	99.4	99.4	99.4	99.4	99.4	99.4	99.5	99.5	99.5	99.5	99.5	99.5
3	34.1	30.8	29.5	28.7	28.2	27.9	27.7	27.5	27.3	27.2	27.1	26.9	26.7	26.6	26.5	26.4	26.3	26.2	26.1
4	21.2	18.0	16.7	16.0	15.5	15.2	15.0	14.8	14.7	14.5	14.4	14.2	14.0	13.9	13.8	13.7	13.7	13.6	13.5
5	16.3	13.3	12.1	11.4	11.0	10.7	10.5	10.3	10.2	10.1	9.89	9.72	9.55	9.47	9.38	9.29	9.20	9.11	9.02
6	13.7	10.9	9.78	9.15	8.75	8.47	8.26	8.10	7.98	7.87	7.72	7.56	7.40	7.31	7.23	7.14	7.06	6.97	6.88
7	12.2	9.55	8.45	7.85	7.46	7.19	6.99	6.84	6.72	6.62	6.47	6.31	6.16	6.07	5.99	5.91	5.82	5.74	5.65
8	11.3	8.65	7.59	7.01	6.63	6.37	6.18	6.03	5.91	5.81	5.67	5.52	5.36	5.28	5.20	5.12	5.03	4.95	4.86
9	10.6	8.02	6.99	6.42	6.06	5.80	5.61	5.47	5.35	5.26	5.11	4.96	4.81	4.73	4.65	4.57	4.48	4.40	4.31
10	10.0	7.56	6.55	5.99	5.64	5.39	5.20	5.06	4.94	4.85	4.71	4.56	4.41	4.33	4.25	4.17	4.08	4.00	3.91
11	9.65	7.21	6.22	5.67	5.32	5.07	4.89	4.74	4.63	4.54	4.40	4.25	4.10	4.02	3.94	3.86	3.78	3.69	3.60
12	9.33	6.93	5.95	5.41	5.06	4.82	4.64	4.50	4.39	4.30	4.16	4.01	3.86	3.78	3.70	3.62	3.54	3.45	3.36
13	9.07	6.70	5.74	5.21	4.86	4.62	4.44	4.30	4.19	4.10	3.96	3.82	3.66	3.59	3.51	3.43	3.34	3.25	3.17
14	8.86	6.51	5.56	5.04	4.69	4.46	4.28	4.14	4.03	3.94	3.80	3.66	3.51	3.43	3.35	3.27	3.18	3.09	3.00
15	8.68	6.36	5.42	4.89	4.56	4.32	4.14	4.00	3.89	3.80	3.67	3.52	3.37	3.29	3.21	3.13	3.05	2.96	2.87
16	8.53	6.23	5.29	4.77	4.44	4.20	4.03	3.89	3.78	3.69	3.55	3.41	3.26	3.18	3.10	3.02	2.93	2.84	2.75
17	8.40	6.11	5.18	4.67	4.34	4.10	3.93	3.79	3.68	3.59	3.46	3.31	3.16	3.08	3.00	2.92	2.83	2.75	2.65
18	8.29	6.01	5.09	4.58	4.25	4.01	3.84	3.71	3.60	3.51	3.37	3.23	3.08	3.00	2.92	2.84	2.75	2.66	2.57
19	8.18	5.93	5.01	4.50	4.17	3.94	3.77	3.63	3.52	3.43	3.30	3.15	3.00	2.92	2.84	2.76	2.67	2.58	2.49
20	8.10	5.85	4.94	4.43	4.10	3.87	3.70	3.56	3.46	3.37	3.23	3.09	2.94	2.86	2.78	2.69	2.61	2.52	2.42
21	8.02	5.78	4.87	4.37	4.04	3.81	3.64	3.51	3.40	3.31	3.17	3.03	2.88	2.80	2.72	2.64	2.55	2.46	2.36
22	7.95	5.72	4.82	4.31	3.99	3.76	3.59	3.45	3.35	3.26	3.12	2.98	2.83	2.75	2.67	2.58	2.50	2.40	2.31
23	7.88	5.66	4.76	4.26	3.94	3.71	3.54	3.41	3.30	3.21	3.07	2.93	2.78	2.70	2.62	2.54	2.45	2.35	2.26
24	7.82	5.61	4.72	4.22	3.90	3.67	3.50	3.36	3.26	3.17	3.03	2.89	2.74	2.66	2.58	2.49	2.40	2.31	2.21
25	7.77	5.57	4.68	4.18	3.85	3.63	3.46	3.32	3.22	3.13	2.99	2.85	2.70	2.62	2.54	2.45	2.36	2.27	2.17
30	7.56	5.39	4.51	4.02	3.70	3.47	3.30	3.17	3.07	2.98	2.84	2.70	2.55	2.47	2.39	2.30	2.21	2.11	2.01
40	7.31	5.18	4.31	3.83	3.51	3.29	3.12	2.99	2.89	2.80	2.66	2.52	2.37	2.29	2.20	2.11	2.02	1.92	1.81
60	7.08	4.98	4.13	3.65	3.34	3.12	2.95	2.82	2.72	2.63	2.50	2.35	2.20	2.12	2.03	1.94	1.84	1.73	1.60
120	6.85	4.79	3.95	3.48	3.17	2.96	2.79	2.66	2.56	2.47	2.34	2.19	2.03	1.95	1.86	1.76	1.66	1.53	1.38
∞	6.63	4.61	3.78	3.32	3.02	2.80	2.64	2.51	2.41	2.32	2.18	2.04	1.88	1.79	1.70	1.59	1.47	1.32	1.00

Degrees of freedom for the denominator

CRITICAL VALUES OF CHI-SQUARE

This table contains the values of χ^2 that corresponds to a specific right-tail area and specific numbers of degrees of freedom df.

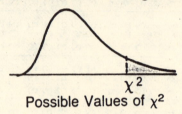

Possible Values of χ^2

DEGREES OF FREEDOM df	RIGHT-TAIL AREA			
	0.10	0.05	0.02	0.01
1	2.706	3.841	5.412	6.635
2	4.605	5.991	7.824	9.210
3	6.251	7.815	9.837	11.345
4	7.779	9.488	11.668	13.277
5	9.236	11.070	13.388	15.086
6	10.645	12.592	15.033	16.812
7	12.017	14.067	16.622	18.475
8	13.362	15.507	18.168	20.090
9	14.684	16.919	19.679	21.666
10	15.987	18.307	21.161	23.209
11	17.275	19.675	22.618	24.725
12	18.549	21.026	24.054	26.217
13	19.812	22.362	25.472	27.688
14	21.064	23.685	26.873	29.141
15	22.307	24.996	28.259	30.578
16	23.542	26.296	29.633	32.000
17	24.769	27.587	30.995	33.409
18	25.989	28.869	32.346	34.805
19	27.204	30.144	33.687	36.191
20	28.412	31.410	35.020	37.566
21	29.615	32.671	36.343	38.932
22	30.813	33.924	37.659	40.289
23	32.007	35.172	38.968	41.638
24	33.196	36.415	40.270	42.980
25	34.382	37.652	41.566	44.314
26	35.563	38.885	42.856	45.642
27	36.741	40.113	44.140	46.963
28	37.916	41.337	45.419	48.278
29	39.087	42.557	46.693	49.588
30	40.256	43.773	47.962	50.892

WILCOXON *T* VALUES

Critical values of T, the Wilcoxon signed rank statistic, where T is the largest integer such that $P(T \leq t/N) \leq \alpha$, the cumulative one-tail probability

N	2 α .15 α.075	.10 .050	.05 .025	.04 .020	.03 .015	.02 .010	.01 .005
4	0						
5	1	0					
6	2	2	0	0			
7	4	3	2	1	0	0	
8	7	5	3	3	2	1	0
9	9	8	5	5	4	3	1
10	12	10	8	7	6	5	3
11	16	13	10	9	8	7	5
12	19	17	13	12	11	9	7
13	24	21	17	16	14	12	9
14	28	25	21	19	18	15	12
15	33	30	25	23	21	19	15
16	39	35	29	28	26	23	19
17	45	41	34	33	30	27	23
18	51	47	40	38	35	32	27
19	58	53	46	43	41	37	32
20	65	60	52	50	47	43	37
21	73	67	58	56	53	49	42
22	81	75	65	63	59	55	48
23	89	83	73	70	66	62	54
24	98	91	81	78	74	69	61
25	108	100	89	86	82	76	68
26	118	110	98	94	90	84	75
27	128	119	107	103	99	92	83
28	138	130	116	112	108	101	91
29	150	140	126	122	117	110	100
30	161	151	137	132	127	120	109
31	173	163	147	143	137	130	118
32	186	175	159	154	148	140	128
33	199	187	170	165	159	151	138
34	212	200	182	177	171	162	148
35	226	213	195	189	182	173	159
40	302	286	264	257	249	238	220
50	487	466	434	425	413	397	373
60	718	690	648	636	620	600	567
70	995	960	907	891	872	846	805
80	1318	1276	1211	1192	1168	1136	1086
90	1688	1638	1560	1537	1509	1471	1410
100	2105	2045	1955	1928	1894	1850	1779

Source: Abridged from Robert L. McCormack, "Extended Tables of the Wilcoxon Matched-Pair Signed Rank Statistic," *Journal of the American Statistical Association*, September 1965, pp. 866–67.

DATA SET 1 — REAL ESTATE

x_1 = Selling price in $000
x_2 = Bedrooms
x_3 = Size of the house in square feet
x_4 = Pool (1 = yes, 0 = no)
x_5 = Distance from center of city
x_6 = Township
x_7 = Garage (1 = yes, 0 = no)
x_8 = Number of bathrooms

x_1	x_2	x_3	x_4	x_5	x_6	x_7	x_8	x_1	x_2	x_3	x_4	x_5	x_6	x_7	x_8
194.9	4	2349	0	17	5	1	2.0	148.0	3	2069	1	19	3	1	2.0
135.1	4	2102	1	19	4	0	2.0	202.4	5	2182	1	16	2	1	3.0
179.3	3	2271	1	12	3	0	2.0	152.6	3	2090	0	9	3	0	1.5
158.2	2	2188	1	16	2	0	2.5	172.0	3	1928	0	16	1	1	1.5
103.6	2	2148	1	28	1	0	1.5	146.9	4	2056	0	19	1	1	1.5
181.8	2	2117	0	12	1	1	2.0	151.9	3	2012	0	20	4	0	2.0
242.4	6	2484	1	15	3	1	2.0	130.1	4	2262	0	24	4	1	2.0
201.3	2	2130	1	9	2	1	2.5	228.0	3	2431	0	21	2	1	3.0
163.8	3	2254	0	18	1	0	1.5	199.4	5	2217	1	8	5	1	3.0
197.5	4	2385	1	13	4	1	2.0	166.5	3	2157	1	17	1	1	2.5
216.6	4	2108	1	14	3	1	2.0	127.1	3	2014	0	16	4	0	2.0
154.8	2	1715	1	8	4	1	1.5	160.6	3	2221	1	15	1	1	2.0
200.6	6	2495	1	7	4	1	2.0	142.7	6	2236	0	14	1	0	2.0
182.3	4	2073	1	18	3	1	2.0	175.1	5	2189	1	20	3	1	2.0
144.0	2	2283	1	11	3	0	2.0	127.7	3	2218	1	23	3	0	2.0
208.4	3	2119	1	16	2	1	2.0	186.2	3	1937	1	12	2	1	2.0
127.9	4	2189	0	16	3	0	2.0	182.2	6	2296	1	7	3	1	3.0
153.7	5	2316	0	21	4	0	2.5	109.2	6	1749	0	12	1	0	2.0
147.3	3	2220	0	10	4	1	2.0	130.4	4	2230	1	15	1	1	2.0
155.0	6	1901	0	15	4	1	2.0	169.2	3	2263	1	17	5	1	1.5
186.9	4	2624	1	8	4	1	2.0	123.3	3	1593	0	19	3	0	2.5
142.9	4	1938	0	14	2	1	2.5	140.3	4	2221	1	24	1	1	2.0
155.0	5	2101	1	20	5	0	1.5	231.2	7	2403	1	13	3	1	3.0
255.8	8	2644	1	9	4	1	2.0	214.7	6	2036	1	21	3	1	3.0
241.7	6	2141	1	11	5	1	3.0	199.9	5	2170	0	11	4	1	2.5
128.2	2	2198	0	21	5	1	1.5	114.3	2	2007	1	13	2	0	2.0
138.5	2	1912	1	26	4	0	2.0	164.5	2	2054	1	9	5	1	2.0
190.5	2	2117	1	9	4	1	2.0	155.3	5	2247	0	13	2	1	2.0
172.6	3	2162	1	14	3	1	1.5	141.4	3	2190	0	18	3	1	2.0
133.6	2	2041	1	11	5	0	2.0	188.4	4	2495	0	15	3	1	2.0
173.3	2	1712	1	19	3	1	2.0	153.7	3	2080	0	10	2	0	2.0
153.4	2	1974	1	11	5	1	2.0	155.3	4	2210	0	19	2	1	2.0
183.5	5	2438	1	16	2	1	2.0	217.8	2	2133	1	13	2	1	2.5
123.1	3	2019	0	16	2	1	2.0	130.6	2	2037	0	17	3	0	2.0
131.2	2	1919	1	10	5	1	2.0	218.0	7	2448	1	8	4	1	2.0
135.3	4	2023	0	14	4	0	2.5	165.9	3	1900	0	6	1	1	2.0
160.0	4	2310	1	19	2	0	2.0	92.6	2	1871	1	18	4	0	1.5
231.2	6	2639	1	7	5	1	2.5								

Appendix K

Data Set 2—1992 Major League Baseball

X_1 = Team
X_2 = Number of games won
X_3 = Team batting average
X_4 = Number of home runs
X_5 = Errors
X_6 = Team earned run average
X_7 = Total team salary
X_8 = League (1 = National, 0 = American)
X_9 = Home surface (1 = artificial, 0 = natural grass)

X_1	X_2	X_3	X_4	X_5	X_6	X_7	X_8	X_9
Team	Wins	Average	Homers	Errors	ERA	Salary	League	Turf
Toronto	96	.263	163	93	3.91	43.326	0	1
Milwaukee	92	.268	82	89	3.43	30.453	0	0
Baltimore	89	.259	148	93	3.79	20.216	0	0
Cleveland	76	.266	127	141	4.11	8.133	0	0
New York Yanks	76	.261	163	114	4.21	35.532	0	0
Detroit	75	.256	182	116	4.60	27.782	0	0
Boston	73	.246	84	139	3.58	42.655	0	0
Oakland	96	.258	142	125	3.73	40.159	0	0
Minnesota	90	.277	104	95	3.70	27.612	0	1
Chicago White Sox	86	.261	110	129	3.82	28.650	0	0
Texas	77	.250	159	154	4.09	28.496	0	0
California	72	.243	88	134	3.84	33.124	0	0
Kansas City	72	.256	75	122	3.81	32.502	0	1
Seattle	64	.263	149	112	4.55	22.445	0	1
Pittsburgh	96	.255	106	101	3.35	31.762	1	1
Montreal	87	.252	102	124	3.25	15.461	1	1
St. Louis	83	.262	94	94	3.38	27.506	1	1
Chicago Cubs	78	.254	104	114	3.39	29.060	1	0
New York Mets	72	.235	93	116	3.66	44.402	1	0
Philadelphia	70	.253	118	131	4.11	24.315	1	1
Atlanta	98	.254	138	109	3.14	31.823	1	0
Cincinnati	90	.260	99	96	3.46	34.684	1	1
San Diego	82	.255	135	115	3.56	29.240	1	0
Houston	81	.246	96	114	3.72	12.747	1	1
San Francisco	72	.244	105	113	3.61	34.029	1	0
Los Angeles	63	.248	72	174	3.41	43.573	1	0